D0699462

EARLY NEGRO AMERICAN WRITERS

EARLY NEGRO
AMERICAN WRITERS

Selections with Biographical and
Critical Introductions

By

BENJAMIN BRAWLEY

PROFESSOR OF ENGLISH, HOWARD UNIVERSITY

Whose vistas show us visions of the dawn.
—PAUL LAURENCE DUNBAR.

Essay Index Reprint Series

Originally published by:

THE UNIVERSITY OF NORTH CAROLINA PRESS

BOOKS FOR LIBRARIES PRESS
FREEPORT, NEW YORK

First Published 1935
Reprinted 1968

Reprinted from a copy in the collections of
The Brooklyn Public Library

STANDARD BOOK NUMBER:

8369-0246-7

LIBRARY OF CONGRESS CATALOG CARD NUMBER:

68-25601

PRINTED IN THE UNITED STATES OF AMERICA

PREFACE

THIS BOOK originated in a desire to render more accessible for the student or general reader some productions in the literature of the Negro in America that were to be found only in special collections. Within recent years there have appeared in the general field not less than five anthologies. These, however, have been restricted almost wholly to the period beginning with Dunbar, and there has been increasing demand for a work dealing with the earlier period and bringing together poems and other compositions that were widely scattered. It is this need that the present collection endeavors to supply.

We at once face the fact that, judged by artistic standards, much of this early writing is weak. Some of it, however, is good, and what is lacking in literary quality is in general more than made up in social interest. It is hoped, accordingly, that the book may be of service to the student of the history of the Negro as well as to one concerned with literary values only.

One could not go far in such an effort as this without being forced to delimit his undertaking. Naturally much that should be included is reflective of the agitation that preceded the Civil War. The years from 1865 to 1895 made strong appeal, especially as they included such a figure as Albery A. Whitman. Even scant representation of the writing and speaking of that period, however, would take one far beyond the original design, so that it has been decided to close with the Civil War.

In the preparation of the biographical and critical sketches I have once more been reminded how much of the writing about representative Negroes has been superficial and inaccurate. Such being the case, it is a pleasure to acknowl-

edge my indebtedness to at least a few books which strive
to give definite facts. Unusually valuable for some subjects
is *The Negro in American History*, by John W. Cromwell;
and *Men of Maryland*, by George P. Bragg, and *Homespun
Heroines*, by Hallie Q. Brown, contain much matter not
easily found elsewhere. Especially do I thank Mr. Charles
Fred Heartman for permission to use two of the poems of
Hammon from Wegelin's edition.

BENJAMIN BRAWLEY

Washington, D. C.,
February 1, 1935.

CONTENTS

EARLY NEGRO AMERICAN WRITERS

INTRODUCTION

It was but natural that the early literature of the Negro in the United States should have a serious tone. Tens of thousands of souls had been wrested from their fatherland; their children were subject to the lash, and there was no immediate hope of a better day. A group might think or feel together, and out of the depth of oppression came the songs of sorrow. Here and there, moreover, some poet with a glimpse of the light might try to give voice to his striving. Before there could be any large achievement, however, or conscious effort in literature or art, the individual soul had to be free. First of all, the chains of bondage had to be broken.

This earnestness of purpose was deepened by other forces at work. From Yorktown to Appomattox the country was in travail, and the Negro was at the heart of the nation's life. Two questions of overwhelming importance pressed for answer. The first was economic, and had to do with the development of new lands and industries: What was to be the ultimate relation of the free labor of the North to the slave labor of the South? With this soon came the moral question: Granted that the labor of the slave might be profitable in new territory, was it right to hold a man in bondage? Could the system of slavery be justified in a great republic? Upon the answers depended the future not only of the Negro but of the country itself.

Meanwhile, far less than is sometimes supposed did the Negro accept the situation. Hundreds of fugitives made their way to the North, and some to Canada. Early in the period word came from Hayti of the deeds of Toussaint L'Ouverture, and within the next generation there were three notable insurrections or attempts at insurrection in the

United States—first, the effort of Gabriel Prosser in Richmond in 1800; second, that of Denmark Vesey in Charleston in 1822; and third, that of Nat Turner in Southampton County, Virginia, in 1831, which was partly successful. The nation had sown the wind; it had now to reap the whirlwind.

Three special matters it might be well to keep in mind as we proceed. The first is that of racial consciousness and organization. Every great war in which the country has engaged has improved the position of the Negro. In the course of the Civil War he was emancipated and he fought to save the Union. In the course of the World War he was employed in industrial plants of the North and in some states began to hold the balance of power. So it was after the Revolution. In the uncertain life of the period some men of initiative saw an unwonted opportunity for coöperative effort. Accordingly, Prince Hall made in Boston a beginning in Negro Masonry; Paul Cuffe, by his protest to the assembly, won the suffrage for the Negro in Massachusetts; and Richard Allen, in Philadelphia, laid the foundation of the African Methodist Episcopal Church.

The second thing is that about the year 1830 a profound change in the life of the Negro took place. Before that date the estate of the black man was so lowly that even personality was sometimes denied; after 1830, however, the Negro was an issue. On January 1, 1831, Garrison founded the *Liberator*, and in his addresses he appealed to the self-respect of the Negro. "Maintain your rights," he said, "in all cases, and at whatever expense. Wherever you are allowed to vote, see that your names are put on the list of voters, and go to the polls." In 1833 the American Anti-Slavery Society was organized; and to the Abolitionists was largely due the rise of Frederick Douglass, William Wells Brown, and several other Negroes of the next one or two decades. There was also inspiration from abroad. Hugo and Mazzini, Macaulay and Mrs. Browning were now on the scene; and in 1833 slavery was abolished in the English dominions. It was a time of furious conflict, but also a time of infinite hope.

A third matter that we may wish to keep in mind is the proposal of colonization. This subject has a long and contradictory history, largely because of the different motives that have actuated men at different times. These extend all the way from missionary interest to the desire to be rid of Negroes who might make trouble. As early as 1773 the Reverend Samuel Hopkins, of Newport, suggested to his friend, the Reverend Ezra Stiles, afterwards president of Yale College, the possibility of educating Negro students who might go as missionaries to Africa. Stiles thought that for the plan to be worth while there should be a colony on the coast of Africa, that at least thirty or forty persons should go, and that the enterprise should have the formal backing of a society organized for the purpose. Two young Negro men sailed from New York in November, 1774; but the Revolutionary War began, and nothing more was done at the time. In 1787 the colony of Sierra Leone was founded under English auspices, ostensibly as a haven for some Negroes who had been discharged from the British Army after the Revolution, and for others who had become free in accordance with the Mansfield Decision of 1772 but were leading in London an uncertain existence. In Virginia, Gabriel's insurrection brought the idea concretely forward, and the House of Delegates passed a resolution that the Governor "be requested to correspond with the President of the United States on the subject of purchasing land without the limits of this state, whither persons obnoxious to the laws or dangerous to the peace of society may be removed." The Governor was James Monroe, and the President was Thomas Jefferson.

Already for fully twenty years Jefferson had considered

the general subject, and he now wrote to Rufus King, minister to England, about coöperation with the English officials for the sending of a number of Negroes to Sierra Leone. "It is material to observe," he remarked, "that they are not felons, or common malefactors, but persons guilty of what the safety of society, under actual circumstances, obliges us to treat as a crime, but which their feelings may represent in a far different shape." By the close of Jefferson's second administration the Northwest, the Southwest, the West Indies, and Sierra Leone had all been thought of as possible fields for the colonization of American Negroes. In 1815 the country was startled by the enterprise of a Negro who had long pondered the situation of his people in America and at length had determined to do something definite in their behalf. Paul Cuffe was a seaman, the captain and owner of his vessel. He had already visited Sierra Leone and made pleasant contacts there. He now took to the colony a total of nine families and thirty-eight persons at an expense to himself of nearly $4,000.

Meanwhile Samuel J. Mills, a young man of the purest altruism, in 1808, as an undergraduate in Williams College, had organized with his fellow students a society whose work later told in the formation of the American Bible Society and the Board of Foreign Missions. Mills continued his theological studies at Andover and then at Princeton, and while at the latter place he established a school for Negroes at Parsippany, thirty miles away. He interested in his work and hopes the Reverend Robert Finley, of Basking Ridge, New Jersey, who called a meeting at Princeton to consider the project of sending Negro colonists to Africa. The meeting was not well attended, but Finley nevertheless felt encouraged to go to Washington in December, 1816, to work for the formation of a national colonization society. On December 21 there was a meeting at which Henry Clay,

Speaker of the House, presided; at another meeting a week
later a constitution was adopted; and on January 1, 1817,
were formally chosen the officers of "The American Society
for Colonizing the Free People of Color of the United
States." This was the organization that led in the founding
of Liberia. Mills, appointed as one of two men who were
to select a place of settlement, died on the way home, a
martyr to missions.

It was observed, however, that Bushrod Washington, the
president of the Society, was a Southern man, that twelve of
the seventeen vice-presidents were Southern men, and that all
of the twelve managers were slaveholders. Accordingly the
new organization created consternation among the Negroes of
the North, among whom there spread a rumor, with good
foundation, that the ultimate aim was to send all the free
people of color in the country back to Africa. Within a few
days there was a meeting in Bethel Church in Philadelphia,
presided over by James Forten and said to have been attended
by three thousand persons. In the resolutions adopted, those
present expressed themselves as viewing "with deep abhorrence" the unmerited stigma cast on the free pople of color
and as determined never to separate themselves voluntarily
from the slave population of the country; and they appointed
a committee to confer with their representative in Congress.
Garrison flayed the Society in the *Liberator* (July 9, 1831),
and in *Thoughts on African Colonization* (1832) developed
at length ten points against it. For some years this continued to be the attitude of the Negroes and the Abolitionists. By 1847, however, Liberia was having difficulties with
England; the Colonization Society, powerless to act except
through the United States Government, said the colonists
should assume all the responsibilities of citizenship; and
Edward Everett, Secretary of State, said that America was
not presuming to settle differences arising between Liberian

and British subjects, "the Liberians being responsible for their own acts." The colony now issued its Declaration of Independence; and thinking American Negroes were thrilled by the motto on the seal of the new republic, "The Love of Liberty Brought Us Here." Three years later, after the enactment of the Fugitive Slave Law, some were disposed to give the whole matter of colonization fresh consideration. It may thus be seen that Martin R. Delany had abundant reason for calling up the question about 1854; and one can also see the line that opposition would naturally take.

When, then, the Negro was faced by such a question as this, when even his representative men were sometimes forced to consider their physical liberty, there was little time or training for what is called polite literature. In George M. Horton and William Wells Brown there might be a little humor; and Brown might make a crude attempt at the novel or the drama; but in general the achievement of the Negro in these fields before the Civil War was negligible. What was not negligible, however, was the story of the individual man who, in spite of all difficulties, was able to press forward and win. Every Negro who escaped from bondage and earned an honest living was an argument against slavery, and, if he became at all prominent, was likely to find encouragement for the telling of his history. The narratives of Douglass, Brown, and Josiah Henson thus went through numerous editions. If now to these autobiographies we add the poems of nine or ten writers, a few essays in serious vein, and the speeches of Douglass and a few other men who were before the public, we shall have the chief works of a literary nature produced by the Negro up to the close of the Civil War.

———————

The first printed production written by a Negro within the present limits of the United States was a poem, *An Evening Thought: Salvation by Christ*, which appeared early in

1761, the author being Jupiter Hammon, the slave of a man on Long Island. One of Hammon's later pieces was addressed to Phillis Wheatley, of Boston, whose first published work, *An Elegiac Poem on the Death of George Whitefield*, appeared in 1770, and whose later career has never ceased to excite wonder and admiration. Both of these early writers were naturally imitative, Hammon finding inspiration in the evangelical hymns of the period, and Phillis Wheatley adhering closely to the school of Pope. About the beginning of the last decade of the century attention was attracted to the isolated genius, Benjamin Banneker, mathematician and astronomer, of Maryland; and the *Interesting Narrative* of Gustavus Vassa appeared in the first of many editions.

Meanwhile, here and there abroad, the Negro rose to distinction in the study or the pursuit of the humanities. As early as the middle of the sixteenth century there was in Spain the notable career of Juan Latino, a teacher in Granada.[1] Anthony William Amo, a native of Guinea, published at Halle in 1738 a philosophical essay written in Latin. Francis Williams, born of free parents in Jamaica about 1700, became the subject of an experiment to test the intellectual capacity of the Negro. After preparatory training he studied at Cambridge, and later was able to write odes in Latin as well as English. Other cases were similar to those of Amo and Williams. The brilliant Russian poet, Aleksandr Sergyeevich Pushkin (1799-1837), had as greatgrandfather an Abyssianian who became a general in the army of Peter the Great. At just about this same time, Alexandre Dumas (1802-1870), a mulatto, entered in France upon his amazing career as novelist and dramatist. Pushkin and Dumas, however, had no real touch with the Negro

[1] Velaurez B. Spratlin, "Juan Latino, Slave and Humanist," *The Crisis*, September, 1932.

in America, and only in a very general way was there any influence in Europe from distinction such as theirs.

The Negro in the United States was more in line with the main tradition of English letters. The imitators of Milton, the poets of the "Graveyard School," and those of the high tide of romanticism influenced William Cullen Bryant, and such brief masterpieces as "Thanatopsis" and "The Past" stamped themselves indelibly upon the public mind. Of similar temper was the work of John Boyd, "a man of color," who is said to have published a collection of his poems in 1834. One of his pieces, "Vanity of Life," was printed in the *Liberator* of February 16, 1833.

VANITY OF LIFE

Thou may'st sit in the green bower of life,
Singing gay as the lark,
But time is bringing on the dark hour of strife,
And joy's last ember-spark
Is burning fast away,
Leaving but ashes and clay!
Thou may'st boast of elegance, wealth, and store—
Palaces and domains;
And to thousands ten, thou may'st add ten more;
But what rewards thy pains?
Health and life are flying,
Nor can wealth save the dying,
Thou may'st live enraptured on beauty's lips,
Tranc'd in am'rous bliss;
But though the balmy redolence thou sipp'st,
That distils from a kiss,
Know Death is even with you,
And participates it too!
Thou may'st exult in vigor, spirits, health,
Unconscious of decay—
But insidious disease saps by stealth,
And wears thee slow away;

Then what of these remains?
Weakness, remorse, and pains.
Thou may'st whirl in dissipation's round,
Inebriate with joy;
Dancing merrily to every tuneful sound,
In wildest revelry;
But Death, with hollow tread,
Lowly shall lay thy head!
Thou may'st boast the statesman's, or scholar's fame,
Proud of immortality—
Dissolved shall be this universal frame,
Learning and arts shall die—
The globe shall perish like a dream,
And darkness merge life's sunny beam.

After the first quarter of the century, the dominant influence in poetry was that of Byron, along with whose sweeping, rhythmic verse may be taken that of Scott. Byron made himself felt for decades in America as well as in England, and in the literature of the Negro he especially affected a group of writers that flourished about the middle of the century—James M. Whitfield, Charles L. Reason, George B. Vashon, James Madison Bell, and, after the Civil War, Albery A. Whitman.

The narratives of Frederick Douglass, William Wells Brown, and Josiah Henson were only the more outstanding of a large group of autobiographies. Prominent among the others were the *Narrative of Sojourner Truth* (Boston, 1850; New York, 1855); *The Autobiography of a Fugitive Negro*, by Samuel Ringgold Ward (London, 1855); *Narrative of the Life and Adventures of Henry Bibb* (New York, 1849); and the *Narrative of Lunsford Lane* (Boston, 1842). In the whole field of history and biography before the Civil War special importance attaches to a work reflecting genuine research, *The Colored Patriots of the American Revolution*, *with Sketches of Several Distinguished Colored Persons: to which is added a Brief Survey of the Condition and Prospects of Colored Americans,* by William Cooper Nell (Boston, 1855).

Paul Cuffe, Prince Hall, Richard Allen, and other leaders in the generation after the Revolution were men of great force of character but very limited training in the schools, and their achievement is accordingly the more remarkable. More and more, however, in the new century there appeared Negroes who had some degree of attainment in scholarship and who were able to bring trained minds to bear upon the problems of their people. Lemuel B. Haynes, a Congregational minister, was not in close touch with the South, as he grew to manhood in New England about the close of the Revolution; but his career is interesting on its own account. He was the son of an African father and a white servant on a Connecticut farm. Ordained in 1785, he served at different times as pastor of four white congregations, his longest period of work at one place being thirty years at Rutland, Vermont; and he published several sermons and pamphlets on theological subjects. John Chavis, described as "a black man of prudence and piety," seems to have received some informal training at Princeton. Later he was permitted to take a regular course of study at Washington Academy, now Washington and Lee University, and in 1801 was commissioned by the General Assembly of the Presbyterians as a missionary to the Negroes. He worked with increasing success and reputation until the Nat Turner insurrection caused the North Carolina legislature to pass in 1832 an act to silence all Negro preachers. As early as 1808, however, he had begun his educational work, having a school for white children in the morning and one for children of color in the evening. Some of the most distinguished men in the history of the state were

his pupils.[2]   In 1827 John B. Russwurm was graduated at
Bowdoin and thus became the first Negro to receive a degree from a college in the United States.   Oberlin was
founded in 1833, and Asa Mahan, when offered the presi-
dency in 1835, let it be known that he would accept only if
Negroes were admitted on equal terms with other students.

About the middle of the century Daniel A. Payne arose
as the real successor of Richard Allen and as a leader destined
to assist his people in an educational as well as a spiritual
way.   Just about 1850 New York Central College, an Abolitionist institution established at McGrawville, New York,
employed three Negro professors—Charles L. Reason,
George B. Vashon, and William G. Allen.   James W. C.
Pennington, a Presbyterian minister of New York, made
several trips to Europe to attend different congresses and received the degree of Doctor of Divinity from the University
of Heidelberg.   Samuel Ringgold Ward, with the assistance
of Gerrit Smith, got sound training in the classics and the-
ology.   He was a black man, six feet in height, and of strong
voice and powerful frame.   As an orator he was second only
to Douglass, and for several years was the pastor of a white
Presbyterian congregation at South Butler, New York. Henry
Highland Garnet studied at the Oneida Institute, which was
established at Whitesboro, New York, by Beriah Green, a
well known Abolitionist.   In 1843, at a convention of Negro
men in Buffalo, he delivered *An Address—to the Slaves of
the United States* which advocated a general strike and was so
incendiary in tone that the majority of those attending were
unwilling to approve it.   Later he had a varied career, and
among his productions was *A Memorial Discourse Delivered
in the Hall of the House of Representatives, Washington,
D. C., on Sabbath, February 12, 1865* (Philadelphia, 1865).

[2] Edgar W. Knight, "Notes on John Chavis," *The North Carolina Historical
Review*, vol. VII, no. 3 (July, 1930), pp. 326-345.

Martin Robison Delany was a restless spirit, but every inch a man, zealously and unselfishly devoted to the welfare of his people.   Alexander Crummell was in Liberia in the years just before the Civil War and rose to his highest distinction after his return to the United States in 1873.

Well known to most of these men and of the highest standing with them was James McCune Smith, who in 1837 returned from the University of Glasgow with the degree of Doctor of Medicine.   In connection with his practice he opened a drug store in New York and helped to train other young men for his profession.   He assisted as editor of *The Colored American* in the early months of 1839, was received into the New York Geographical Society, and was one of the five men appointed to draft a constitution for the Statistic Institute.   Payne says[3] that he was called to Wilberforce when that institution was established and given the choice of any chair he might wish to take, and after he had selected anthropology, the post and a home were held in reserve for him for twelve months, in the course of which time he died of heart disease.   Smith left no one great work, and the scattered writings that we have hardly represent him adequately, though all are in a strong, clear style.   His standing with his contemporaries is seen from the fact that he wrote the introductions for Douglass' *My Bondage and My Freedom* and Garnet's *Memorial Discourse*.   One may also find in the *Liberator*[4] a speech before the American Anti-Slavery Society and two letters on "Freedom and Slavery for Africans" first contributed to the *Tribune;* and in the *Anglo-African Magazine*[5] such a paper as that on "Civilization: Its Dependence on Physical Circumstances."   In connection with him it is also worth while to note a special Abolitionist publication to

[3] *Recollections of Seventy Years*, Nashville, 1888, pp. 324-326.
[4] June 1, 1838, and February 16 and 23, 1844.
[5] January, 1859.

which we are indebted for some selections from the writers of the period that are not available elsewhere. This was *Autographs for Freedom*, an annual edited by Julia Griffiths, secretary of the Rochester Ladies' Anti-Slavery Society. Two volumes were issued, for 1853 and 1854, and each was a book of ordinary size. To the first, Smith contributed a paper, "John Murray (of Glasgow)," a tribute to a Scotch Abolitionist, and to the second a paragraph entitled "Freedom—Liberty," which well represents his style.

Freedom—Liberty

Freedom and Liberty are synonyms. Freedom is an essence; Liberty, an accident. Freedom is born with a man; Liberty may be conferred on him. Freedom is progressive; Liberty is circumscribed. Freedom is the gift of God; Liberty, the creature of society. Liberty may be taken away from a man; but, on whatsoever soul Freedom may light, the course of that soul is thenceforth onward and upward; society, customs, laws, armies, are but as wythes in its giant grasp, if they oppose, instruments to work its will, if they assent. Human kind welcome the birth of a free soul with reverence and shoutings, rejoicing in the advent of a fresh off-shoot of the Divine Whole, of which this is but a part.

At the outbreak of the Civil War two questions affecting the Negro overshadowed all others, those of his freedom and his employment as a soldier. Before the conflict was over both were answered in the affirmative; and at Port Hudson and Fort Wagner, Fort Pillow and Petersburg, Negro soldiers gave sterling proof of their valor. In the North the conviction grew that men who had served so bravely deserved well at the hands of the nation, and in Congress there was a feeling that if the South could once more take its place in the life of the Union, certainly the Negro soldier should have the rights of citizenship. In Syracuse, New York, however,

beginning on October 4, 1864, there was held a convention
of Negro men that threw interesting light on the problems of
the period.   At this gathering John Mercer Langston was
temporary chairman, Frederick Douglass was president, and
Henry Highland Garnet, James W. C. Pennington, George
B. Vashon, George L. Ruffin, and Ebenezer D. Bassett were
among the delegates.   There was a fear that some of the
things that seemed to have been gained by the war might not
actually be realized; and grave question was raised by a recent
speech in which Seward, Secretary of State, had said that when
the insurgents laid down their arms, all war measures, including those which affected slavery, would cease.   The convention thanked the President and the Thirty-seventh Congress
for revoking a prohibitory law with regard to the carrying
of mail by Negroes, for abolishing slavery in the District of
Columbia, for recognizing Hayti and Liberia, and for the
military order retaliating for the unmilitary treatment ac-
corded Negro soldiers by the Confederate officers; and especially it thanked Senator Sumner "for his noble efforts to
cleanse the statute books of the nation from every stain of in-
equality against colored men."   At the same time it resolved
to send a petition to Congress to ask that the rights of the
country's Negro patriots in the field be respected, and that the
Government cease to set an example to those in arms against
it by making invidious distinctions as to pay, labor, and promotion.   Finally the convention insisted that any such things as
the right to own real estate, to testify in courts of law, and
to sue and be sued, were mere privileges so long as general
political liberty was withheld, and asked frankly not only
for the formal and complete abolition of slavery in the United
States, but also for the complete franchise in all the states
then in the Union and in all that might come into the Union
thereafter.   In general, the men who assembled at this time

showed a very clear conception of the problems facing the Negro and the country in 1864.

They and some others also had deep insight into things two years later when the country had entered upon the period of readjustment. One of the most brilliant and active young men of the time was James Lynch, who from February 24, 1866, to June 15, 1867, was editor of *The Christian Recorder* in Philadelphia. The career of Lynch shows how easy it was for the Negro minister of ability to be drawn into politics at the close of the war. He was born in Baltimore on January 8, 1839, and in his youth had good educational advantages. In 1858 he joined the Presbyterian Church in New York, but soon thereafter was accepted by the African Methodist Episcopal Conference in Indiana. He transferred to Baltimore, and in 1863 went to South Carolina to labor in the towns near the coast. He was a member of the South Carolina Conference organized by Bishop Payne in 1865. Then came the sixteen months as editor of *The Christian Recorder*, in which capacity he made thoughtful comment on the events of the day. Later he was with the Freedmen's Bureau under General Howard in Mississippi, and in 1871 was elected Secretary of State. The strain of the political campaign, however, prostrated him, and he died December 18, 1872.[6] One of his editorials is so discerning in outlook and so clear in statement that we give it entire.

TRYING MOMENT FOR THE COLORED PEOPLE
(1866)

It frequently occurs in the lives of individuals that there comes a period when it is necessary to summon all they have of intellect, wisdom, physical power, and the aid of friends, in order to

[6] Daniel A. Payne, *The Semi-Centenary and the Retrospection of the African Methodist Episcopal Church*, Baltimore, 1866, pp. 157-172, and Richard R. Wright, Jr., *Centennial Encyclopaedia of the African Methodist Episcopal Church*, Philadelphia, 1916, p. 153.

meet some great crisis. This is no less true of nations and communities than of individuals. Such a period occurs now, in the history of the colored people of the United States. Since the close of the great civil war, their relations to political government have changed. Public sentiment has undergone a revolution. All this has been for the better. Though we have not a clear sky, the clouds have parted. Though we ever and anon have our light of hope hid behind them, yet we catch the gleam of many shining rays.

Our Colored Representatives enter the Executive Mansion, and in dignified and manly manner present our cause to the President of the United States,—recount our grievances and claim redress. The President stands before them, making a plea in behalf of his own fidelity, and struggling in embarrassed apology for not obeying the dictates of simple justice.[7]

A delegation of colored men are acknowledged, conferred and counselled with, by the most eminent legislators in Congress, and their every word is hurried along the telegraphic wires, and commented upon by the press. Nearly two-thirds of the members in each branch of Congress are pledged to legislate in behalf of our natural and political rights.

As an indication of the favorable state of public sentiment at the North, let us note the fact that millions of dollars have been raised and expended to educate and provide for the Freedmen of the South. Who of us can reflect upon all this, without perceiving that our race has grander opportunities for progress and improvement *now* than they ever had; and that responsibilities rest upon us, which we were never before called upon to assume?

It is true also, that there is a party rising—not increasing in numbers, but improving in discipline, unity, and tactics—whose great mission is to crush out our hopes of elevation. This party will bring to bear upon our faults a telescope, and give the world a magnified picture. *The World,* a copperhead newspaper, well

---

[7] This has reference to the recent appearance before President Andrew Johnson of a delegation consisting of Frederick Douglass, George Downing, and other prominent men in behalf of Negro suffrage.

remarks that the position of this party is that of an "army of observation."

The opposition of our enemies, and the expectation created among the great "cloud of witnesses" that behold us by the opportunities we enjoy, make the present moment a trying one for us. We have entered upon a new life in this nation. The circumstances by which we have been surrounded in the past, especially in the slave states, have not been such as to develop manhood. The laws of those states ignored it; and to obey the laws, we had to ignore our own manhood too. If we enjoyed security against outrage and injury, it was because we enjoyed some sympathy among the ruling class. Our domestic peace and comfort depended entirely upon our continued appeal to sympathy. If a man be not allowed to claim a thing as his right, he must do the next best thing—beg for it as a gift. We have always been beggars for justice, beggars for sympathy, because bound hand and foot by American tyranny. But this has well nigh come to an end, and the grand era is near at hand, when we shall everywhere cease to present ourselves as objects of pity, but as the fit subjects of respect.

There are two ways by which we are to get our rights. The first is, to continually present our claim to the nation, and the second is to continue to prove ourselves capable of making as good use of all the political privileges which white citizens enjoy, as they do themselves. We have proved this already, in our loyalty and sacrifices during the terrible civil war; but we must add proof to proof, that our very existence may be a living protest against the injustice that would proscribe us.

There is a danger that in looking with anxiety at our contest for political equality, and the enjoyment of civil rights, and in our indignation at those who would withhold them from us, we may forget, or not pay sufficient attention to our *individual* improvement, morally, socially, and intellectually. It is not alone in the Halls of Congress or Legislatures, on the platform and in the pulpit, that American prejudice is most successfully fought.

The colored man who owns a farm and cultivates it well, and carries produce to market, makes a plea for his race far more effectual than the tongue of the most eloquent orator. A colored man standing in the door of his own blacksmith shop, with a leather apron on, is doing as much to elevate the race as the man in public station.

No race of people inferior in numbers or power to another race, can live with them on terms of equality, unless they have the same great current of thought and feeling—unless they imbibe the spirit of the age. The present age in America is pre-eminently a practical and working age. The people's attention is in the work of developing the resources of the country; they are after sinking shafts and hoisting to the surface precious and useful metals, tunnelling mountains, yoking hills together, and spanning streams with bridges. They believe in individual accumulation, and glory in the increasing wealth of the nation. Colored men, now that they have commenced thinking and acting for themselves, must be found in all the different branches of mechanism and labor, in agriculture and in commerce.

American oppression taught us that we were fit only for plantation hands and servants. Now that it is fast crumbling away, let us teach the world that we have the power and the disposition to enter into every branch of labor or mechanism that is required to make the physical resources of the world serve the demands of a civilization that is standing in the meridian blaze of the nineteenth century.

JUPITER HAMMON

Jupiter Hammon seems to have been born between 1720 and 1730, and to have died soon after 1800; but there is no definite evidence on either point. He was first owned by Henry Lloyd, who lived on Long Island. On the death of this master in 1763, Hammon went with the portion of the estate that fell to Joseph, one of four sons. When Joseph Lloyd died in the course of the Revolutionary War, he passed into the service of John Lloyd, Jr., a grandson; and he was with the family in Hartford, Conn., while the British were in possession of Long Island. He was a dutiful servant, so highly esteemed by the Lloyds that they assisted him in placing his verses before the public.

Hammon grew into manhood in the years when the Wesleyan revival was making itself felt in England and America, and he was strongly influenced by the evangelical hymns of Charles Wesley, John Newton, and William Cowper. Early in 1761 was printed as a broadside in New York "An Evening Thought. Salvation by Christ, with Penetential Cries: Composed by Jupiter Hammon, a Negro belonging to Mr. Lloyd, of Queen's Village, on Long Island, the 25th of December, 1760." This was the first composition by a Negro printed within the present limits of the United States. The second production was "An Address to Miss Phillis Wheatly," dated Hartford, August 4, 1778. This consisted of twenty-one four-line stanzas and was also in broadsheet form. Then appeared "An Essay on the Ten Virgins" (1779), of which no copy seems to have been preserved, and "A Winter Piece" (Hartford, 1782). This latter production was for the most part a sermon in prose, but on the last two pages was "A Poem for Children, with Thoughts on Death." "An Evening's Improvement," written toward the close of the war, has special autobiographical interest, containing a poetical dialogue entitled "The Kind Master and the Dutiful Servant."

Somewhat apart from Hammon's other efforts is a prose production, "An Address to the Negroes of the State of New

York," originally presented to the members of the African Society in the City of New York September 24, 1786, and printed early in 1787. This shows the writer as feeling it his personal duty to bear slavery with patience, but as strongly opposed to the system and as urging that young Negroes be manumitted. Hammon had to receive editorial assistance before the Address could be issued, but the style is evidently his own. There was an immediate reprinting in Philadelphia by order of the Pennsylvania Society for Promoting the Abolition of Slavery, and there was a third edition after the author's death. Because of his personal submission to slavery and his generally conciliatory attitude, Hammon was not quite in line with such independent and aggressive Negro leaders as Richard Allen and Prince Hall, who were already on the scene; and he passed into oblivion when he died. Only within recent years has there been a revival of interest in his achievement. It is worth while to note, however, that in his will dated 1795 John Lloyd, Jr., ordered that certain of his slaves be set free on arriving at the age of twenty-eight; and the Address doubtless had something to do with the fact that in 1799 the state of New York took formal action looking toward the gradual emancipation of all slaves within her borders.

One who reads Hammon to-day must remember that he was a slave working without the advantage of formal education and basing his rhythm on the strongly accented measures of the hymns that he heard. Only thus can allowance be made for the faulty syntax, the forced rhymes, and the strained metrical effects to be found in his work. He was content to express his pious musing in such forms as he knew, and he at least has the virtue of earnestness. The authoritative edition is *Jupiter Hammon, American Negro Poet; Selections from his writings and a bibliography,* by Oscar Wegelin. Printed for Charles Fred Heartman, New York, 1915. As was said in the Preface, we are indebted to Mr. Heartman for permission to print the two poems given below.

An Evening Thought: Salvation by Christ, with Penetential Cries

Salvation comes by Christ alone,
    The only Son of God;
Redemption now to every one,
    That love his holy Word.

Dear Jesus, we would fly to Thee,
    And leave off every Sin,
Thy tender Mercy well agree;
    Salvation from our King;

Salvation comes now from the Lord,
    Our victorious King.
His holy Name be well ador'd,
    Salvation surely bring.

Dear Jesus, give thy* Spirit now,
    Thy Grace to every Nation,
That han't the Lord to whom we bow,
    The Author of Salvation.

Dear Jesus, unto Thee we cry,
    Give us the Preparation;
Turn not away thy tender Eye;
    We seek thy true Salvation.

Salvation comes from God we know,
    The true and only One;
It's well agreed and certain true,
    He gave his only Son.

Lord, hear our penetential Cry:
    Salvation from above;
It is the Lord that doth supply,
    With his Redeeming Love.

* *They* in original text.

Dear Jesus, by thy precious Blood,
　　The World Redemption have:
Salvation now comes from the Lord,
　　He being thy captive slave.

Dear Jesus, let the Nations cry,
　　And all the People say,
Salvation comes from Christ on high,
　　Haste on Tribunal Day.

We cry as Sinners to the Lord,
　　Salvation to obtain;
It is firmly fixt his holy Word,
　　Ye shall not cry in vain.

Dear Jesus, unto Thee we cry,
　　And make our Lamentation:
O let our Prayers ascend on high;
　　We felt thy Salvation.

Lord, turn our dark benighted Souls;
　　Give us a true Motion,
And let the Hearts of all the World,
　　Make Christ their Salvation.

Ten Thousand Angels cry to Thee,
　　Yea, louder than the Ocean.
Thou art the Lord, we plainly see;
　　Thou art the true Salvation.

Now is the Day, excepted* Time;
　　The Day of Salvation;
Increase your Faith, do not repine:
　　Awake ye, every Nation.

Lord, unto whom now shall we go,
　　Or seek a safe Abode?

---

* Thus; evidently intended for *accepted.*

Thou hast the Word Salvation Too,
  The only Son of God.

Ho! every one that hunger hath,
  Or pineth after me,
Salvation be thy leading Staff,
  To set the Sinner free.

Dear Jesus, unto Thee we fly;
  Depart, depart from Sin,
Salvation doth at length supply,
  The Glory of our King.

Come, ye Blessed of the Lord,
  Salvation greatly given;
O turn your Hearts, accept the Word,
  Your Souls are fit for Heaven.

Dear Jesus, we now turn to Thee,
  Salvation to obtain;
Our Hearts and Souls do meet again,
  To magnify thy Name.

Come, holy Spirit, Heavenly Dove,
  The Object of our Care;
Salvation doth increase our Love;
  Our Hearts hath felt thy fear.

Now Glory be to God on High,
  Salvation high and low;
And thus the Soul on Christ rely,
  To Heaven surely go.

Come, Blessed Jesus, Heavenly Dove,
  Accept Repentance here;
Salvation give, with tender Love;
  Let us with Angels share.   Finis.

A Dialogue Intitled the Kind Master and the
Dutiful Servant, as Follows:

Master.

Come my servant, follow me,
  According to thy place;
And surely God will be with thee,
  And send thee heav'nly grace.

Servant.

Dear Master, I will follow thee,
  According to thy word,
And pray that God may be with me,
  And save thee in the Lord.

Master.

My Servant, lovely is the Lord,
  And blest those servants be,
That truly love his holy word,
  And thus will follow me.

Servant.

Dear Master, that's my whole delight,
  Thy pleasure for to do;
As far as grace and truth's in sight,
  Thus far I'll surely go.

Master.

My Servant, grace proceeds from God,
  And truth should be with thee;
Whence e'er you find it in his word,
  Thus far come follow me.

Servant.

Dear Master, now without controul,
  I quickly follow thee;
And pray that God would bless thy soul,
  His heav'nly place to see.

Master.

My Servant, Heaven is high above,
    Yea, higher than the sky:
I pray that God would grant his love,
    Come follow me thereby.

Servant.

Dear Master, now I'll follow thee,
    And trust upon the Lord;
The only safety that I see,
    Is Jesus' holy word.

Master.

My Servant, follow Jesus now,
    Our great victorious King;
Who governs all both high and low,
    And searches things within.

Servant.

Dear Master, I will follow thee,
    When praying to our King;
It is the Lamb I plainly see,
    Invites the sinner in.

Master.

My Servant, we are sinners all,
    But follow after grace;
I pray that God would bless thy soul,
    And fill thy heart with grace.

Servant.

Dear Master, I shall follow then,
    The voice of my great King;
As standing on some distant land,
    Inviting sinners in.

Master.

My servant, we must all appear,
    And follow then our King;
For sure he'll stand where sinners are,
    To take true converts in.

Servant.

Dear Master, now if Jesus calls,
    And sends his summons in;
We'll follow saints and angels all,
    And come unto our King.

Master.

My servant, now come pray to God,
    Consider well his call;
Strive to obey his holy word,
    That Christ may love us all.

A Line on the Present War.

Servant.

Dear Master, now it is a time,
    A time of great distress;
We'll follow after things divine,
    And pray for happiness.

Master.

Then will the happy day appear,
    That virtue shall increase;
Lay up the sword and drop the spear,
    And Nations seek for peace.

Servant.

Then shall we see the happy end,
    Tho' still in some distress;
That distant foes shall act like friends,
    And leave their wickedness.

Master.

We pray that God would give us grace,
　　And make us humble too;
Let ev'ry Nation seek for peace,
　　And virtue make a show.

Servant.

Then we shall see the happy day,
　　That virtue is in power;
Each holy act shall have its sway,
　　Extend from shore to shore.

Master.

This is the work of God's own hand,
　　We see by precepts given;
To relieve distress and save the land,
　　Must be the pow'r of heav'n.

Servant.

Now glory be unto our God,
　　Let ev'ry nation sing;
Strive to obey his holy word,
　　That Christ may take them in.

Master.

Where endless joys shall never cease,
　　Blest Angels constant sing;
The glory of their God increase,
　　Hallelujahs to their King.

Servant.

Thus the Dialogue shall end,
　　Strive to obey the word;
When ev'ry Nation acts like friends,
　　Shall be the sons of God.

Believe me now, my Christian friends,
　　Believe your friend call'd Hammon:
You cannot to your God attend,
　　And serve the God of Mammon.

If God is pleased by his own hand
　　To relieve distresses here;
And grant a peace throughout the* land,
　　'Twill be a happy year.

'Tis God alone can give us peace;
　　It's not the pow'r of man:
When virtuous pow'r shall increase,
　　'Twill beautify the land.

Then shall we rejoice and sing
　　By pow'r of virtue's word,
Come, sweet Jesus, heav'nly King,
　　Thou art the Son of God.

When virtue comes in bright array,
　　Discovers ev'ry sin;
We see the dangers of the day,
　　And fly unto our King.

Now glory be unto our God,
　　All praise be justly given;
Let ev'ry soul obey his word,
　　And seek the joy of heav'n.　Finis.

* *The* is repeated in original version; obviously a printer's error.

PHILLIS WHEATLEY

PHILLIS WHEATLEY was born very probably in 1753. She was first seen in America as a delicate little girl on a slave ship that came from Senegal to Boston in 1761. Mrs. Susannah Wheatley, wife of John Wheatley, a tailor, desired to have a girl whom she might train to be a special servant for her declining years, and she was attracted by the bright eye and the gentle demeanor of the child that had just come from Africa. The young slave was purchased, taken home, and given the name Phillis. When she began to be known to the world she used also the name of the family to which she belonged.

Mrs. Wheatley was a woman of unusual piety and culture, and King Street on which she lived was then as noted for its residences as it is now, under the name of State Street, famous for its banking houses. When Phillis entered the home the family consisted of four persons, Mr. and Mrs. Wheatley, their son Nathaniel, and their daughter Mary. Nathaniel and Mary were twins, born May 4, 1743. There were three other children, Sarah, John, and Susannah, but all of these died in early youth. Mary Wheatley accordingly was the only daughter of the family that Phillis knew to any extent, and she was eighteen years old when her mother brought the child to the house. Observing the ease with which the young attendant assimilated knowledge, Mrs. Wheatley and her daughter began to teach her, giving special attention to instruction in the Scriptures and in morals. Within sixteen months from the time of her arrival in Boston Phillis was able to read fluently the most difficult parts of the Bible, and in course of time, thanks to the tutelage of Mary Wheatley, her learning consisted of a little astronomy, some ancient and modern geography, a little ancient history, and an appreciative acquaintance with the most important Latin classics. Pope's translation of Homer was her favorite English classic, and before long she too began to make verses. More and more she came to be regarded by Mrs. Wheatley as a daughter or companion rather than as a slave; and, as she proved to have a talent for writing occasional verse, she became "a kind of poet-laureate in the domestic circles of Boston." In her room she was specially permitted to have heat and a light, because her constitution was delicate, and in order that she might write down her thoughts as they came to her rather than trust them to memory.

Such for some years was the life of Phillis Wheatley. In 1770 appeared the first of her productions to be seen in print, "A Poem, by Phillis, a Negro Girl, in Boston, On the Death of the Reverend George Whitefield." This was addressed to the Countess of Huntingdon, whom Whitefield had served as chaplain, and to the orphan children of Georgia whom he had befriended. Early in the next year came to the young writer her first real sorrow; on January 31 Mary Wheatley left the old home to become the wife of the Reverend John Lathrop, pastor of the Second Church in Boston. On August 18 of this year, 1771, "Phillis, the servant of Mr. Wheatley" became a communicant of the Old South Meeting House, it being said later that "her membership in Old South was an exception to the rule that slaves were not baptized into the church." Meanwhile her health began to fail, and by the spring of 1773 her condition was such as to give her friends genuine concern. The family physician advised that she try the air of the sea. As Nathaniel Wheatley was just then going to England on business, it was decided that she should go in his care. The two sailed in May. Not desiring to have her young friend appear in England as a slave, however, Mrs. Wheatley saw to it that before she left she was formally manumitted.

The poem on Whitefield served well as an introduction to the Countess of Huntingdon. Through the influence of this noblewoman the young author met other ladies, and now it was that a peculiar gift of hers shone to advantage. To the recommendations of a strange history, ability to write verses, and the solicitude of friends, she added the art of brilliant conversation. Presents were showered upon her. One that has been preserved is a copy of the 1770 Glasgow folio edition of *Paradist Lost*, given by Brook Watson, Lord Mayor of London. It happened, however, that the young visitor had not arrived at the most fashionable season, and the ladies of the circle of the Countess of Huntingdon desired that she remain long enough to be presented at the court of George III. Mrs. Wheatley, however, had become ill; she longed for her old companion; and Phillis could not be persuaded to delay her return. Before she left England, however, arrangements were made for the publication of her book, *Poems on Various Subjects, Religious and Moral.* While the little volume does not of course contain the later scattered poems, it is the only collection ever brought together by Phillis Wheatley, and the book by which she is known.

In 1775, while the siege of Boston was in progress, the young author wrote a letter to General George Washington enclosing a complimentary poem. Washington replied graciously and later received her very courteously at his headquarters in Cambridge. This was an event not soon to be forgotten. In general, however, it may be said that the visit to England marked the highest point in the career of Phillis Wheatley, and that after it her piety and faith were put to their severest test. Mrs. Wheatley died in March, 1774, and the old home was finally broken up by the death of Mr. John Wheatley in March, 1778. In September of the latter year Mary Wheatley, Mrs. Lathrop, also died. Nathaniel was living abroad. Meanwhile, in April, Phillis was persuaded to become the wife of John Peters, whom she described in a letter to a friend as "a very clever man, complaisant and agreeable." It was not long, however, before she realized that she was married to a ne'er-do-well at a time when even an industrious man found it hard to make a living. Failing health, increasing poverty, and the course of the war made her more and more uncertain as to the future, and she finally earned her board by drudgery in a cheap lodging-house. She died December 5, 1784. Two of her three children had died before her, and the third slept with its mother in death.

As has been suggested, the chief literary model of Phillis Wheatley was Alexander Pope; but one must not forget in this connection the precision that she gained from direct acquaintance with the greater Latin authors. The ease with which she was able to chisel the heroic couplet when no more than sixteen or eighteen years of age, was amazing; and the diction—"fleecy care," "tuneful nine," "feather'd vengeance"—is constantly in the pseudo-classic tradition. What one misses in the poems of Phillis Wheatley is the personal note. Like others who were of the school of Pope, she was objective in her point of view, and of all the elegies that she wrote hardly one is a genuine lyric. She was intensely religious, however, and if she had come on the scene forty years later, when the romantic writers had given a new tone to English poetry, she might have been much greater; but even with this speculation we have to remember that she ever exercised restraint, with a sense of the fitness of things.

At the time when she appeared Phillis Wheatley was regarded as a prodigy. Her vogue, however, was more than temporary, and the 1793, 1802, and 1816 editions of her poems found ready sale. If after 1816 interest in her work declined, it greatly revived at the time of the anti-slavery agitation, when anything indicating ability on the part of the Negro was received with eagerness. When then Margaretta Matilda Odell, a descendant of the Wheatley family, republished *Poems on Various Subjects* with a memoir in 1834, there was such a demand for the book that two more editions were called for within the next four years. Within the last two decades there has been further interest, with new editing and critical appraisal.

The bibliography of Phillis Wheatley is now a study in itself. See *The Negro in Literature and Art,* by the present editor, third edition, New York, 1930, pp. 219-221, and *Phillis Wheatley: A Critical Attempt and a Bibliography of her Writings,* by Charles Fred Heartman, New York, 1915. For further study of life and work see *The Negro in Literature and Art,* pp. 15-37; also *The Negro Author,* by Vernon Loggins, New York, 1931, pp. 16-29. Importance attaches to the *Letters,* edited by Charles Deane, Boston, 1864, and along with this work to *Phillis Wheatley: Poems and Letters,* edited by Charles Fred Heartman, New York, 1915. Most of the letters that are preserved were written to Obour Tanner, a friend living in Newport, R. I. Evidence for 1753 as the birth year seems fairly adequate. The poem on Whitefield published in 1770 said on the title-page that the author was seventeen years old, and the formal notice of her death in 1784 said that she was thirty-one. The copy of *Paradise Lost* given by the Lord Mayor of London, is now in the library of Harvard University. At the top of one of the first pages, in the handwriting of Phillis Wheatley herself, are the words: "Mr. Brook Watson to Phillis Wheatley, London, July, 1773." At the bottom of the same page, in the handwriting of another, probably Dudley L. Pickman, are the words: "This book was given by Brook Watson formerly Lord Mayor of London to Phillis Wheatley & after her death was sold in payment of her husband's debts. It is now presented to the Library of Harvard University at Cambridge, by Dudley L. Pickman of Salem. March, 1824." In this connection it will be observed that the poet spelled her first name P-h-i-l-l-i-s. The poem "His Excellency General Washington" first appeared in the *Pennsylvania Magazine* for April, 1776, while Thomas Paine was editor. "Liberty and Peace" was first issued in Boston in 1784 as a leaflet of four pages. From an advertisement in *The Evening Post and the General Advertiser* of Boston it appears that there was a proposal to bring out a second volume by Phillis Wheatley, this to be dedicated to Benjamin Franklin. The war was on, however, subscriptions were slow, and the plan did not materialize. While the titles of thirty-three poems are given, only two of those mentioned are preserved to us.

Of the poems given below, all except the last two are from *Poems on Various Subjects* (London, 1773). "To the University of Cambridge, in New England," which begins with a note of apology and which internal evidence would place two or three years before most of the other poems, is one of the few pieces in which the author touches upon her own experience. A similar note had been struck in the juvenile poem, "On Being Brought from Africa to America," and it is also in the one "To the Right Honorable William, Earl of Dartmouth." "An Hymn to the Morning" and "An Hymn to the Evening" especially represent the pseudo-classic influence, while "On Imagination" is not only the best in this vein but probably from any standpoint the strongest poem in the book. "Niobe in Distress for her Children Slain by

Apollo" represents the interest in the Latin classics; and "To S. M., a Young African Painter, on Seeing his Works" is, with the exception of the lines "On Being Brought from Africa to America," the only poem in the book prompted by a Negro subject. Except in the title, however, even this contains not a single reference to race. Phillis Wheatley lived more than a hundred years before the Negro as such was to receive serious literary treatment, and for the time being she could only follow such models as she knew.

The text of the selections from *Poems on Various Subjects* is in general that of the 1773 edition with the spelling and the punctuation of those of 1834 and 1835. The first edition uses such forms as *sooth* for *soothe, out-strecht* for *outstretched, deign'd* for *deigned, dies* for *dyes,* and *shall thou dread* for *shalt thou dread;* and the punctuation is especially faulty. On such points the later editions are better. At the same time the 1834, 1835, and some other late editions are not impeccable, as they make too frequent use of the exclamation point; and some of them unfortunately omit line 17 of the poem "To the University of Cambridge, in New England." The present readings also keep such forms as *show'rs, flow'ry,* and *ethereal* in the first edition. The text of "His Excellency George Washington" is that of the *Pennsylvania Magazine,* vol. II, p. 193 (April, 1776). "Liberty and Peace," originally printed in Boston, 1784, was later made more accessible by inclusion in Duyckinck's *Cyclopaedia of American Literature,* New York, 1855.

To the University of Cambridge, in New England

While an intrinsic ardor prompts to write,
The Muses promise to assist my pen.
'T was not long since I left my native shore,
The land of errors and Egyptian gloom:
Father of mercy! 't was thy gracious hand
Brought me in safety from those dark abodes.

Students, to you 'tis given to scan the heights
Above, to traverse the ethereal space,
And mark the systems of revolving worlds.
Still more, ye sons of science, ye receive
The blissful news by messengers from heaven,
How Jesus' blood for your redemption flows.
See him, with hands outstretched upon the cross!
Immense compassion in his bosom glows;
He hears revilers, nor resents their scorn.
What matchless mercy in the Son of God!
When the whole human race by sin had fall'n,
He deigned to die, that they might rise again,
And share with him, in the sublimest skies,
Life without death, and glory without end.

Improve your privileges while they stay,
Ye pupils; and each hour redeem, that bears
Or good or bad report of you to heaven.
Let sin, that baneful evil to the soul,
By you be shunned; nor once remit your guard:
Suppress the deadly serpent in its egg.
Ye blooming plants of human race divine,
An Ethiop tells you, 't is your greatest foe;
Its transient sweetness turns to endless pain,
And in immense perdition sinks the soul.

On the Death of the Rev. Mr. George Whitefield

Hail, happy saint! on thine immortal throne,
Possest of glory, life, and bliss unknown:
We hear no more the music of thy tongue;
Thy wonted auditories cease to throng.
Thy sermons in unequalled accents flowed,

And ev'ry bosom with devotion glowed;
Thou didst, in strains of eloquence refined,
Inflame the heart, and captivate the mind.
Unhappy, we the setting sun deplore,
So glorious once, but ah! it shines no more.

Behold the prophet in his towering flight!
He leaves the earth for heaven's unmeasured height,
And worlds unknown receive him from our sight.
There Whitefield wings with rapid course his way,
And sails to Zion through vast seas of day.
Thy prayers, great saint, and thine incessant cries,
Have pierced the bosom of thy native skies.
Thou, moon, hast seen, and all the stars of light,
How he has wrestled with his God by night.
He prayed that grace in ev'ry heart might dwell;
He longed to see America excel;
He charged its youth that ev'ry grace divine
Should with full lustre in their conduct shine.
That Saviour, which his soul did first receive,
The greatest gift that ev'n a God can give,
He freely offered to the numerous throng,
That on his lips with list'ning pleasure hung.

"Take him, ye wretched, for your only good,
"Take him, ye starving sinners, for your food;
"Ye thirsty, come to this life-giving stream,
"Ye preachers, take him for your joyful theme;
"Take him, my dear Americans," he said,
"Be your complaints on his kind bosom laid:
"Take him, ye Africans, he longs for you;
"Impartial Saviour is his title due:
"Washed in the fountain of redeeming blood,
"You shall be sons, and kings, and priests to God."

Great Countess,* we Americans revere
Thy name, and mingle in thy grief sincere;
New England deeply feels, the orphans mourn,
Their more than father will no more return.
    But though arrested by the hand of death,
Whitefield no more exerts his lab'ring breath,
Yet let us view him in th' eternal skies,
Let ev'ry heart to this bright vision rise;
While the tomb, safe, retains its sacred trust,
Till life divine reanimates his dust.

To the Right Honorable William, Earl of Dartmouth, His Majesty's Secretary of State for North America

Hail, happy day! when, smiling like the morn,
Fair Freedom rose, New England to adorn:
The northern clime, beneath her genial ray,
Dartmouth! congratulates thy blissful sway;
Elate with hope, her race no longer mourns,
Each soul expands, each grateful bosom burns,
While in thine hand with pleasure we behold
The silken reins, and Freedom's charms unfold.
Long lost to realms beneath the northern skies,
She shines supreme, while hated faction dies:
Soon as appeared the goddess long desired,
Sick at the view she languished and expired;
Thus from the splendors of the morning light
The owl in sadness seeks the caves of night.

No more, America, in mournful strain,
Of wrongs and grievance unredressed complain;
No longer shalt thou dread the iron chain

* The Countess of Huntingdon, to whom Mr. Whitefield was chaplain.

Which wanton Tyranny, with lawless hand,
Had made, and with it meant t' enslave the land.

Should you, my lord, while you peruse my song,
Wonder from whence my love of Freedom sprung,
Whence flow these wishes for the common good,
By feeling hearts alone best understood,
I, young in life, by seeming cruel fate
Was snatched from Afric's fancied happy seat:
What pangs excruciating must molest,
What sorrows labor in my parent's breast!
Steeled was that soul, and by no misery moved,
That from a father seized his babe beloved:
Such, such my case. And can I then but pray
Others may never feel tyrannic sway?

For favors past, great Sir, our thanks are due,
And thee we ask thy favors to renew,
Since in thy power, as in thy will before,
To soothe the griefs which thou didst once deplore.
May heavenly grace the sacred sanction give
To all thy works, and thou forever live,
Not only on the wings of fleeting Fame,
Though praise immortal crowns the patriot's name,
But to conduct to heaven's refulgent fane,
May fiery coursers sweep th' ethereal plain,
And bear thee upwards to that blest abode,
Where, like the prophet, thou shalt find thy God.

An Hymn to the Morning

Attend my lays, ye ever honored Nine,
Assist my labors, and my strains refine;
In smoothest numbers pour the notes along,
For bright Aurora now demands my song.

Aurora hail! and all the thousand dies,
Which deck thy progress through the vaulted skies:
The morn awakes, and wide extends her rays,
On ev'ry leaf the gentle zephyr plays;
Harmonious lays the feathered race resume,
Dart the bright eye, and shake the painted plume.

Ye shady groves, your verdant bloom display,
To shield your poet from the burning day:
Calliope, awake the sacred lyre,
While thy fair sisters fan the pleasing fire.
The bowers, the gales, the variegated skies,
In all their pleasures in my bosom rise.

See in the east, th' illustrious king of day!
His rising radiance drives the shades away—
But oh! I feel his fervid beams too strong,
And scarce begun, concludes the abortive song.

An Hymn to the Evening

Soon as the sun forsook the eastern main,
The pealing thunder shook the heavenly plain;
Majestic grandeur! From the zephyr's wing,
Exhales the incense of the blooming spring.
Soft purl the streams, the birds renew their notes,
And through the air their mingled music floats.

Through all the heavens what beauteous dyes are
    spread!
But the west glories in the deepest red:
So may our breasts with ev'ry virtue glow,
The living temples of our God below!

Filled with the praise of him who gives the light,
And draws the sable curtains of the night,

Let placid slumbers soothe each weary mind,
At morn to wake, more heavenly, more refined;
So shall the labours of the day begin
More pure, more guarded from the snares of sin.

Night's leaden sceptre seals my drowsy eyes;
Then cease, my song, till fair Aurora rise.

On Imagination

Thy various works, imperial queen, we see;
How bright their forms! how decked with pomp by
        thee!
Thy wond'rous acts in beauteous order stand,
And all attest how potent is thine hand.

From Helicon's refulgent heights attend,
Ye sacred choir, and my attempts befriend:
To tell her glories with a faithful tongue,
Ye blooming graces, triumph in my song.
Now here, now there, the roving Fancy flies,
Till some loved object strikes her wand'ring eyes,
Whose silken fetters all the senses bind,
And soft captivity involves the mind.

Imagination! who can sing thy force?
Or who describe the swiftness of thy course?
Soaring through air to find the bright abode,
Th' empyreal palace of the thundering God,
We on thy pinions can surpass the wind,
And leave the rolling universe behind:
From star to star the mental optics rove,
Measure the skies, and range the realms above.
There in one view we grasp the mighty whole,
Or with new worlds amaze the unbounded soul.

Though Winter frowns, to Fancy's raptured eyes
The fields may flourish, and gay scenes arise;
The frozen deeps may burst their iron bands,
And bid their waters murmur o'er the sands.
Fair Flora may resume her fragrant reign,
And with her flow'ry riches deck the plain;
Sylvanus may diffuse his honours round,
And all the forests may with leaves be crowned;
Show'rs may descend, and dews their gems disclose,
And nectar sparkle on the blooming rose.

Such is thy power, nor are thine orders vain,
O thou, the leader of the mental train;
In full perfection all thy works are wrought,
And thine the sceptre o'er the realms of thought;
Before thy throne the subject-passions bow,
Of subject-passions sov'reign ruler Thou;
At thy command joy rushes on the heart,
And through the glowing veins the spirits dart.

Fancy might now her silken pinions try
To rise from earth, and sweep the expanse on high;
From Tithon's bed now might Aurora rise,
Her cheeks all glowing with celestial dyes,
While a pure stream of light o'erflows the skies.
The monarch of the day I might behold,
And all the mountains tipt with radiant gold,
But I reluctant leave the pleasing views,
Which Fancy dresses to delight the Muse;
Winter austere forbids me to aspire,
And northern tempests damp the rising fire;
They chill the tides of Fancy's flowing sea,*—
Cease then, my son, cease then th' unequal lay.

* In the eighteenth century the sound of *a* in a word like this was a common
pronunciation. In *The Rape of the Lock* (III, 7-8) Pope has the lines:
Here thou, great Anna! whom three realms obey,
Dost sometimes counsel take—and sometimes tea.

NIOBE IN DISTRESS FOR HER CHILDREN SLAIN BY APOLLO
From Ovid's Metamorphoses, Book 6th, and from a View
of the Painting of Mr. Richard Wilson.

Apollo's wrath, to man the dreadful spring
Of ills innum'rous, tuneful goddess, sing!
Thou who didst first the ideal pencil give,
And taught the painter in his works to live,
Inspire with glowing energy of thought
What Wilson painted, and what Ovid wrote.
Muse! lend thine aid, nor let me sue in vain,
Though last and meanest of the rhyming train!
Oh! guide my pen in lofty strains to show
The Phrygian queen, all beautiful in woe.

'Twas where Maeonia spreads her wide domain
Niobe dwelt, and held her potent reign:
See in her hand the regal sceptre shine,
The wealthy heir of Tantalus, divine,
He most distinguished by Dodonean Jove,
To approach the tables of the gods above:
Her grandsire Atlas, who with mighty pains
Th' ethereal axis on his neck sustains:
Her other grandsire on the throne on high
Rolls the loud pealing thunder thro' the sky.

Her spouse, Amphion, who from Jove too springs,
Divinely taught to sweep the sounding strings.

Seven sprightly sons the royal bed adorn,
Seven daughters, beauteous as the rising morn;
As when Aurora fills the ravished sight,
And decks the orient realms with rosy light,
From their bright eyes the living splendors play,
Nor can beholders bear the flashing ray.

Wherever, Niobe, thou turn'st thine eyes,
New beauties kindle and new joys arise!
But thou hadst far the happier mother proved,
If this fair offspring had been less beloved:
What if their charms exceed Aurora's teint,
No words could tell them, and no pencil paint;
Thy love, too vehement, hastens to destroy
Each blooming maid, and each celestial boy.

Now Manto comes, endued with mighty skill,
The past to explore, the future to reveal.
Through Thebes' wide streets Tiresia's daughter
    came,
Divine Latona's mandate to proclaim:
The Theban maids to hear the order ran,
When thus Maeonia's prophetess began:

"Go, Thebans! great Latona's will obey,
"And pious tribute at her altars pay:
"With rites divine, the Goddess be implored,
"Nor be her sacred offspring unadored."
Thus Manto spoke. The Theban maids obey,
And pious tribute to the Goddess pay.
The rich perfumes ascend the waving spires,
And altars blaze with consecrated fires;
The fair assembly moves with graceful air,
And leaves of laurel bind the flowing hair.

Niobe comes with all her royal race,
With charms unnumbered, and superior grace:
Her Phrygian garments of delightful hue,
Inwove with gold, refulgent to the view;
Beyond description beautiful, she moves
Like heavenly Venus, 'midst her smiles and loves.
She views around the supplicating train,

And shakes her graceful head with stern disdain,
Proudly she turns around her lofty eyes,
And thus reviles celestial deities:

"What madness drives the Theban ladies fair
"To give their incense to surrounding air?
"Say, why this new-sprung deity preferred?
"Why vainly fancy your petitions heard?
"Or say why Coeus' offspring is obeyed,
"While to my goddesship no tribute 's paid?
"For me no altars blaze with living fires,
"No bullock bleeds, no frankincense transpires,
"Though Cadmus' palace, not unknown to fame,
"And Phrygian nations all revere my name.
"Where'er I turn my eyes vast wealth I find.
"Lo! here an empress with a goddess joined.
"What! shall a Titaness be deified,
"To whom the spacious earth a couch denied?
"Nor heaven, nor earth, nor sea received your queen,
"Till pitying Delos took the wand'rer in.
"Round me what a large progeny is spread!
"No frowns of fortune has my soul to dread.
"What if indignant she decrease my train?
"More than Latona's number will remain.
"Then hence, ye Theban dames, hence haste away,
"No longer offerings to Latona pay;
"Regard the orders of Amphion's spouse,
"And take the leaves of laurel from your brows."

Niobe spoke. The Theban maids obeyed,
Their brows unbound, and left the rites unpaid.

The angry goddess heard, then silence broke
On Cynthus' summit, and indignant spoke:
"Phoebus! behold thy mother in disgrace,

"Who to no goddess yields the prior place,
"Except to Juno's self, who reigns above,
"The spouse and sister of the thundering Jove.
"Niobe, sprung from Tantalus, inspires
"Each Theban bosom with rebellious fires:
"No reason her imperious temper quells,
"But all her father in her tongue rebels;
"Wrap her own sons, for her blaspheming breath,
"Apollo! wrap them in the shades of death."

Latona ceased, and ardent thus replies
The God whose glory decks the expanded skies.

"Cease thy complaints; mine be the task assigned
"To punish and to scourge the rebel mind."

This Phoebe joined. They wing their instant
        flight;
Thebes trembled as th' immortal powers alight.
With clouds encompassed, glorious Phoebus stands,
The feathered vengeance quivering in his hands.

Near Cadmus' walls a plain extended lay,
Where Thebes' young princes passed in sport the
        day;
There the bold coursers bounded o'er the plains,
While their great masters held the golden reins.
Ismenus first, the racing pastime led,
And ruled the fury of his flying steed.
"Ah me!" he sudden cries, with shrieking breath,
While in his breast he feels the shaft of death;
He drops the bridle on his courser's mane,
Before his eyes in shadows swims the plain;
He, the first-born of great Amphion's bed,
Was struck the first, first mingled with the dead.

Then didst thou, Sipylus, the language hear
Of fate portentous whistling in the air;
As when th' impending storm the sailor sees,
He spreads his canvass to the favoring breeze;
So to thine horse thou gav'st the golden reins,
Gav'st him to rush impetuous o'er the plains:
But ah! a fatal shaft from Phoebus' hand
Smites through thy neck and sinks thee on the sand.

Two other brothers were at wrestling found,
And in their pastime clasped each other round:
A shaft that instant from Apollo's hand
Transfixed them both and stretched them on the
    sand:
Together they their cruel fate bemoaned,
Together languished and together groaned:
Together, too, the unbodied spirits fled,
And sought the gloomy mansions of the dead.

Alphenor saw, and trembling at the view,
Beat his torn breast, that changed its snowy hue.
He flies to raise them in a kind embrace;
A brother's fondness triumphs in his face:
Alphenor fails in this fraternal deed;
A dart despatched him (so the fates decreed):
Soon as the arrow left the deadly wound,
His issuing entrails smoked upon the ground.

What woes on blooming Damasichon wait!
His sighs portend his near impending fate.
Just where the well-made leg begins to be,
And the soft sinews form the supple knee,
The youth, sore wounded by the Delian god,
Attempts to extract the crime-avenging rod;
But while he strives the will of fate to avert,

Divine Apollo sends a second dart;
Swift through his throat the feathered mischief flies;
Bereft of sense, he drops his head and dies.
Young Ilioneus, the last, directs his prayer,
And cries, "My life, ye gods celestial, spare."
Apollo heard, and pity touched his heart,
But ah! too late, for he had sent the dart:
Thou, too, oh Ilioneus doomed to fall,
The fates refuse that arrow to recall.

On the swift wings of ever-flying Fame,
To Cadmus' palace soon the tidings came.
Niobe heard, and with indignant eyes
She thus expressed her anger and surprise:
"Why is such privilege to them allowed?
"Why thus insulted by the Delian god?
"Dwells there such mischief in the powers above?
"Why sleeps the vengeance of immortal Jove?"
For now Amphion, too, with grief oppressed,
Had plunged the deadly dagger in his breast.
Niobe now, less haughty than before,
With lofty head directs her steps no more.
She, who late told her pedigree divine,
And drove the Thebans from Latona's shrine,
How strangely changed! yet beautiful in woe,
She weeps, nor weeps unpitied by the foe.
On each pale corse the wretched mother, spread,
Lay overwhelmed with grief, and kissed her dead,
Then raised her arms, and thus, in accents slow,
"Be sated, cruel goddess, with my woe!
"If I've offended, let these streaming eyes,
"And let this seven-fold funeral suffice:
"Ah! take this wretched life you deign to save;
"With them I too am carried to the grave:

"Rejoice triumphant, my victorious foe,
"But show the cause from whence your triumphs
    flow.
"Though I unhappy mourn these children slain,
"Yet greater numbers to my lot remain."

She ceased, the bow-string twanged with awful sound,
Which struck with terror all th' assembly round,
Except the queen, who stood unmoved alone,
By her distresses more presumptuous grown.
Near the pale corses stood their sisters fair,
In sable vestures and dishevelled hair;
One, while she draws the fatal shaft away,
Faints, falls, and sickens in the light of day.
To soothe her mother, lo! another flies,
And blames the fury of the inclement skies,
And, while her words a filial pity show,
Struck dumb—indignant seeks the shades below.
Now from the fatal place, another flies,
Falls in her flight, and languishes and dies.
Another on her sister drops in death;
A fifth in trembling terror yields her breath;
While the sixth seeks some gloomy cave in vain,
Struck with the rest, and mingled with the slain.
One only daughter lives, and she the least;
The queen close clasped the daughter to her breast.
"Ye heavenly powers, ah! spare me one," she cried,
"Ah! spare me one," the vocal hills replied:
In vain she begs, the Fates her suit deny;
In her embrace she sees her daughter die.

*"The queen, of all her family bereft,
"Without or husband, son, or daughter left,
"Grew stupid at the shock. The passing air

* This verse to the end is the work of another hand. (Note in first edition.)

"Made no impression on her stiff'ning hair.
"The blood forsook her face: amidst the flood
"Poured from her cheeks, quite fixed her eye-balls
    stood.
"Her tongue, her palate, both obdurate grew,
"Her curdled veins no longer motion knew;
"The use of neck, and arms, and feet was gone,
"And even her bowels hardened into stone:
"A marble statue now the queen appears,
"But from the marble steal the silent tears."

To S. M.,* A Young African Painter On Seeing His Works

To show the lab'ring bosom's deep intent,
And thought in living characters to paint,
When first thy pencil did those beauties give,
And breathing figures learnt from thee to live,
How did those prospects give my soul delight,
A new creation rushing on my sight!
Still, wondrous youth! each noble path pursue;
On deathless glories fix thine ardent view:
Still may the painter's and the poet's fire,
To aid thy pencil and thy verse conspire!
And may the charms of each seraphic theme
Conduct thy footsteps to immortal fame!
High to the blissful wonders of the skies
Elate thy soul, and raise thy wishful eyes.
Thrice happy, when exalted to survey
That splendid city, crowned with endless day,
Whose twice six gates on radiant hinges ring:
Celestial Salem blooms in endless spring.
Calm and serene thy moments glide along,

* Scipio Moorhead.

And may the muse inspire each future song!
Still, with the sweets of contemplation blessed,
May peace with balmy wings your soul invest!
But when these shades of time are chased away,
And darkness ends in everlasting day,
On what seraphic pinions shall we move,
And view the landscapes in the realms above!
There shall thy tongue in heavenly murmurs flow,
And there my muse with heavenly transport glow;
No more to tell of Damon's tender sighs,
Or rising radiance of Aurora's eyes;
For nobler themes demand a nobler strain,
And purer language on the ethereal plain.
Cease, gentle Muse! the solemn gloom of night
Now seals the fair creation from my sight.

His Excellency General Washington

Celestial choir! enthron'd in realms of light,
Columbia's scenes of glorious toils I write.
While freedom's cause her anxious breast alarms,
She flashes dreadful in refulgent arms.
See mother earth her offspring's fate bemoan,
And nations gaze at scenes before unknown!
See the bright beams of heaven's revolving light
Involved in sorrows and the veil of night!
The goddess comes, she moves divinely fair,
Olive and laurel binds her golden hair:
Wherever shines this native of the skies,
Unnumber'd charms and recent graces rise.
Muse! bow propitious while my pen relates
How pour her armies through a thousand gates;
As when Eolus heaven's fair face deforms,
Enwrapped in tempest and a night of storms;

Astonish'd ocean feels the wild uproar,
The refluent surges beat the sounding shore,
Or thick as leaves in Autumn's golden reign,
Such, and so many, moves the warrior's train.
In bright array they seek the work of war,
Where high unfurl'd the ensign waves in air.
Shall I to Washington their praise recite?
Enough thou know'st them in the fields of fight.
Thee, first in place and honours,—we demand
The grace and glory of thy martial band.
Fam'd for thy valour, for thy virtues more,
Here every tongue thy guardian aid implore!
One century scarce performed its destin'd round,
When Gallic powers Columbia's fury found;
And so may you, whoever dares disgrace
The land of freedom's heaven-defended race!
Fix'd are the eyes of nations on the scales,
For in their hopes Columbia's arm prevails.
Anon Britannia droops the pensive head,
While round increase the rising hills of dead.
Ah! cruel blindness to Columbia's state!
Lament thy thirst of boundless power too late.
Proceed, great chief, with virtue on thy side,
Thy every action let the goddess guide.
A crown, a mansion, and a throne that shine,
With gold unfading, *Washington*, be thine.

LIBERTY AND PEACE

Lo! freedom comes. Th' prescient muse foretold,
All eyes th' accomplish'd prophecy behold:
Her port describ'd, "She moves divinely fair,
Olive and laurel bind her golden hair."
She, the bright progeny of Heaven, descends,

And every grace her sovereign step attends;
For now kind Heaven, indulgent to our prayer,
In smiling peace resolves the din of war.
Fix'd in Columbia her illustrious line,
And bids in thee her future councils shine.
To every realm her portals open'd wide,
Receives from each the full commercial tide.
Each art and science now with rising charms,
Th' expanding heart with emulation warms.
E'en great Britannia sees with dread surprise,
And from the dazzling splendors turns her eyes.
Britain, whose navies swept th' Atlantic o'er,
And thunder sent to every distant shore;
E'en thou, in manners cruel as thou art,
The sword resign'd, resume the friendly part.
For Gallia's power espous'd Columbia's cause,
And new-born Rome shall give Britannia laws,
Nor unremember'd in the grateful strain,
Shall princely Louis' friendly deed remain;
The generous prince th' impending vengeance eyes,
Sees the fierce wrong and to the rescue flies.
Perish that thirst of boundless power, that drew
On Albion's head the curse to tyrants due.
But thou appeas'd submit to Heaven's decree,
That bids this realm of freedom rival thee.
Now sheathe the sword that bade the brave atone
With guiltless blood for madness not their own.
Sent from th' enjoyment of their native shore,
Ill-fated—never to behold her more.
From every kingdom on Europa's coast
Throng'd various troops, their glory, strength, and
        boast.
With heart-felt pity fair Hibernia saw
Columbia menac'd by the Tyrant's law:

On hostile fields fraternal arms engage,
And mutual deaths, all dealt with mutual rage:
The muse's ear hears mother earth deplore
Her ample surface smoke with kindred gore:
The hostile field destroys the social ties,
And everlasting slumber seals their eyes.
Columbia mourns, the haughty foes deride,
Her treasures plunder'd and her towns destroy'd:
Witness how Charlestown's curling smokes arise,
In sable columns to the clouded skies.
The ample dome, high-wrought with curious toil,
In one sad hour the savage troops despoil.
Descending peace the power of war confounds;
From every tongue celestial peace resounds:
As from the east th' illustrious king of day,
With rising radiance drives the shades away,
So freedom comes array'd with charms divine,
And in her train commerce and plenty shine.
Britannia owns her independent reign,
Hibernia, Scotia, and the realms of Spain;
And great Germania's ample coast admires
The generous spirit that Columbia fires.
Auspicious Heaven shall fill with fav'ring gales,
Where'er Columbia spreads her swelling sails:
To every realm shall peace her charms display,
And heavenly freedom spread her golden ray.

GUSTAVUS VASSA

GUSTAVUS VASSA was not, strictly speaking, an American Negro; nevertheless he spent considerable time in bondage in this country, and his book was so frequently reprinted in the United States that he might well be considered in this connection. He was born in 1745 in Benin, a country west of the main channel of the lower Niger, forming part of Southern Nigeria. When he was eleven years of age, as we are told in the selection below, he was seized by kidnappers and after various adventures placed on a ship to be taken to America. He served for a while on a plantation in Virginia; then he was with a British naval officer, who helped him to get an education; and at length he worked on plantations and on small vessels going to the West Indies as the property of a Philadelphia merchant. This last master was considerate, helped him to save money to purchase his freedom, and otherwise acted as his friend and adviser. Later Vassa traveled extensively as a ship's steward, was converted to Methodism, and settled in England to engage in antislavery effort. In 1790 he presented to Parliament a petition for the suppression of the slave trade. He died about 1801.

The Interesting Narrative of the Life of Oloudah Equiano, or Gustavus Vassa first appeared in two volumes in London in 1789. From a stilted introductory flourish and a formal argument near the close it appears that the author received some editorial assistance, and it is highly improbable that he selected the laudatory title. The heart of the work, however, is his own, and his narrative has a continuous flow, an unaffected style, and a pictorial quality that not only carry conviction but that actually enthrall the reader. The book was exceedingly successful; within five years it was in the eighth edition. Its very ingenuousness gave power to its human appeal. To an edition issued at Halifax in 1813 was added as an appendix *Poems on Various Subjects*, by Phillis Wheatley.

Kidnapping and Enslavement

(Being Chapter II of *The Interesting Narrative*)

I hope the reader will not think I have trespassed on his patience in introducing myself to him, with some account of the manners and customs of my country. They had been implanted in me with great care, and made an impression on my mind which time could not erase, and which all the adversity and variety of fortune I have since experienced served only to rivet and record; for, whether the love of one's country be real or imaginary, or a lesson of reason, or an instinct of nature, I still look back with pleasure on the first scenes of my life, though that pleasure has been for the most part mingled with sorrow.

I have already acquainted the reader with the time and place of my birth. My father, besides many slaves, had a numerous family, of which seven lived to grow up, including myself and a sister, who was the only daughter. As I was the youngest of the sons, I became, of course, the greatest favorite with my mother, and was always with her; and she used to take particular pains to form my mind. I was trained up from my earliest years in the arts of agriculture and war: my daily exercise was shooting and throwing javelins; and my mother adorned me with emblems, after the manner of our greatest warriors. In this way I grew up till I was turned the age of eleven, when an end was put to my happiness in the following manner:—Generally, when the grown people in the neighborhood were gone far in the fields to labour, the children assembled together in some of the neighbors' premises to play; and commonly some of us used to get up a tree to look out for any assailant or kidnapper that might come upon us; for they sometimes took those opportunities of our parents' absence, to attack and carry off as many as they could seize. One day, as I was watching at the top of a tree in our yard, I saw one of those people come into the yard of our next neighbor but one, to kidnap, there being many stout young people in it. Immediately, on this, I gave the alarm of the rogue, and he was surrounded by the stoutest of them, who entangled him with cords, so that he could not escape till some of the grown people came and secured him. But alas! ere long, it was my fate to be thus attacked, and to be carried off, when none of our grown people were nigh. One day, when all our people were gone out to their works as usual, and only I and my dear sister were left to mind the house, two men and a woman got over our walls, and in a moment seized us both; and without giving us time to cry out, or make resistance, they stopped our mouths and ran off with us into the nearest wood. Here they tied our hands, and continued to carry us as far as they could, till night came on, when we reached a small house, where the robbers halted for refreshment, and spent the night. We were then unbound, but were unable to take any food; and, being quite overpowered by fatigue and grief, our only relief was some sleep, which allayed our misfortune for a short time. The next morning we left the house, and continued traveling all the day. For a long time we had kept the woods, but at last we came into a road which I believed I knew. I now had some hopes of being delivered; for we had advanced but a little way when I discovered some people at a distance, on which I began to cry out for their assistance; but my cries had no other effect than to make them tie me faster and stop my mouth, and then they put me into a large sack. They also stopped my sister's mouth and tied her hands; and in this manner we proceeded till we were out of the sight of these people.—When we went to rest the following night they offered us some victuals, but we refused them; and the only comfort we had was in being in one another's arms all that night, and bathing each other with our

tears. But alas! we were soon deprived of even the small comfort of weeping together. The next day proved a day of
greater sorrow than I had yet experienced; for my sister and I
were then separated, while we lay clasped in each other's
arms: it was in vain that we besought them not to part us; she
was torn from me, and immediately carried away, while I was
left in a state of distraction not to be described. I cried and
grieved continually; and for several days did not eat any
thing but what they forced into my mouth. At length, after
many days traveling, during which I had often changed masters, I got into the hands of a chieftain, in a very pleasant
country. This man had two wives and some children, and
they all used me extremely well, and did all they could to
comfort me; particularly the first wife, who was something
like my mother. Although I was a great many days journey
from my father's house, yet these people spoke exactly the
same language with us. This first master of mine, as I may
call him, was a smith, and my principal employment was working his bellows, which was the same kind as I had seen in my
vicinity. They were in some respects not unlike the stoves
here in gentlemen's kitchens; and were covered over with
leather; and in the middle of that leather a stick was fixed,
and a person stood up, and worked it, in the same manner as
is done to pump water out of a cask with a hand pump.
I believe it was gold he worked, for it was of a lovely bright
yellow colour, and was worn by the women on their wrists
and ancles. I was there I suppose about a month, and they at
last used to trust me some little distance from the house.
This liberty I used in embracing every opportunity to inquire
the way to my own home: and I also sometimes, for the same
purpose, went with the maidens, in the cool of the evenings,
to bring pitchers of water from the springs for the use of
the house. I had also remarked where the sun rose in the
morning, and set in the evening, as I had travelled along;

and I had observed that my father's house was towards the rising of the sun. I therefore determined to seize the first opportunity of making my escape, and to shape my course for that quarter; for I was quite oppressed and weighed down by grief after my mother and friends; and my love of liberty, ever great, was strengthened by the mortifying circumstance of not daring to eat with the free-born children, although I was mostly their companion.—While I was projecting my escape one day, an unlucky event happened, which quite disconcerted my plan, and put an end to my hopes. I used to be sometimes employed in assisting an elderly woman slave to cook and take care of the poultry; and one morning while I was feeding some chickens, I happened to toss a small pebble at one of them, which hit it on the middle, and directly killed it. The old slave, having soon after missed the chicken, inquired after it; and on my relating the accident, (for I told her the truth, because my mother would never suffer me to tell a lie), she flew into a violent passion, threatened that I should suffer for it; and, my master being out, she immediately went and told her mistress what I had done. This alarmed me very much, and I expected an instant flogging, which to me was uncommonly dreadful; for I had seldom been beaten at home. I therefore resolved to fly; and accordingly I ran into a thicket that was hard by, and hid myself in the bushes. Soon afterwards my mistress and the slave returned, and, not seeing me, they searched all the house, but not finding me, and I not making answer when they called to me, they thought I had run away, and the whole neighborhood was raised in the pursuit of me. In that part of the country (as well as ours) the houses and villages were skirted with woods or shrubberies, and the bushes were so thick, that a man could readily conceal himself in them, so as to elude the strictest search. The neighbors continued the whole day looking for me, and several times many of them came within a few yards of the place where I lay hid. I expected every moment, when I heard a rustling among the trees, to be found out, and punished by my master; but they never discovered me, though they were often so near that I even heard their conjectures as they were looking about for me; and I now learned from them that any attempt to return home would be hopeless. Most of them supposed I had fled towards home; but the distance was so great, and the way so intricate, that they thought I could never reach it, and that I should be lost in the woods. When I heard this I was seized with a violent panic, and abandoned myself to despair. Night too began to approach, and aggravated all my fears. I had before entertained hopes of getting home, and had determined when it should be dark to make the attempt; but I was now convinced that it was fruitless, and began to consider that, if possibly I could escape all other animals, I could not those of the human kind; and that, not knowing the way, I must perish in the woods.—Thus was I like the hunted deer:

—"Ev'ry leaf, and ev'ry whisp'ring breath
"Convey'd a foe, and ev'ry foe a death."

I heard frequent rustlings among the leaves; and being pretty sure they were snakes, I expected every instant to be stung by them.—This increased my anguish; and the horror of my situation became now quite insupportable. I at length quitted the thicket, very faint and hungry, for I had not eaten or drank anything all the day, and crept to my master's kitchen, from whence I set out at first, and which was an open shed, and laid myself down in the ashes with an anxious wish for death to relieve me from all my pains. I was scarcely awake in the morning, when the old woman slave, who was the first up, came to light the fire, and saw me in the fireplace. She was very much surprised to see me, and could scarcely believe her own eyes. She now promised to intercede for me, and went for her master, who soon after came, and having lightly reprimanded me, ordered me to be taken care of, and not ill treated.

Soon after this my master's only daughter and child by his first wife sickened and died, which affected him so much that for some time he was almost frantic, and really would have killed himself, had he not been watched and prevented. However, in a small time afterwards he recovered and I was again sold. I was now carried to the left of the sun's rising, through many dreary wastes and dismal woods, amidst the hideous roaring of wild beasts.—The people I was sold to used to carry me very often, when I was tired, either on their shoulders or on their backs. I saw many convenient well-built sheds along the road, at proper distances, to accommodate the merchants and travellers, who lay in those buildings along with their wives, who often accompany them; and they always go well armed.

From the time I left my own nation I always found somebody that understood me till I came to the sea coast. The languages of different nations did not totally differ, nor were they so copious as those of the Europeans, particularly the English. They were therefore easily learned; and while I was journeying thus through Africa, I acquired two or three different tongues. In this manner I had been travelling for a considerable time, when one evening to my great surprise, whom should I see brought to the house where I was but my dear sister? As soon as she saw me she gave a loud shriek, and ran into my arms. I was quite overpowered: neither of us could speak, but, for a considerable time, clung to each other in mutual embraces, unable to do anything but weep. Our meeting affected all who saw us; and indeed I must acknowledge, in honour of those sable destroyers of human rights, that I never met with any ill treatment, or saw

any offered to their slaves, except tying them, when necessary to keep them from running away. When these people
knew we were brother and sister, they indulged us to be
together; and the man, to whom I supposed we belonged,
lay with us, he in the middle, while she and I held one
another by the hands across his breast all night; and thus
for awhile we forgot our misfortunes in the joy of being
together; but even this small comfort was soon to have an
end; for scarcely had the fatal morning appeared, when she
was again torn from me for ever! I was now more miserable, if possible, than before. The small relief which her
presence gave me from pain was gone, and the wretchedness
of my situation was redoubled by my anxiety after her fate,
and my apprehensions lest her sufferings should be greater
than mine, when I could not be with her to alleviate them.
Yes, thou dear partner of my childish sports! thou sharer
of my joys and sorrows! happy should I have ever esteemed
myself to encounter every misery for you, and to procure
your freedom by the sacrifice of my own! Though you were
early forced from my arms, your image has been always
rivetted in my heart, from which neither *time nor fortune*
have been able to remove it: so that, while the thoughts of
your suffering have dampened my prosperity, they have
mingled with adversity and increased its bitterness.—To that
Heaven which protects the weak from the strong, I commit
the care of your innocence and virtues, if they have not already
received their full reward, and if your youth and delicacy
have not long since fallen victims to the violence of the
African trader, the pestilential stench of a Guinea ship, the
seasoning in the European colonies, or the lash and lust of a
brutal and unrelenting overseer.

I did not long remain after my sister. I was again sold,
and carried through a number of places, till after travelling
a considerable time, I came to a town called Tinmah, in the

most beautiful country I had yet seen in Africa. It was extremely rich, and there were many rivulets which flowed through it, and supplied a large pond in the centre of the town, where the people washed. Here I first saw and tasted cocoa nuts, which I thought superior to any nuts I had ever tasted before; and the trees which were loaded were also interspersed among the houses, which had commodious shades adjoining, and were in the same manner as ours, the insides being neatly plastered and whitewashed. Here I also saw and tasted for the first time, sugar cane. Their money consisted of little white shells, the size of the finger nail. I was sold here for one hundred and seventy-two of them, by a merchant who lived and brought me there. I had been about two or three days at his house, when a wealthy widow, a neighbor of his, came there one evening, and brought with her an only son, a young gentleman about my own age and size. Here they saw me; and having taken a fancy to me, I was bought of the merchant, and went home with them. Her house and premises were situated close to one of those rivulets I have mentioned, and were the finest I ever saw in Africa: they were very extensive, and she had a number of slaves to attend her. The next day I was washed and perfumed, and when meal time came, I was led into the presence of my mistress, and ate and drank before her with her son. This filled me with astonishment; and I could scarce help expressing my surprise that the young gentleman should suffer me, who was bound, to eat with him who was free; and not only so, but that he would not at any time either eat or drink till I had taken first, because I was the eldest, which was agreeable to our custom. Indeed, everything here, and all their treatment of me, made me forget that I was a slave. The language of these people resembled ours so nearly, that we understood each other perfectly. They had also the same customs as we. There were likewise slaves daily to attend us, while my young master and I, with other boys, sported with our darts and bows and arrows, as I had been used to do at home. In this resemblance to my former happy state, I passed about two months; and I now began to think I was to be adopted into the family, and was beginning to be reconciled to my situation, and to forget by degrees my misfortunes, when all at once the delusion vanished; for, without the least previous knowledge, one morning early, while my dear master and companion was still asleep, I was awakened out of my reverie to fresh sorrow, and hurried away even amongst the uncircumcised.

Thus at the very moment I dreamed of the greatest happiness, I found myself most miserable; and it seemed as if fortune wished to give me this taste of joy only to render the reverse more poignant.—The change I now experienced, was as painful as it was sudden and unexpected. It was a change indeed, from a state of bliss to a scene which is inexpressible by me, as it discovered to me an element I had never before beheld, and till then had no idea of, and wherein such instances of hardship and cruelty occurred, as I can never reflect on but with horror.

All the nations and people I had hitherto passed through, resembled our own in their manners, customs and language; but I came at length to a country, the inhabitants of which differed from us in all those particulars. I was very much struck with this difference, especially when I came among a people who did not circumcise, and ate without washing their hands. They cooked also in iron pots, and had European cutlasses and cross bows, which were unknown to us, and fought with their fists among themselves. Their women were not so modest as ours, for they ate and drank, and slept with their men. But, above all, I was amazed to see no sacrifices or offerings among them. In some of these places the people ornamented themselves with scars, and likewise filed their teeth very sharp. They wanted sometimes to ornament me in the same manner, but I would not suffer them; hoping that I might some time be among a people who did not thus disfigure themselves, as I thought they did. At last I came to the banks of a large river which was covered with canoes, in which the people appeared to live with their household utensils, and provisions of all kinds. I was beyond measure astonished at this, as I had never before seen any water larger than a pond or a rivulet: and my surprise was mingled with no small fear when I was put into one of these canoes, and we began to paddle and move along the river. We continued going on thus till night, when we came to land, and made fires on the banks, each family by themselves; some dragged their canoes on shore, others stayed and cooked in theirs, and laid in them all night. Those on the land had mats, of which they made tents, some in the shape of little houses; in these we slept; and after the morning meal, we embarked again and proceeded as before. I was often very much astonished to see some of the women, as well as the men, jump into the water, dive to the bottom, come up again, and swim about.—Thus I continued to travel, sometimes by land, sometimes by water, through different countries and various nations, till, at the end of six or seven months after I had been kidnapped, I arrived at the sea coast. It would be tedious and uninteresting to relate all the incidents which befell me during this journey, and which I have not yet forgotten; of the various hands I passed through, and the manners and customs of all the different people among whom I lived. I shall therefore only observe, that in all the places where I was, the soil was exceedingly rich; the pumpkins, eadas, plaintains, yams, etc., were in great abundance, and of incredible size. There were also vast quantities of different gums, though not used for any purpose, and every where a great deal of tobacco. The cotton even grew quite wild, and there was plenty of red-wood. I saw no mechanics whatever in all the way, except such as I have mentioned. The chief employment in all these countries was agriculture, and both the males and females, as with us, were brought up to it, and trained in the arts of war.

The first object which saluted my eyes when I arrived on the coast, was the sea, and a slave ship, which was then riding at anchor, and waiting for its cargo. These filled me with astonishment, which was soon converted into terror, when I was carried on board. I was immediately handled, and tossed up to see if I were sound, by some of the crew; and I was now persuaded that I had gotten into a world of bad spirits, and that they were going to kill me. Their complexions, too, differing so much from ours, their long hair, and the language they spoke, (which was very different from any I had ever heard) united to confirm me in this belief. Indeed, such were the horrors of my views and fears at the moment, that, if ten thousand worlds had been my own, I would have freely parted with them all to have exchanged my condition with that of the meanest slave in my own country. When I looked round the ship too, and saw a large furnace of copper boiling, and a multitude of black people of every description chained together, every one of their countenances expressing dejection and sorrow, I no longer doubted of my fate; and quite overpowered with horror and anguish, I fell motionless on the deck and fainted. When I recovered a little, I found some black people about me, who I believed were some of those who had brought me on board, and had been receiving their pay; they talked to me in order to cheer me, but all in vain. I asked them if we were not to be eaten by those white men with horrible looks, red faces and long hair. They told me I was not: and one of the crew brought me a small portion of spirituous liquor in a wine glass, but, being afraid of him, I would not take it out of his hand. One of the blacks, therefore, took it from him and gave it to me, and I took a little down my palate, which, instead of reviving me, as they thought it would, threw me into the greatest consternation at the strange feeling it produced, having never tasted any such liquor before. Soon after this, the blacks who brought me on board went off, and left me abandoned to despair.

I now saw myself deprived of all chance of returning to my native country, or even the least glimpse of hope of gaining the shore, which I now considered as friendly; and I even wished for my former slavery in preference to my present situation, which was filled with horrors of every kind, still heightened by my ignorance of what I was to undergo. I was not long suffered to indulge my grief; I was soon put down under the decks, and there I received such a salutation in my nostrils as I had never experienced in my life: so that, with the loathsomeness of the stench and crying together, I became so sick and low that I was not able to eat, nor had I the least desire to taste any thing. I now wished for the last friend, death, to relieve me; but soon, to my grief, two of the white men offered me eatables; and, on my refusing to eat, one of them held me fast by the hands, and laid me across, I think the windlass, and tied my feet, while the other flogged me severely. I had never experienced any thing of this kind before, and although not being used to the water, I naturally feared that element the first time I saw it, yet, nevertheless, could I have got over the nettings, I would have jumped over the side, but I could not; and besides, the crew used to watch us very closely who were not chained down to the decks, lest we should leap into the water; and I have seen some of these poor African prisoners most severely cut, for attempting to do so, and hourly whipped for not eating. This indeed was often the case with myself. In a little time after, amongst the poor chained men, I found some of my own nation, which in a small degree gave ease to my mind. I inquired of these what was to be done with us? They gave me to understand, we were to be carried to these white people's country to work for them. I then was a little revived, and thought, if it were no worse than working, my situation was not so desperate; but still I feared I should be put to death, the white people looked and acted, as I thought, in so savage a manner; for I had never seen among any people such instances of brutal cruelty; and this not only shown towards us blacks, but also to some of the whites themselves. One white man in particular I saw, when we were permitted to be on deck, flogged so unmercifully with a large rope near the foremast, that he died in consequence of it; and they tossed him over the side as they would have done a brute. This made me fear these people the more; and I expected nothing less than to be treated in the same manner. I could not help expressing my fears and apprehensions to some of my countrymen; I asked them if these people had no country, but lived in this hollow place? (the ship) they told me they did not, but came from a distant one. "Then," said I, "how comes it in all our country we never heard of them?" They told me because they lived so very far off. I then asked where were their women? had they any like themselves? I was told they had. "And why," said I, "do we not see them?" They answered, because they were left behind. I asked how the vessel could go? they told me they could not tell; but that there was cloth put upon the masts by the help of the ropes I saw, and then the vessel went on; and the white men had some spell or magic they put in the water when they liked in order to stop the vessel. I was exceedingly amazed at this account, and really thought they were spirits. I therefore wished much to be from amongst them, for I expected they would sacrifice me; but my wishes were vain, for we were so quartered that it was impossible for any of us to make our escape.

While we stayed on the coast I was mostly on deck; and one day, to my great astonishment, I saw one of these vessels coming in with the sails up. As soon as the whites saw it, they gave a great shout, at which we were amazed; and the more so, as the vessel appeared larger by approaching nearer. At last, she came to an anchor in my sight, and when the anchor was let go, I and my countrymen who saw it, were lost in astonishment to observe the vessel stop—and were now convinced it was done by magic. Soon after this the other ship got her boats out, and they came on board of us, and the people of both ships seemed very glad to see each other.—Several of the strangers also shook hands with us black people, and made motions with their hands, signifying, I suppose, we were to go to their country, but we did not understand them.

At last, when the ship we were in, had got in all her cargo, they made ready with many fearful noises, and we were all put under deck, so that we could not see how they managed the vessel. But this disappointment was the least of my sorrow. The stench of the hold while we were on the coast was so intolerably loathsome, that it was dangerous to remain there for any time, and some of us had been permitted to stay on the deck for the fresh air; but now that the whole ship's cargo were confined together, it became absolutely pestilential. The closeness of the place, and the heat of the climate, added to the number in the ship, which was so crowded that each had scarcely room to turn himself, almost suffocated us. This produced copious perspirations, so that the air soon became unfit for respiration, from a variety of loathsome smells, and brought on a sickness among the slaves, of which many died—thus falling victims to the improvident avarice, as I may call it, of their purchasers.

This wretched situation was again aggravated by the falling of the chains, now become insupportable; and the filth of the necessary tubs, into which the children often fell, and were almost suffocated. The shrieks of the women, and the groans of the dying, rendered the whole a scene of horror almost inconceivable. Happily perhaps, for myself, I was soon reduced so low here that it was thought necessary to keep me almost always on deck; and from my extreme youth I was not put in fetters. In this situation I expected every hour to share the fate of my companions, some of whom were almost daily brought upon the deck at the point of death, which I began to hope would soon put an end to my miseries. Often did I think many of the inhabitants of the deep much more happy than myself. I envied them the freedom they enjoyed, and as often wished I could change my condition for theirs. Every circumstance I met with, served only to render my state more painful, and heightened my apprehensions, and my opinion of the cruelty of the whites.

One day they had taken a number of fishes; and when they had killed and satisfied themselves with as many as they thought fit, to our astonishment, who were on deck, rather than give any of them to us to eat, as we expected, they tossed the remaining fish into the sea again, although we begged and prayed for some as well as we could, but in vain; and some of my countrymen, being pressed by hunger, took an opportunity, when they thought no one saw them, of trying to get a little privately; but they were discovered, and the attempt procured them some very severe floggings. One day, when we had a smooth sea and moderate wind, two of my wearied countrymen who were chained together, (I was near them at the time,) preferring death to such a life of misery, somehow made through the nettings and jumped into the sea: immediately, another quite dejected fellow, who, on account of his illness, was suffered to be out of irons, also followed their example; and I believe many more would very soon have done the same, if they had not been prevented by the ship's crew, who were instantly alarmed. Those of us that were the most active, were in a moment put down under the deck, and there was such a noise and confusion amongst the people of the ship as I never heard before, to stop her and get the boat out to go after the slaves. However, two of the wretched were drowned, but they got the other, and afterwards flogged him unmercifully, for thus attempting to prefer death to slavery. In this manner we continued to undergo more hardships than I can now relate, hardships which are inseparable from this accursed trade. Many a time we were near suffocation from the want of fresh air, which we were often without for whole days together. This and the stench of the necessary tubs, carried off many.

During our passage, I first saw flying fishes, which surprised me very much; they used frequently to fly across the ship, and many of them fell on the deck. I also now first saw the use of the quadrant; I had often with astonishment seen the mariners make observations with it, and I could not think what it meant. They at last took notice of my surprise; and one of them, willing to increase it, as well as to gratify my curiosity, made me one day look through it. The clouds appeared to me to be land, which disappeared as they passed along. This heightened my wonder; and I was now more persuaded than ever, that I was in another world, and that every thing about me was magic. At last, we came in sight of the island of Barbadoes, at which the whites on board gave a great shout, and made many signs of joy to us. We did not know what to think of this; but as the vessel drew nearer, we plainly saw the harbor, and other ships of different kinds and sizes, and we soon anchored amongst them, off Bridgetown. Many merchants and planters now came on board, though it was in the evening. They put us in separate parcels, and examined us attentively. They also made us jump, and pointed to the land, signifying we were to go there. We thought by this, we should be eaten by these ugly men, as they appeared to us; and, when soon after we were all put down under the deck again, there was much dread and trembling among us, and nothing but bitter cries to be heard all the night from these apprehensions, insomuch that at last the white people got some old slaves from the land to pacify us. They told us we were not to be eaten, but to work, and were soon to go on land, where we should see many of our country people. This report eased us much. And sure enough, soon after we were landed, there came to us Africans of all languages.

We were conducted immediately to the merchant's yard, where we were all pent up together, like so many sheep in a fold, without regard to sex or age. As every object was new to me, everything I saw filled me with surprise. What struck me first, was that the houses were built with bricks and stories, and in every other respect different from those I had seen in Africa; but I was still more astonished on seeing people on horseback. I did not know what this could mean; and, indeed, I thought these people were full of nothing but magical arts. While I was in this astonishment, one of my fellow-prisoners spoke to a countryman of his, about the horses, who said they were the same kind they had in their country. I understood them, though they were from a distant part of Africa; and I thought it odd I had not seen any horses there; but afterwards, when I came to converse with different Africans, I found they had many horses amongst them, and much larger than those I then saw.

We were not many days in the merchant's custody, before we were sold after their usual manner, which is this:—On a signal given, (as the beat of a drum,) the buyers rush at once into the yard where the slaves are confined, and make choice of that parcel they like best.   The noise and clamor with which this is attended, and the eagerness visible in the countenance of the buyers, serve not a little to increase the apprehension of terrified Africans, who may well be supposed to consider them as the ministers of that destruction to which they think themselves devoted.   In this manner, without scruple, are relations and friends separated, most of them never to see each other again.   I remember in the vessel in which I was brought over, in the men's apartment, there were several brothers, who, in the sale, were sold in different lots; and it was very moving on this occasion, to see and hear their cries at parting.   O, ye nominal Christians! might not an African ask you—Learned you this from your God, who says unto you, Do unto all men as you would men should do unto you?   Is it not enough that we are torn from our country and friends, to toil for your luxury and lust of gain? Must every tender feeling be likewise sacrificed to your avarice?   Are the dearest friends and relations, now renderd more dear by their separation from their kindred, still to be parted from each other, and thus prevented from cheering the gloom of slavery, with the small comfort of being together, and mingling their sufferings and sorrows?   Why are parents to lose their children, brothers their sisters, or husbands their wives?   Surely, this is a new refinement in cruelty, which, while it has no advantage to atone for it, thus aggravates distress, and adds fresh horrors even to the wretchedness of slavery.

BENJAMIN BANNEKER

BEFORE ONE can understand the ancestry and career of Benjamin Banneker, it is necessary for him to go back in thought not only to the eighteenth century but even to the latter years of the seventeenth, when settlements only a few miles from the Atlantic coast were still being made and when white servitude was a common system of labor in the colonies. When Banneker was born, Baltimore was but a struggling village of thirty houses, and the Revolution was still forty-five and the cotton-gin sixty years in the future. One must remember too that in this case he has to deal not only with a mastermind, not only with a genius achieving results with the scantiest materials, but also with a philosopher and humanitarian, one with keen insight into the physical universe and deep understanding of the mystery of life.

Some years before the close of the seventeenth century, Molly Welsh, a young English woman working on a farm, was accused of stealing a pail of milk. It appears that a cow kicked over the pail; nevertheless Molly was sold under the system of indenture, transported to Maryland, and forced to serve for seven years. At length she became free, and she purchased a small farm. This she tended with such diligence that in 1692 she was able to purchase two Negro men who had just been brought from Africa. One of the two, Banaky, a prince in his native land, was described as not such a good worker as his companion, but as intelligent, of agreeable presence, dignified manner, and contemplative habits. In course of time Molly Welsh liberated both men and married Banaky. Of the marriage there were four children. One, a daughter, Mary, in 1730 was married to Robert, a native African who had become free and who preferred to adopt his wife's surname rather than take that of the man to whom he had belonged. Again there were four children. The oldest, and the only son, was Benjamin, born November 9, 1731. In the earlier years the surname was variously given not only as *Banaky*, but also as *Banneky* and *Bannaker*. By the time, however, it came to the most famous member of the family, it had become fixed as *Banneker*.

Robert Banneker was a man of energy and thrift. When his son was six years old he purchased for 17,000 pounds of tobacco a farm of one hundred and twenty acres ten miles from Baltimore. Within the next few years Benjamin attended a private school not far away and received at least the fundamentals of an education. When he was twenty-seven years of age his father died, and upon him fell full responsibility for the farm, which with its fruit trees, its fine lot of cattle, and its well stocked apiary, became known as one of the best in the section. While still a young man, having observed the movement of a watch, he made a clock that not only kept good time but that struck the hours—the first of the sort made in the country. This naturally interested the neighbors, who had already been impressed by his unusual ability in making calculations.

Thus the years passed until the inventor was forty years of age, and not yet had he found opportunity to develop his best powers. In 1772, however, steps were taken for the erection of the flour mills of Ellicott City near his home, and he was intensely interested in the actual construction of the buildings in the following year. The proprietors, who happened to be Quakers, were friendly with him and bought from his farm many provisions for their workmen. In 1787 George Ellicott, having observed Banneker's interest in mathematics, loaned to him Ferguson's *Astronomy*, Mayer's *Tables*, and Leadbetter's *Lunar Tables*, with some astronomical instruments, giving at the time no suggestion that might further his instruction. Banneker on his own initiative so thoroughly mastered the books that in course of time he was able to point out errors in them. A new world was opened before him, and he now reversed his habits, studying the stars at night and sleeping so much in the day that the neighbors said be was growing lazy and neglecting his farm. Under his new inspiration he also showed his strength of character in that, having previously become somewhat addicted to strong drink, he now overcame the habit completely. In 1789, when commissioners were appointed for the surveying of the Federal Territory, later known as the

District of Columbia, at the suggestion of Andrew Ellicott he became a member of the group. In 1791 he began the issuing of his almanacs, the first being that for the year 1792 and the series continuing until 1802. He wrote a dissertation on bees and calculated the locust plague as recurrent in seventeen year cycles. Having divided his property into tenancies and become dissatisfied with these, he sold the land to the Ellicotts for an annuity of £12 based on the market value of the land and his expectancy of life, reserving only a residence for himself. He lived eight years longer than he calculated, and this has more than once been remarked as the only time he made such a mistake in figuring. The Ellicotts, however, faithfully kept the contract to the end.

Banneker never married. In his maturity he was described as "a large man of noble appearance, with venerable hair, wearing a coat of superfine drab broad cloth," and again as "of black complexion, medium stature, of uncommonly soft and gentlemanly manners and of pleasing colloquial powers." Though not a member of any church, he sometimes attended the meetings of the Society of Friends; and he liked good music. His straightforward look gave every suggestion of the seeker for truth. In his later years and for decades after he passed, he was frequently referred to both at home and abroad as proof of the intellectual capacity of the Negro; thus Jefferson, then Secretary of State, to whom he sent a letter along with a copy of his almanac, said in reply: "Nobody wishes more than I do to seek such proofs as you exhibit, that nature has given to our black brethren talents equal to those of the other colors of men." He died in Octber, 1806, having willed his important papers to George Ellicott.

There are two original sources of information about the life of Banneker. One is a sketch in the almanac for 1792, reproduced, with some modifications, in that for 1793, and the other is the collection of papers left with the Ellicotts, together with such other information as was in the possession of that family. The sketch was written by another prominent man who was a friend of the astronomer, James McHenry (1753-1816), military surgeon and politician, who was born in Ireland but who removed to America in 1771 and, after service in the war as assistant secre-

tary to Washington and major on the staff of Lafayette, was for
two terms, 1781-85 1791-96, member of the Maryland Senate,
in 1787 member of the Constitutional Convention in Philadelphia,
and finally Secretary of War under Washington and Adams.
The information to be gained from the papers and from members
of the Ellicott family is summed up in *A Sketch of the Life of
Benjamin Banneker from notes taken in 1836*, read by J. Saurin
Norris before the Maryland Historical Society October 5, 1854,
and *Banneker*, the *Afric-American Astronomer*, from the post-
humous papers of Martha E (llicott) Tyson, edited by her daughter, Philadelphia, 1884. Early articles, good in spirit but not
impeccable in details, were written by Moncure D. Conway in the
Atlantic Monthly, vol. XI (January, 1863), pp. 79-84, and L.
Maria Child in *The Freedmen's Book*, Boston, 1865, pp. 14-23;
similar in quality was the *Memoir of Benjamin Banneker*, read
before the Maryland Historical Society, by John H. B. Latrobe,
Baltimore, 1845. See also sketch by John W. Cromwell in *The
Negro in American History*, Washington, 1914, pp. 86-97;
"The Negro, Benjamin Banneker: Astronomer and Mathemati-
cian," by P. Lee Phillips, in Records of the Columbia Historical
Society, vol. XX, Washington, 1917, pp. 114-120; "Benjamin
Banneker, the Negro Mathematician and Astronomer," by Henry
E. Baker, Washington, 1918, reprinted from the *Journal of
Negro History*, vol. III, no. 2 (April, 1918); and *Banneker, the
Afro-American Astronomer*, from data collected by Will W.
Allen, assisted by Daniel Murray, Washington, 1921. Banneker
is also treated in Henri Grégoire's *De la littérature des nègres*,
1808, which appeared in an English version in Brooklyn, 1810.
The letter to the Secretary of State was published as *Copy of a
Letter from Benjamin Banneker to the Secretary of State, with
his Answer*, Philadelphia, 1792. "A Plan of Peace-Office for the
United States" originally appeared in the almanac for 1793, and
in more recent years was made accessible by Phillips. In the latter
portion this, like some other efforts for peace in modern times, was
rather fantastic; but in general the Plan may be said to have
anticipated both the formation of the Department of the Interior
and such effort as that of the League of Nations. In its opposition

to capital punishment it shows the author as thoroughly in line with the humanitarian temper of his day and as standing for some of the principles advocated by the English radical, William Godwin, whose notable work, *An Enquiry concerning Political Justice*, also appeared in 1793.

LETTER TO THE SECRETARY OF STATE

Maryland, Baltimore County, August 19, 1791.

Sir,

I am fully sensible of the greatness of the freedom I take with you on the present occasion; a liberty which seemed scarcely allowable, when I reflected on that distinguished and dignified station in which you stand, and the almost general prejudice which is so prevalent in the world against those of my complexion.

It is a truth too well attested, to need proof here, that we are a race of beings, who have long laboured under the abuse and censure of the world; that we have long been looked upon with an eye of contempt; and considered rather as brutish than human, and scarcely capable of mental endowments.

I hope I may safely admit, in consequence of the report which has reached me, that you are a man far less inflexible in sentiments of this nature, than many others; that you are measurably friendly, and well disposed towards us; and that you are willing to lend your aid and assistance for our relief from those many distresses, and numerous calamities, to which we are reduced.

If this is founded in truth, I apprehend you will embrace every opportunity to eradicate that train of absurd and false ideas and opinions, which so generally prevail with respect to us: and that your sentiments are concurrent with mine, which are, that one universal Father hath given being to us

all; that He hath not only made us all of one flesh, but that
He hath also, without partiality, afforded us all the same sensations, and endowed us all with the same faculties; and that,
however variable we may be in society or religion, however
diversified in situation or in colour, we are all of the same
family, and stand in the same relation to Him.

If these are sentiments of which you are fully persuaded,
you cannot but acknowledge, that it is the indispensable duty
of those who maintain for themselves the rights of human
nature, and who profess the obligations of Christianity, to extend their powers and influence to the relief of every part of
the human race, from whatever burden or oppression they
may unjustly labour under, and this, I apprehend, a full conviction of the truth and obligation of these principles should
lead all to.

I have long been convinced, that if your love for yourselves, and for those inestimable laws which preserved to you
the rights of human nature, was founded on sincerity you
could not but be solicitous, that every individual, of whatever
rank or distinction, might with you equally enjoy the blessings thereof; neither could you rest satisfied short of the
most active effusion of your exertions, in order to their promotion* from any state of degradation, to which the unjusti-
fiable cruelty and barbarism of men may have reduced them.

I freely and cheerfully acknowledge, that I am of the
African race, and in that colour which is natural to them, of
the deepest dye; and it is under a sense of the most profound
gratitude to the Supreme Ruler of the Universe, that I now
confess to you, that I am not under that state of tyrannical
thraldom, and inhuman captivity, to which many of my
brethren are doomed, but that I have abundantly tasted of the
fruition of those blessings, which proceed from that free
and unequalled liberty with which you are favoured; and

* Thus.

which I hope you will willingly allow you have mercifully received, from the immediate hand of that Being from whom proceedeth every good and perfect gift.

Suffer me to recall to your mind that time, in which the arms of the British crown were exerted, with every powerful effort, in order to reduce you to a state of servitude: look back, I entreat you, on the variety of dangers to which you were exposed; reflect on that period in which every human aid appeared unavailable, and in which even hope and fortitude wore the aspect of inability to the conflict, and you cannot but be led to a serious and grateful sense of your miraculous and providential preservation; you cannot but acknowledge, that the present freedom and tranquillity which you enjoy, you have mercifully received, and that it is the peculiar blessing of heaven.

This, Sir, was a time when you clearly saw into the injustice of a state of Slavery, and in which you had just apprehensions of the horrors of its condition. It was then that your abhorrence thereof was so excited, that you publicly held forth this true and invaluable doctrine, which is worthy to be recorded and remembered in all succeeding ages: "We hold these truths to be self-evident, that all men are created equal; that they are endowed by their Creator with certain inalienable rights, and that among these are life, liberty, and the pursuit of happiness."

Here was a time in which your tender feelings for yourselves had engaged you thus to declare; you were then impressed with proper ideas of the great violation of liberty, and the free possession of those blessings, to which you were entitled by nature; but, sir, how pitiable it is to reflect, that although you were so fully convinced of the benevolence of the Father of Mankind and of his equal and impartial distribution of these rights and privileges which he hath conferred upon them, that you should at the same time counteract his mercies, in detaining by fraud and violence, so numerous a part of my brethren under groaning captivity and cruel oppression, that you should at the same time be found guilty of that most criminal act, which you professedly detested in others, with respect to yourselves.

Your knowledge of the situation of my brethren is too extensive to need a recital here; neither shall I presume to prescribe methods by which they may be relieved, otherwise than by recommending to you and all others, to wean yourselves from those narrow prejudices which you have imbibed with respect to them, and as Job proposed to his friends, 'put your soul in their soul's stead'; thus shall your hearts be enlarged with kindness and benevolence towards them; and thus shall you need neither the direction of myself or others, in what manner to proceed herein.

And now, sir, although my sympathy and affection for my brethren hath caused my enlargement thus far, I ardently hope, that your candour and generosity will plead with you in my behalf, when I state that it was not originally my design; but having taken up my pen in order to present a copy of an almanac which I have calculated for the succeeding year, I was unexpectedly led thereto.

This calculation is the production of my arduous study, in my advanced stage of life; for having long had unbounded desires to become acquainted with the secrets of nature, I have had to gratify my curiosity herein through my own assiduous application to astronomical study, in which I need not recount to you the many difficulties and disadvantages which I have had to encounter.

And although I had almost declined to make my calculation for the ensuing year, in consequence of the time which I had alloted for it being taken up at the federal territory, by the request of Mr. Andrew Ellicott, yet I industriously applied myself thereto, and hope I have accomplished it with correctness and accuracy. I have taken the liberty to direct a copy to you, which I humbly request you will favourably receive; and although you may have the opportunity of perusing it after its publication, yet I desire to send it to you in manuscript previous thereto, that thereby you might not only have an earlier inspection, but that you might also view it in my own handwriting.

And now, sir, I shall conclude, and subscribe myself, with the most profound respect,

Your most obedient humble servant,

Benjamin Banneker.

A Plan of Peace-Office for the United States

Among the many defects which have been pointed out in the federal constitution by its antifederal enemies, it is much to be lamented that no person has taken notice of its total silence upon the subject of an office of the utmost importance to the welfare of the United States, that is, an office for promoting and preserving perpetual peace in our country.

It is to be hoped that no objection will be made to the establishment of such an office, while we are engaged in a war with the Indians, for as the War-Office of the United States was established in time of peace, it is equally reasonable that a Peace-Office should be established in time of war.

The plan of this office is as follows:

I. Let a Secretary of Peace be appointed to preside in this office, who shall be perfectly free from all the present absurd and vulgar European prejudices upon the subject of government; let him be a genuine republican and a sincere Christian, for the principles of republicanism and Christianity are no less friendly to universal and perpetual peace, than they are to universal and equal liberty.

II. Let a power be given to this Secretary to establish

and maintain free schools in every city, village, and township of the United States; and let him be made responsible for the talents, principles, and morals of all his schoolmasters. Let the youth of our country be carefully instructed in reading, writing, and arithmetic, and in the doctrines of a religion of some kind; the Christian religion should be preferred to all others; for it belongs to this religion exclusively to teach us not only to cultivate peace with all men, but to forgive, nay more—to love our very enemies. It belongs to it further to teach us that the Supreme Being alone possesses a power to take away human life, and that we rebel against his laws whenever we undertake to execute death in any way whatever upon any of his creatures.

III. Let every family in the United States be furnished at the public expense, by the Secretary of this office, with a copy of an American edition of the Bible. This measure has become the more necessary in our country, since the banishment of the Bible, as a school-book, from most of the schools in the United States. Unless the price of this book be paid for by the public, there is reason to fear that in a few years it will be met with only in courts of justice or in magistrates' offices; and should the absurd mode of establishing truth by kissing this sacred book fall into disuse, it may probably, in the course of the next generation, be seen only as a curiosity on a shelf in Mr. Peale's museum.*

IV. Let the following sentences be inscribed in letters of gold over the door of every home in the United States:

THE SON OF MAN CAME INTO THE WORLD,

NOT TO DESTROY MEN'S LIVES, BUT TO SAVE THEM.

* Charles Wilson Peale (1741-1827) was an American painter born in Maryland. He studied with J. S. Copley in Boston and Benjamin West in London. In the course of the Revolution he painted many portraits of Washington and other officers. In 1785 the discovery of the bones of a mastodon gave him the idea of founding a museum, which he opened in Philadelphia in 1802. He was also instrumental in founding the Pennsylvania Academy of Fine Arts, the first of its kind in the United States.

V. To inspire a veneration for human life, and an horror at the shedding of human blood, let all those laws be repealed which authorize juries, judges, sheriffs, or hangmen to assume the resentments of individuals, and to commit murder in cold blood in any case whatever. Until this reformation in our code of penal jurisprudence takes place, it will be in vain to attempt to introduce universal and perpetual peace in our country.

VI. To subdue that passion for war which education, added to human depravity, has made universal, a familiarity with the instruments of death, as well as all military shows, should be carefully avoided. For which reason, militia laws should everywhere be repealed and military dresses and military titles should be laid aside: reviews tend to lessen the horrors of a battle by connecting them with the charms of order; militia laws generate idleness and vice, and thereby produce the wars they are said to prevent; military dresses fascinate the mind of young men, and lead them from serious and useful professions; were there no uniforms, there would probably be no armies; lastly, military titles feed vanity, and keep up ideas in the mind which lessen a sense of the folly and miseries of war.

In the seventh and last place, let a large room, adjoining the federal hall, be appointed for transacting the business and preserving all the records of this office. Over the door of this room let there be a sign, on which the figures of a lamb, a dove, and an olive-branch should be painted, together with the following inscriptions in letters of gold:

PEACE ON EARTH—GOOD-WILL TO MAN.
AH! WHY SHOULD MEN FORGET THAT THEY ARE BRETHREN?

Within this apartment let there be a collection of plough-shares and pruning-hooks made out of swords and spears; and on each of the walls of the apartment the following pictures as large as life:

1. A lion eating straw with an ox, and an adder playing upon the lips of a child.

2. An Indian boiling his venison in the same pot with a citizen of Kentucky.

3. Lord Cornwallis and Tippo Saib, under the shade of a sycamore tree in the East Indies, drinking Madeira wine out of the same decanter.

4. A group of French and Austrian soldiers dancing, arm in arm, under a bower erected in the neighborhood of Mons.

5. A St. Domingo planter, a man of color, and a native of Africa, legislating together in the same colonial assembly.

To complete the entertainment of this delightful apartment, let a group of young ladies, clad in white robes, assemble every day at a certain hour, in a gallery to be erected for the purpose, and sing odes, and hymns, and anthems in praise of the blessings of peace.

One of these songs should consist of the following beautiful lines of Mr. Pope:

> Peace o'er the world her olive wand extends,
> And white-rob'd innocence from heaven descends;
> All crimes shall cease, and ancient frauds shall fail,
> Returning justice lifts aloft her scale.

RICHARD ALLEN AND ABSALOM JONES

IN THE course of the year 1793 there was in Philadelphia an epidemic of yellow fever that paralyzed the life of the city and that influenced more than one work in American literature. Charles Brockden Brown employed the theme in his novel *Arthur Mervyn*, Longfellow used it near the close of *Evangeline*, and Philip Freneau, at the time editor of the *National Gazette* in the city, was forced to suspend publication of his periodical. When the pestilence was at its height, the request was made of the Negro citizens to come forward, attend the sick and bury the dead, as it was supposed by many that they were immune from the disease. The unheard-of request naturally appalled them at first, but Richard Allen and Absalom Jones accepted the challenge, and their service at this time must ever rank with the heroic deeds of the country's history. In the conduct of their work they faced many practical difficulties, and in spite of their sacrificial effort, when all was over they were misrepresented, as a man named Matthew Carey published a *Short Account of the Malignant Fever*, in which he said that the Negroes should have done much more and charged much less than they did. To this Allen and Jones made a devastating reply in their pamphlet, *A Narrative of the Proceedings of the Black People during the Late Awful Calamity in Philadelphia; and a Refutation of Some Censures Thrown upon Them in Some Late Publications* (1794), selections from which are given below. As the work of men who had grown up in bondage and who received no assistance in their statement, the *Narrative* is not without grammatical lapses; but no attempt has been made to edit it, as nothing should alter its ingenuous tone or mar its rugged strength.

Richard Allen was born a slave in Philadelphia in February, 1760. While still young he was sold to a farmer near Dover, Del., and later was converted under Methodist influence. As a young man he began to preach. His master let him conduct services in his home, was himself converted, and coöperated with him in his effort to secure his freedom. By cutting wood, working in a brickyard, and serving as a wagoner in the later years of the Revolution, Allen was able to purchase his liberty on September 3, 1783. He traveled through the eastern part of Pennsylvania and the neighboring states, and at the first general conference of the Methodist Episcopal Church, in Baltimore, 1784, he was regarded as a promising young minister. He received appointments from Bishop Francis Asbury, and, having removed to Philadelphia in 1786, occasionally preached at St. George's Methodist Episcopal Church. Meanwhile he conducted prayer-meetings among the Negroes. When in 1787 there was trouble about the seating in St. George's, he and his friends withdrew and in April organized the Free African Society, which became the nucleus of formal effort by Negroes in both the Methodist and the Episcopalian denominations. Those who remained Methodists and went with Allen organized Bethel Church, dedicated in 1794. The union of this congregation with similar ones in places not far away resulted in 1816 in the forming of a distinct denomination, the African Methodist Episcopal Church, of which Allen became the first bishop. He was a member of the committee appointed at the great meeting in Philadelphia in January, 1817, to convey to Joseph Hopkinson, member of Congress from the city, the sentiment of the gathering against colonization, and a letter on the subject written to *Freedom's Journal* (November 2, 1827) will be found quoted in David Walker's *Appeal*. Richard Allen was a man of deep piety, the strictest integrity, and indomitable perseverance; and his moral influence was unbounded. He died March 26, 1831, and it was said that the immense concourse of people gathered to do honor to him exceeded anything of the kind ever before witnessed in the country. See *The Life, Experience, and Gospel Labors of the Rt. Rev. Richard Allen* (1880); sketch in *Centennial Encyclopedia of the African Methodist Episcopal Church,* by R. R. Wright, Philadelphia, 1916; article by Carter G. Woodson in *Dictionary of American Biography,* and this author's *The History of the Negro Church,* Washington, 1921, pp. 73-78; *The Negro Author,* by Vernon Loggins, New York, 1931, pp. 56-62; and, in the present volume, the important reference by David Walker in his *Appeal*, article IV.

Absalom Jones was born a slave in Sussex, Del., November 6, 1746. When he was still very young his master took him from the field to wait on him in the house, and even in these early years he had the good sense to save the pennies that were given to him by visitors from time to time. He bought a primer, a spelling-book, and a Testament, and in general sought to spend his leisure hours to advantage. In 1762, when he was sixteen years of age, his mother, his five brothers, and a sister were sold (not all together, it seems), and he was taken to Philadelphia by his new master. His work was to help in a store and to carry out goods. He was diligent in improving himself and for a short while at least, with his master's permission, he attended night school. In 1770 he married a woman who was also a slave. By his own efforts and some contributions from the Friends he won her freedom on payment of £30, and his own liberty he finally secured in 1784. Henceforth he made rapid progress in education and civic interest, and he figured prominently in the incident that caused Richard Allen and other Negroes to leave St. George's Methodist Episcopal Church one Sunday in 1787, as it was he whom an usher sought to pull from his knees during prayer. Those members of the Free African Society who did not remain Methodists followed him in the organization of St. Thomas's, the African Episcopal Church. Jones himself was ordained as a clergyman August 6, 1795, and he thus became the first Negro rector in the United States. After the faithful discharge of his duties at St. Thomas's for twenty-two years, he died February 13, 1818. See *History of the Afro-American Group of the Episcopal Church*, by George F. Bragg, Baltimore, 1922, especially pp. 47-74.

A Narrative of the Proceedings of the Black People During the Late Awful Calamity in Philadelphia

In consequence of a partial representation of the conduct of the people who were employed to nurse the sick, in the late calamitous state of the city of Philadelphia, we are so-licited, by a number of those who feel themselves injured thereby, and by the advice of several respectable citizens, to step forward and declare facts as they really were; seeing that from our situation, on account of the charge we took upon us, we had it more fully and generally in our power, to know and observe the conduct and behaviour of those that were so employed.

Early in September, a solicitation appeared in the public papers, to the people of colour to come forward and assist the distressed, perishing, and neglected sick; with a kind of assurance, that people of our colour were not liable to take the infection. Upon which we and a few others met and consulted how to act on so truly alarming and melancholy an occasion. After some conversation, we found a freedom to go forth, confiding in him who can preserve in the midst of a burning fiery furnace, sensible that it was our duty to do all the good we could to our suffering fellow mortals. We set out to see where we could be useful. The first we visited was a man in Emsley's-Alley, who was dying, and his wife lay dead at the time in the house, there were none to assist but two poor helpless children. We administered what relief we could, and applied to the overseers of the poor to have the woman buried. We visited upwards of twenty families that day—there were scenes of woe indeed! The Lord was pleased to strengthen us, and remove all fear from us, and disposed our hearts to be as useful as possible.

In order the better to regulate our conduct, we called on the mayor next day, to consult with him how to proceed, so as to be most useful. The first object he recommended was a strict attention to the sick, and the procuring of nurses. This was attended to by Absalom Jones and William Gray; and, in order that the distressed might know where to apply, the mayor advised the public that upon application to them they would be supplied. Soon after, the mortality increasing, the difficulty of getting a corpse taken away, was such, that few were willing to do it, when offered great rewards. The black people were looked to. We then offered our services in the public papers, by advertising that we would remove the dead and procure nurses. Our services were the production of real sensibility;—we sought no fee nor reward, until the increase of the disorder rendered our labour so arduous that we were not adequate to the service we had assumed. The mortality increasing rapidly, obliged us to call in the assistance of five* hired men, in the awful discharge of interring the dead. They, with great reluctance, were prevailed upon to join us. It was very uncommon, at this time, to find any one that would go near, much more, handle, a sick or dead person.

Mr. Carey, in page 106 of his third edition, has observed, that, "for the honor of human nature, it ought to be recorded, that some of the convicts in the gaol, a part of the term of whose confinement had been remitted as a reward for their peaceable, orderly behaviour, voluntarily offered themselves as nurses to attend the sick at Bush-hill; and have, in that capacity, conducted themselves with great fidelity, &c". Here it ought to be remarked, (although Mr. Carey hath not done it) that two thirds of the persons, who rendered these essential services, were people of colour, who, on the application of the elders of the African church, (who met to consider what they could do for the help of the sick) were liberated, on condition of their doing the duty of nurses at the hospital at Bushhill; which they as voluntarily accepted to do, as they did faithfully discharge, this severe and disagreeable duty.— May the Lord reward them, both temporally and spiritually.

When the sickness became general, and several of the physicians died, and most of the survivors were exhausted by sickness or fatigue; that good man, Dr. Rush, called us more immediately to attend upon the sick, knowing we could both

* Two of whom were Richard Allen's brothers.

bleed; he told us we could increase our utility, by attending to his instructions, and accordingly directed us where to procure medicine duly prepared, with proper instruction, how to administer them, and at what stages of the disorder to bleed; and when we found ourselves incapable of judging what was proper to be done, to apply to him, and he would, if able, attend them himself, or send Edward Fisher, his pupil, which he often did; and Mr. Fisher manifested his humanity, by an affectionate attention for their relief.—This has been no small satisfaction to us; for, we think, that when a physician was not attainable, we have been the instruments, in the hand of God, for saving the lives of some hundreds of our suffering fellow mortals.

We feel ourselves sensibly aggrieved by the censorious epithets of many, who did not render the least assistance in the time of necessity, yet are liberal of their censure of us, for the prices paid for our services, when no one knew how to make a proposal to any one that wanted to assist them. At first we made no charge, but left it to those we served in removing their dead, to give what they thought fit—we set no price, until the reward was fixed by those we had served. After paying the people we had to assist us, our compensation is much less than many will believe.

(At this point Allen and Jones give a detailed statement of receipts and expenditures to show that all the cash that they had received had not been nearly sufficient to pay for the coffins they had purchased and the special labor employed; in addition they state that they had buried hundreds of poor persons and strangers, for which service they had neither asked nor received compensation. Then they continue as follows.)

We feel ourselves hurt most by a partial, censorious paragraph in Mr. Carey's second edition, of his account of the sickness, &c. in Philadelphia; pages 76 and 77, where he asperses the blacks alone, for having taken the advantage of the distressed situation of the people. That some extravagant prices were paid, we admit; but how came they to be demanded? the reason is plain. It was with difficulty persons could be had to supply the wants of the sick, as nurses; —applications became more and more numerous, the consequence was, when we procured them at six dollars per week, and called upon them to go where they were wanted, found they were gone elsewhere; here was a disappointment; upon enquiring the cause, we found, they had been allured away by others who offered greater wages, until they got from two to four dollars per day. We had no restraint upon the people. It was natural for people in low circumstances to accept a voluntary, bounteous reward; especially under the loathsomness many of the sick, when nature shuddered at the thought of the infection, and the task assigned was aggravated by lunacy, and being left much alone with them. Had Mr. Carey been solicited to such an undertaking, for hire, *Query*, "what would *he* have demanded?" but Mr. Carey, although chosen a member of that band of worthies who have so eminently distinguished themselves by their labours, for the relief of the sick and helpless—yet, quickly after his election, left them to struggle with their arduous and hazardous task, by leaving the city. It is true Mr. Carey was no hireling, and had a right to flee, and upon his return, to plead the cause of those who fled; yet we think, he was wrong in giving so partial and injurious an account of the black nurses. . . .

We wish not to offend, but when an unprovoked attempt is made, to make us blacker than we are, it becomes less necessary to be over cautious on that account; therefore we shall take the liberty to tell of the conduct of some of the whites.

We know six pounds was demanded by, and paid to, a white woman, for putting a corpse into a coffin; and forty

dollars was demanded, and paid to four white men, for bringing it down the stairs.

(Here are given three pages of other incidents of the epidemic.)

It is unpleasant for us to make these remarks, but justice
to our colour demands it.   Mr. Carey pays William Gray and
us a compliment; he says, our services and others of their
colour, have been very great &c.   By naming us, he leaves
these others, in the hazardous state of being classed with those
who are called the "vilest." . . . We have many unprovoked
enemies, who begrudge us the liberty we enjoy, and are glad
to hear of any complaint against our colour, be it just or
unjust; in consequence of which we are more earnestly endeavoring all in our power, to warn, rebuke, and exhort our
African friends, to keep a conscience void of offence towards
God and man; and, at the same time, would not be backward
to interfere, when stigmas or oppression appear pointed at, or
attempted against them, unjustly; and, we are confident, we
shall stand justified in the sight of the candid and judicious
for such conduct.

*   *   *   *   *   *   *

Notwithstanding the compliment Mr. Carey hath paid
us, we have found reports spread of our taking between one,
and two hundred beds, from houses where people died; such
slanderers as these who propagate such wilful lies are dangerous, although unworthy notice.   We wish if any person
hath the least suspicion of us, they would endeavour to bring
us to the punishment which such atrocious conduct must deserve; and by this means, the innocent will be cleared from
reproach, and the guilty known.

We shall now conclude with the following old proverb,

which we think applicable to those of our colour who exposed
their lives in the late afflicting dispensation:—

> God and a soldier, all men do adore,
> In time of war, and not before;
> When the war is over, and all things righted,
> God is forgotten, and the soldier slighted.

PRINCE HALL

PRINCE HALL was born probably in 1748, the son of an English father and a mulatto woman of Barbadoes. In March, 1765, when seventeen years of age, he worked his way from Bridgetown, the capital of the island, to Boston. Arriving in Massachusetts he was soon impressed by the lowly estate of the Negro people, their lack of opportunity and the indignities visited upon them; and he threw himself wholeheartedly into anything pertaining to their welfare. Physically small and of refined features and bearing, he would seem hardly to have been adapted to the leadership of untutored people in a dark day; but he had great moral force and the power to win the allegiance of men. He was led to enter the Methodist ministry, and he took a positive stand on all questions relating to freedom and equality before the law. In 1775, after vain attempts to get recognition from the American Masonic bodies, Prince Hall and fourteen of his black brethren were initiated in a British army lodge attached to a regiment stationed near Boston. On March 2, 1784, these men applied to the Grand Lodge of England for a warrant. This was issued to "African Lodge, No. 459," with Prince Hall as master, September 29, 1784. Various delays befell the warrant, however, so that it was not actually received before April 29, 1787. The lodge was then duly organized on May 6, and from this beginning developed the idea of Masonry among the Negroes of America. Hall lived until December 7, 1807. He was in no sense a man of letters, but the selection below may give some idea of the quality of his public utterances. See *Prince Hall and his Followers*, by George W. Crawford, New York, 1914, and *Negro Masonry*, by William H. Upton, Cambridge, 1899.

Extract from a Charge

Delivered to the African Lodge, June 24th, 1797,
at Menotomy (now West Cambridge), Mass.

Beloved Brethren of the African Lodge:

It is now five years since I delivered a charge to you on
some parts and points of masonry. As one branch or superstructure of the foundation, I endeavored to show you the
duty of a mason to a mason, and of charity and love to all
mankind, as the work and image of the great God and the
Father of the human race. I shall now attempt to show you
that it is our duty to sympathize with our fellowmen under
their troubles, and with the families of our brethren who
are gone, we hope, to the Grand Lodge above.

We are to have sympathy, said he; but this, after all, is
not to be confined to parties or colors, nor to towns or states,
nor to a kingdom, but to the kingdoms of the whole earth,
over whom Christ the King is head and grand master for
all distress.

Among these numerous sons and daughters of distress,
let us see our friends and brethren; and first let us see *them*
dragged from their native country, by the iron hand of
tyranny and oppression, from their dear friends and connections, with weeping eyes and aching hearts, to a strange land,
and among a strange people, whose tender mercies are cruel,
—and there to bear the iron yoke of slavery and cruelty, till
death, as a friend, shall relieve them. And must not the
unhappy condition of these, our fellow-men, draw forth our
hearty prayers and wishes for their deliverance from those
merchants and traders, whose characters you have described
in Revelation xviii, 11-13? And who knows but these same
sort of traders may, in a short time, in like manner bewail the
loss of the African traffic, to their shame and confusion? The
day dawns now in some of the West Indian Islands. God

can and will change their condition and their hearts, too, and let Boston and the world know that He hath no respect of persons, and that the bulwark of envy, pride, scorn and contempt, which is so visible in some, shall fall.

Jethro, an Ethiopian, gave instructions to his son-in-law, Moses, in establishing government. Exodus XVIII, 22-24. Thus Moses was not ashamed to be instructed by a black man. Philip was not ashamed to take a seat beside the Ethiopian Eunuch, and to instruct him in the gospel. The Grand Master Solomon was not ashamed to hold conference with the Queen of Sheba. Our Grand Master Solomon did not divide the living child, whatever he might do with the dead one; neither did he pretend to make a law to forbid the parties from having free intercourse with one another, without the fear of censure, or be turned out of the synagogue.

Now, my brethren, nothing is stable; all things are changeable. Let us seek those things which are sure and steadfast, and let us pray God that, while we remain here, he would give us the grace of patience, and strength to bear up under all our troubles, which at this day, God knows, we have our share of. Patience, I say; for were we not possessed of a great measure of it, we could not bear up under the daily insults we meet with in the streets of Boston, much more on public days of recreation. How at such times are we shamefully abused, and that to such a degree, that we may truly be said to carry our lives in our hands, and the arrows of death are flying about our heads. Helpless women have their clothes torn from their backs. . . . And by whom are these disgraceful and abusive actions committed? Not by the men born and bred in Boston,—they are better bred; but by a mob or horde of shameless, low-lived, envious, spiteful persons—some of them, not long since, servants in gentlemen's kitchens, scouring knives, horse-tenders, chaise-drivers. I was told by a gentleman who saw the filthy behavior in the Com-

mon, that, in all places he had been in, he never saw so cruel
behavior in all his life; and that a slave in the West Indies,
on Sundays or holidays, enjoys himself and friends without
molestation. Not only this man, but many in town, who
have seen their behavior to us, and that, without provocation,
twenty or thirty cowards have fallen upon one man. (O,
the patience of the blacks!) 'Tis not for want of courage in
you, for they know that they do not face you man for man;
but in a mob, which we despise, and would rather suffer wrong
than to do wrong, to the disturbance of the community, and
the disgrace of our reputation; for every good citizen doth
honor to the laws of the State where he resides.

My brethren, let us not be cast down under these and
many other abuses we at present are laboring under,—for
the darkest hour is just before the break of day. My brethren,
let us remember what a dark day it was with our African
brethren, six years ago, in the French West Indies. Nothing
but the snap of the whip was heard, from morning to evening.
Hanging, breaking on the wheel, burning, and all manner
of tortures, were inflicted on those unhappy people. But,
blessed be God, the scene is changed. They now confess that
God hath no respect of persons, and therefore, receive them
as their friends and treat them as brothers. Thus doth
Ethiopia stretch forth her hand from slavery, to freedom
and equality.

PETER WILLIAMS

ABOUT THE close of the eighteenth century several strong Negro men came into prominence in different places along the Atlantic seaboard. Reference has already been made to Richard Allen, Prince Hall, and Benjamin Banneker. In Philadelphia James Forten was just beginning his career as a sailmaker and prominent man of business; and James Derham, born a slave in Philadelphia, purchased his freedom and removed to New Orleans, where he was both skillful and successful in his work as a physician. Of all of these men no one was more unselfish or more intelligent in his effort than Paul Cuffe, whose high sense of rectitude and philanthropic spirit made his life a challenge to all who came after him. As we are told further below, three achievements stand to his credit: the winning of the suffrage for the Negro in Massachusetts, the establishment of a school in his community, and the actual testing of the practicability of colonization. He left a fortune of $20,000.

Peter Williams was the son of a father of the same name who was prominent in the organizing of Methodism among the Negroes of New York. He himself was born about 1780 and lived until 1840. He learned rapidly as a child and, in spite of his father's affiliation, was trained for the Episcopal priesthood. In 1820 he was ordained a clergyman and appointed rector of St. Philip's Church in New York, which position he held until his death. For years he was very highly regarded, but his prestige declined after the beginning of the convention movement among Negro men about 1830. When Paul Cuffe took several families to Sierra Leone in 1815, largely at his own expense, an earnest individual was endeavoring to find a way out of a difficult problem. The organization of the American Colonization Society, however, a year later, just as Cuffe himself was passing off the scene, radically changed matters; and thoughtful Negro men felt that they now had to deal with a concerted effort on the part of slaveholders to get the free Negroes out of the country in order that their own slave property might be secure. They denounced the Society accordingly, but the desire of Williams not to offend the higher powers in his church by an aggressive attitude led him to take a weak stand and to that extent to lose the heart of his people. Three of his addresses are extant. *An Oration on the Abolition of the Slave Trade* was printed as a pamphlet in 1808. It is in an ejaculatory and rhetorical style that by no means shows the author at his best. *A Discourse, Delivered on the Death of Capt. Paul Cuffe* was an address before the New York African Institution in the African Methodist Episcopal Zion Church, October 21, 1817. This begins in a high-flown and stilted style but after a page or two develops into a clearcut account of the career of the famous seaman. The *Discourse Delivered for the Benefit of the Coloured Community of Wilberforce, in Upper Canada,* printed in 1830, is a thoughtful piece of work but incidentally gave ground for the objection that has already been remarked.

The selection that follows from *A Discourse, Delivered on the Death of Capt. Paul Cuffe* omits the formal opening and the close of the address, throwing emphasis on the middle portion. This part is not only valuable as showing us the speaker at his best but as giving us the only first hand account we have of the life of a great and good man.

A Discourse Delivered on the Death of Captain Paul Cuffe

Were I required to delineate a character of distinguished greatness, I would not seek, as my original, one whose blood has been ennobled through a long line of ancestry, who has had all the advantages of fortune, education, wealth and friends to push him forward; but for one who, from a state of poverty, ignorance and obscurity, through a host of difficulties, and with an unsullied conscience, by the native energy of his mind, has elevated himself to wealth, to influence, to respectability and honour; and being thus elevated, conducts

himself with meekness and moderation, and devotes his time
and talents to pious and benevolent purposes. Such an one's
character deserves to be drawn by the ablest artist, and to be
placed up on high for public imitation and esteem; nay, the
portrait should be placed in our bosoms, and worn as a
sacred treasure ever near to the heart. Such an one was
Paul Cuffe, the son of a poor African, whom the hand of
unfeeling avarice had dragged from home and connections,
and consigned to rigorous and unlimited bondage; subjected
to all the disadvantages which unreasonable prejudice heaps
upon that class of men; destitute of the means of early education; and more frequently struggling under the frowns of
fortune than basking in her smiles: by perseverance, prudence
and laudable enterprise, he raised himself to wealth and respectability: and, having attained that eminence, he so distinguished himself by his amiable and upright deportment,
and his zealous exertions in the cause of humanity and religion, that he became, not only an object of general notice and
regard throughout the civilized world, but even the untutored tribes, that inhabit the regions of Ethiopia, learnt to consider him as a father and a friend.

If ever there was necessity for me to apologize to an
audience for my inadequacy to my subject, I feel it so on
the present occasion. I knew the man. I had the honour
of an intimacy with him; and having from the first moment
of my acquaintance an exalted opinion of his worth, which
time and a more thorough knowledge of him has served to
heighten and confirm, I cannot but regret my inability to
present him to you, *as he was*. In the minds of those who
were acquainted with him, my deficiencies will be readily
supplied by their recollections; but of those who knew him
not, I must beg that they will consider what will now be
offered, not as a finished picture, but as the rude outlines
of the character of a man who was truly great.

In his person, Capt. Cuffe was large and well proportioned. His countenance was serious but mild. His speech
and habit, plain and unostentatious. His deportment, dignified and prepossessing; blending gravity with modesty and
sweetness, and firmness with gentleness and humility. His
whole exterior indicated a man of respectability and piety.
Such would a stranger have supposed him to be at the first
glance.

To convey a further idea of him, it is necessary to recur
to his history. He was born in the year 1759, on one of
the Elizabeth Islands, near New Bedford. His parents had
ten children—four sons and six daughters. He was the youngest of the sons. His father died when he was about 14 years
of age, at which time he had learnt but little more than his
alphabet; and having from thence, with his brothers, the
care of his mother and sisters devolving upon him, he had
but little opportunity for the acquisitions of literature. Indeed, he never had any schooling, but obtained what learning
he had by his own indefatigable exertions, and the scanty aids
which he occasionally received from persons who were friendly towards him. By these means, however, he advanced to a
considerable proficiency in arithmetic, and skill in navigation.
Of his talent for receiving learning, we may form an estimate
from the fact, that he acquired such a knowledge of navigation in two weeks as enabled him to command his vessel
in the voyages which he made to Russia, to England, to Africa, to the West India Islands, as well as to a number of
different ports in the southern section of the United States.
His mind, it appears, was early inclined to the pursuits of
commerce. Before he was grown to manhood, he made several voyages to the West Indies, and along the American
coast. At the age of 20, he commenced business for himself,
in a small open boat. With this, he set out trading to the
neighboring towns and settlements; and, though Providence

seemed rather unpropitious to him at first, by perseverance, prudence and industry, his resources were so blessed with an increase, that, after a while, he was enabled to obtain a good sized schooner. In this vessel he enlarged the sphere of his action; trading to more distant places, and in articles requiring a larger capital; and thus, in the process of time, he became owner of one brig, afterwards of 2, then he added a ship, and so on until 1806, at which time he was possessed of one ship, two brigs, and several smaller vessels, besides considerable property in houses and lands.

In this part of his history, though not the most interesting, we may discover one of those distinguished traits of character, which rendered him so eminently useful, i.e., a steady perseverance in laudable undertakings, which overcomes obstacles apparently insurmountable, and attains its objects while others fall back in despair.

*   *   *   *   *   *   *

In the year 1780, Capt. C. being just then of age, was with his brother John, called on by the collector to pay his personal tax. At that time the coloured people of Massachusetts were not considered as entitled to the right of suffrage, or to any of the privileges peculiar to citizens. A question immediately arose with them, whether it was constitutional for them to pay taxes, while they were deprived of the rights enjoyed by others who paid them? They concluded, it was not; and, though the sum was small, yet considering it as an imposition affecting the interests of the people of colour throughout the state, they refused to pay it. The consequence was, a law-suit, attended with so much trouble and vexatious delay, that they finally gave it up, by complying with the requisitions of the collector. They did not, however, abandon the pursuit of their rights; but at the next session of the Legislature, presented a petition, praying that they might have the rights, since they had to bear the burden of citizenship; and though there was much reason to doubt of its success, yet it was granted, and all the free coloured people of the state, on paying their taxes, were considered, from thenceforth, as entitled to all the privileges of citizens. For this triumph of justice and humanity over prejudice and oppression, not only the coloured people of Massachusetts, but every advocate of correct principle, owes a tribute of respect and gratitude to John and Paul Cuffe.

In 1797, Capt. Cuffe, lamenting that the place in which he lived was destitute of a school for the instruction of youth; and anxious that his children should have a more favorable opportunity of obtaining education than he had had, proposed to his neighbors to unite with him in erecting a school-house. This, though the utility of the object was undeniable, was made the cause of so much contention, (probably on account of his colour) that he resolved at length to build a school-house on his own land, and at his own expense. He did so, and when finished, gave them the use of it gratis, satisfying himself with seeing it occupied for the purposes contemplated. I would not draw a contrast, brethren. The neighbors, no doubt, have long since atoned for their conduct on this occasion in a generous sorrow. But let not prejudice denounce such a man as possessed of an inferior soul.

But it was in his active commiseration in behalf of his African brethren, that he shone forth most conspicuously as a man of worth. Long had his bowels yearned over their degraded, destitute, miserable condition. He saw, it is true, many benevolent men engaging in releasing them from bondage, and pouring into their minds the light of literature and religion, but he saw also the force of prejudice operating so powerfully against them, as to give but little encouragement to hope that they could ever rise to respectability and usefulness, unless it were in a state of society where they would have greater incentives to improvement, and more favorable opportunities than would probably be ever afforded them where the bulk of the population are whites.

Under this impression, he turned his thoughts to the British settlement at Sierra Leona; and in 1811, finding his property sufficient to warrant the undertaking, and believing it to be his duty to appropriate part of what God had given him to the benefit of his and our unhappy race, he embarked on board of his own brig, manned entirely by persons of colour, and sailed to the land of his forefathers, in the hope of benefitting its natives and descendants.

Arrived at the colony, he made himself acquainted with its condition, and held a number of conversations with the governor and principal inhabitants; in which he suggested a number of important improvements. Among other things, he recommended the formation of a society for the purposes of promoting the interests of its members and of the colonists in general; which measure was immediately adopted, and the society named "The Friendly Society of Sierra Leona." From thence he sailed to England, where, meeting with every mark of attention and respect, he was favored with an opportunity of opening his views to the board of managers of the African Institution, who cordially acquiescing in all his plans, gave him authority to carry over from the U. States a few coloured persons of good character, to instruct the colonists in agriculture and the mechanical arts. After this he returned to Sierra Leona, carrying with him some goods as a consignment to the Friendly Society, to encourage them in the way of trade; which having safely delivered, and given them some salutary instructions, he set sail and returned again to his native land.

Thus terminated his first mission to Africa; a mission fraught with the most happy consequences; undertaken from the purest motives of benevolence; and solely at his own expense and risk.

Returned to the bosom of his family and friends, where every comfort awaited his command, he could not think of enjoying repose while he reflected that he might, in any degree, administer to the relief of the multitudes of his brethren, who were groaning under the yoke of bondage, or groping in the dark and horrible night of heathenish superstition and ignorance. Scarcely had the first transports of rejoicing, at his return, time to subside, before he commenced his preparations for a second voyage; not discouraged by the labours and dangers he had past, and unmindful of the ease which the decline of life requires, and to which his long continued and earnest exertions gave him a peculiar claim. In the hope of finding persons of the description given by the African Institution, he visited most of the large cities in the union, held frequent conferences with the most reputable men of colour, and also with those among the whites who had distinguished themselves as the friends of the Africans; and recommended to the coloured people to form associations for the furtherance of the benevolent work in which he was engaged. The results were, the formation of two societies, one in Philadelphia, and the other in New York, and the discovery of a number of proper persons, who were willing to go with him and settle in Africa. But unfortunately, before he found himself in readiness for the voyage, the war commenced between this country and Great Britain. This put a bar in the way of his operations, which he was so anxious to remove, that he travelled from his home at Westport, to the city of Washington, to solicit the government to favor his views, and to let him depart and carry with him those persons and their effects whom he had engaged to go and settle in Sierra Leona. He was, however, unsuccessful in the attempt. His general plan was highly and universally approbated, but the policy of the government would not admit of such an intercourse with an enemy's colony.

He had now no alternative but to stay at home and wait the event of the war. But the delay, thus occasioned, instead of being suffered to damp his ardor, was improved by him to the maturing of his plans, and extending his correspondence, which already embraced some of the first characters in Great Britain and America. After the termination of the war, he with all convenient speed prepared for his departure, and in Dec. 1815, he took on board his brig 38 persons of the dispersed race of Africa; and after a voyage of 55 days, landed them safely on the soil of their progenitors.

It is proper here to remark that Capt. C. in his zeal for the welfare of his brethren, had exceeded the instructions of the institution at London. They had advised him not to carry over, in the first instance, more than 6 or 8 persons; consequently, he had no claim on them for the passage and other expenses attending the removal of any over that number. But this he had previously considered, and generously resolved to bear the burden of the expense himself, rather than any of those whom he had engaged should be deprived of an opportunity of going where they might be so usefully employed. He moreover foresaw, that when these persons were landed at Sierra Leona, it would be necessary to make such provision for the destitute as would support them until they were enabled to provide for themselves.

For this also he had to apply to his own resources, so that in this voyage he expended out of his own private funds, between three and four thousand dollars, for the benefit of the colony.

* * * * * * *

Such was his public character. Such was the warmth of his benevolence, the activity of his zeal, and the extent of his labours, in behalf of the African race. Indeed his whole life may be said to have been spent in their service. To their benefit he devoted the acquisitions of his youth, the time of his later years, and even the thoughts of his dying pillow.

As a private man, he was just and upright in all his dealings, an affectionate husband, a kind father, a good neighbor, and a faithful friend. Pious without ostentation, and warmly attached to the principles of Quakerism, he manifested, in all his deportment, that he was a true disciple of Jesus; and cherished a charitable disposition to professors of every denomination, who walked according to the leading principles of the gospel. Regardless of the honors and pleasures of the world, in humble imitation of his divine master, he went from place to place doing good, looking not for his reward among men, but in the favor of his Heavenly Father. Thus walking in the ways of piety and usefulness, in the smiles of an approving conscience, and the favor of God, he enjoyed, through life, an unusual serenity and satisfaction of mind, and when the fatal messenger arrived to cut the bonds of mortality, it found him in peace, ready and willing to depart. In that solemnly interesting period, when nature with him was struggling in the pangs of dissolution, such a calmness and serenity overspread his soul, and manifested itself in his countenance and actions, that the heart of the greatest reprobate, at beholding him, would have responded the wish "Let me die the death of the righteous, and let my last end be like his."

GEORGE MOSES HORTON

GEORGE MOSES HORTON was born in 1797 in Northampton County, N. C., the slave of William Horton. About 1803 his master removed to Chatham County, where he died in 1815. George then passed to James Horton, son of William, at whose death in 1832 he became the property of Hall Horton, a son. Hall Horton had the reputation of being a hard master, but he soon realized that George was not a good hand on the farm and permitted him to go to Chapel Hill and hire his time at twenty-five or fifty cents a day. The young man had an alert mind and was almost entirely self-taught. He studied the alphabet from scraps of paper, secured possession of a spelling-book, and learned to read largely by studying the hymns that he committed to memory. Separate ones of his poems began to find their way into print, and in 1829 was published in Raleigh a booklet, *The Hope of Liberty*, from the sale of which it was thought that a sum might be realized sufficient to purchase the freedom of the author and transport him to Liberia. About this time Horton was on fire with aspiration and ambition. His hopes were doomed to disappointment, however, and for the next thirty years he settled down at Chapel Hill, working as a janitor and executing little commissions in verse from the students. For twenty-five cents he would supply a poem of moderate warmth, but if a gentleman wished to send to a young lady an effusion of exceptional fervor, fifty cents would be the fee. He married a slave belonging to Franklin Snipes and in course of time became the father of two children, a son and a daughter. Slowly but surely also deterioration worked its will. The poet took to drink and he lost something of the "high seriousness" that once uplifted him. He wrote more and more in the vein of merriment or banter, dwelt again and again on the fickleness of woman, and, capitalizing in verse the distress of himself and his family, he appealed to the students at the university to "lend a helping hand to the old, unfortunate bard." To their credit it must be said that the stu-

dents responded liberally.   Sometimes there was a new ray of
hope.   We read of other collections of poems in these years; and
Miss Mary Youngs Cheney, of Connecticut, later Mrs. Horace
Greeley, having heard of Horton while teaching in Warrenton,
spoke of him to the famous editor, so that some lines entitled "The
Poet's Petition" appeared in the *New York Tribune*.   Then came
the Civil War.   In 1865 Horton went to Philadelphia with a
United States Cavalry officer, Captain Will H. S. Banks, of the
9th Michigan Cavalry Volunteers, to whose lines he had escaped.
From the records of the Banneker Institute we learn that "a
special meeting of the institution was held on the evening of
August 31, 1866, the object being to receive Mr. George Horton,
of North Carolina, a poet of considerable genius, it was claimed.
The possibility of publishing his book was submitted to Mr. John
H. Smythe, but found too expensive."   The poet died in Philadelphia in or about 1883.   He is described as having been "of
medium height, dark but not black," of courteous manner, and of
good character.

Horton's most distinctive contribution is to be found in his
first collection, *The Hope of Liberty*.   The little book of twenty-
two pages reveals any number of technical faults; at the same
time it has an earnestness of tone that the author never duplicated.
Horton had neither the sure taste nor the careful training of
Phillis Wheatley, but with his bolder imagination and his more
varied effort in versification, he sometimes gave the suggestion of
more power.   *The Hope of Liberty* was reprinted in Philadephia
in 1837 as *Poems by a Slave* and under this title was again printed
and bound with the 1838 edition of the poems of Phillis Wheatley.
Copies of other editions are exceedingly rare, if indeed they are
in existence at all; but at Harvard University is a copy of *Poetical
Works* (Hillsborough, N. C., 1845) and at the Athenaeum in
Boston one of *Naked Genius* (Raleigh, N. C., 1865).   One hears
also of an autobiography and collection issued in Boston in 1852,
and of other editions or collections in 1850 and 1854.   The
1845 edition was used by N. I. White and W. C. Jackson for
An Anthology of Verse by American Negroes (Durham, 1924)
and is discussed on pages 222-223.   *Naked Genius* is considerably

larger than *The Hope of Liberty*, containing one hundred and sixty pages, and its contents are more miscellaneous. In the second title in the book, "George Moses Horton, Myself," the poet is unblushingly subjective; but there is in the lines a seriousness of feeling considerably beyond what one would expect from the title. "The Woodman and the Money Hunter" gives some comparison of country life and the striving for wealth in the city, also some reflection of Horton's own life as a huntsman in the woods of North Carolina. "The Creditor to his Proud Debtor" is in light vein, as are other pieces in the book; and there are poems on prominent figures in the Civil War, Confederate as well as Union, representative ones being those on Jackson and Grant. The president of the Confederacy is satirized in "Jefferson in a Tight Place," in which he is likened to a fox caught in the hunt, with pointed reference to the disguise in which he is said to have sought to escape. All in all, *Naked Genius* contains much that is bright, much that is entertaining; but it hardly impresses the reader as having the message that is to be found, with all the crudities, in *The Hope of Liberty*.

Of the pieces that follow, all are taken from *The Hope of Liberty* except the last, which is from *Naked Genius*. For further study of the poet see the volumes mentioned, also *History of the University of North Carolina*, by Kemp P. Battle, 2 vols., Raleigh, 1907, 1912 (vol. I, pp. 603-605); "An American Man of Letters: George Horton, the Negro Poet," by Collier Cobb, first published in full in *The North Carolina Review*, October 3, 1909, and *The University of North Carolina Magazine*, October, 1909, and several times reprinted as a pamphlet; "George Moses Horton: Slave Poet," by Stephen B. Weeks, in *The Southern Workman*, Vol. 43, p. 571 (October, 1914); and *The Negro Author*, by Vernon Loggins, New York, 1931, pp. 107-117.

EXPLANATION

(Prefixed to *The Hope of Liberty*)

George, who is the author of the following Poetical effusions, is a Slave, the property of Mr. James Horton, of Chatham County,

North Carolina.   He has been in the habit, some years past, of
producing poetical pieces, sometimes on suggested subjects, to
such persons as would write them while he dictated.   Several
compositions of his have already appeared in the Raleigh Register.
Some have made their way into the Boston Newspapers, and have
evoked expressions of approbation and surprise.   Many persons
have now become much interested in the promotion of his prospects, some of whom are elevated in office and literary attainments.
They are solicitous that efforts at length be made to obtain by
subscription, a sum sufficient for his emancipation, upon the condition of his going in the vessel which shall first afterwards sail for
Liberia.   It is his earnest and only wish to become a member of
that Colony, to enjoy its privileges, and apply his industry and
mental abilities to the promotion of its prospects and his own.   It
is upon these terms alone, that the efforts of those who befriend
his views are intended to have a final effect.

   To put to trial the plan here urged in his behalf, the paper
now exhibited is published.   Several of his productions are con-
tained in the succeeding pages.   Many more might have been
added, which would have swelled into a larger size.   They would
doubtless be interesting to many, but it is hoped that the specimens
here inserted will be sufficient to accomplish the object of the publication.   Expense will thus be avoided, and the money better employed in enlarging the sum applicable for his emancipation.—It
is proposed, that in every town or vicinity where contributions
are made, they may be put into the hands of some person, who
will humanely consent to receive them, and give notice to Mr.
Weston R. Gales, in Raleigh, of the amount collected.   As soon
as it is ascertained that the collections will accomplish the object,
it is expected that they will be transmitted without delay to Mr.
Weston R. Gales.   But should they ultimately prove insufficient,
they will be returned to subscribers.

   None will imagine it possible that pieces produced as these
have been, should be free from blemish in composition or taste.
The author is now 32 years of age, and has always laboured in
the field on his master's farm, promiscuously with the few others
which Mr. Horton owns, in circumstances of the greatest possible

simplicity.   His master says he knew nothing of his poetry but
as he heard of it from others.   George knows how to read, and
is now learning to write.   All his pieces are written down by
others; and his reading, which is done at night, and at the usual
intervals allowed to slaves, has been much employed on poetry,
such as he could procure, this being the species of composition most
interesting to him.   It is thought best to print his productions
without correction, that the mind of the reader may be in no un-
certainty as to the originality and genuineness of every part.   We
shall conclude this account of George, with an assurance that he
has been ever a faithful, honest and industrious slave.   That
his heart has felt deeply and sensitively in this lowest possible condition of human nature, will easily be believed, and is impressively
confirmed by one of his stanzas.

> Come, melting Pity, from afar,
> And break this vast enormous bar
>   Between a wretch and thee;
> Purchase a few short days of time
> And bid a vassal soar sublime,
>   On wings of Liberty.

Raleigh, July 2, 1829.

On Liberty and Slavery

Alas! and am I born for this,
    To wear this slavish chain?
Deprived of all created bliss,
    Through hardship, toil, and pain!

How long have in bondage lain,
    And languished to be free!
Alas! and must I still complain—
    Deprived of liberty.

Oh, Heaven! and is there no relief
    This side the silent grave—

To soothe the pain—to quell the grief
  And anguish of a slave?

Come, Liberty, thou cheerful sound,
  Roll through my ravished ears,
Come, let my grief in joys be drowned,
  And drive away my fears.

Say unto foul oppression, Cease:
  Ye tyrants rage no more,
And let the joyful trump of peace,
  Now bid the vassal soar.

Soar on the pinions of that dove
  Which long has cooed for thee,
And breathed her notes from Afric's grove,
  The sound of Liberty.

Oh, Liberty! thou golden prize,
  So often sought by blood—
We crave thy sacred sun to rise,
  The gift of nature's God!

Bid Slavery hide her haggard face,
  And barbarism fly:
I scorn to see the sad disgrace
  In which enslaved I lie.

Dear Liberty! upon thy breast,
  I languish to respire;
And like the Swan unto her nest,
  I'd to thy smiles retire.

Oh, blest asylum—heavenly balm!
  Unto thy boughs I flee—
And in thy shades the storm shall calm,
  With songs of Liberty!

The Slave's Complaint

Am I sadly cast aside,
On misfortunes's rugged tide?
Will the world my pains deride
    Forever?

Must I dwell in Slavery's night,
And all pleasure take its flight,
Far beyond my feeble sight,
    Forever?

Worst of all, must hope grow dim,
And withhold her cheering beam?
Rather let me sleep and dream
    Forever!

Something still my heart surveys,
Groping through this dreary maze;
Is it Hope?—then burn and blaze
    Forever!

Leave me not a wretch confined,
Altogether lame and blind—
Unto gross despair consigned,
    Forever!

Heaven! in whom can I confide?
Canst thou not for all provide?
Condescend to be my guide
    Forever:

And when this transient life shall end,
Oh, may some kind, eternal friend
Bid me from servitude ascend,
    Forever!

On Hearing of the Intention of a Gentleman
to Purchase the Poet's Freedom

When on life's ocean first I spread my sail,
I then implored a mild auspicious gale;
And from the slippery strand I took my flight,
And sought the peaceful haven of delight.

Tyrannic storms arose upon my soul,
And dreadful did their mad'ning thunders roll;
The pensive muse was shaken from her sphere,
And hope, it vanished in the clouds of fear.

At length a golden sun broke through the gloom,
And from his smiles arose a sweet perfume—
A calm ensued, and birds began to sing,
And lo! the sacred muse resumed her wing.

With frantic joy she chaunted as she flew,
And kiss'd the clement hand that bore her through;
Her envious foes did from her sight retreat,
Or prostrate fall beneath her burning feet.

'Twas like a proselyte, allied to Heaven—
Or rising spirits' boast of sins forgiven,
Whose shout dissolves the adamant away,
Whose melting voice the stubborn rocks obey.

'Twas like the salutation of the dove,
Borne on the zephyr through some lonesome grove,
When Spring returns, and Winter's chill is past,
And vegetation smiles above the blast.

'Twas like the evening of a nuptial pair,
When love pervades the hour of sad despair—
'Twas like fair Helen's sweet return to Troy,
When every Grecian bosom swell'd with joy.

The silent harp which on the osiers hung,
Was then attuned, and manumission sung;
Away by hope the clouds of fear were driven,
And music breathed my gratitude to Heaven.

Hard was the race to reach the distant goal,
The needle oft was shaken from the pole;
In such distress who could forbear to weep?
Toss'd by the headlong billows of the deep!

The tantalizing beams which shone so plain,
Which turned my former pleasures into pain—
Which falsely promised all the joys of fame,
Gave way, and to a more substantial flame.

Some philanthropic souls as from afar,
With pity strove to break the slavish bar;
To whom my floods of gratitude shall roll,
And yield with pleasure to their soft control.

And sure of Providence this work begun—
He shod my feet this rugged race to run;
And in despite of all the swelling tide,
Along the dismal path will prove my guide.

Thus on the dusky verge of deep despair,
Eternal Providence was with me there;
When pleasure seemed to fade on life's gay dawn,
And the last beam of hope was almost gone.

ON SPRING

Hail, thou auspicious vernal dawn!
Ye birds, proclaim the winter's gone,
    Ye warbling minstrels sing;
Pour forth your tribute as ye rise,
And thus salute the fragrant skies
    The pleasing smiles of Spring.

Coo sweetly, oh thou harmless Dove,
And bid thy mate no longer rove
   In cold, hybernal vales;
Let music rise from every tongue,
Whilst winter flies before the song,
   Which floats on gentle gales.

Ye frozen streams dissolve and flow
Along the valley, sweet and slow;
   Divested fields be gay;
Ye drooping forests bloom on high,
And raise your branches to the sky,
   And thus your charms display.

Thou world of heat—thou vital source,
The torpid insects feel thy force,
   Which all with life supplies;
Gardens and orchards richly bloom,
And send a gale of sweet perfume,
   To invite them as they rise.

Near where the crystal waters glide,
The male of birds escorts his bride,
   And twitters on the spray;
He mounts upon his active wing,
To hail the bounty of the Spring,
   The lavish pomp of May.

Inspiring month of youthful Love,
How oft we in the peaceful grove,
   Survey the flowery plume;
Or sit beneath the sylvan shade,
Where branches wave above the head,
   And smile on every bloom.

Exalted month, when thou art gone,
May Virtue then begin the dawn
  Of an eternal Spring?
May raptures kindle on my tongue,
And start a new, eternal song,
  Which ne'er shall cease to ring!

LOVE

Whilst tracing thy visage, I sink in emotion,
  For no other damsel so wond'rous I see;
Thy looks are so pleasing, thy charms so amazing,
  I think of no other, my true-love, but thee.

With heart-burning rapture I gaze on thy beauty,
  And fly like a bird to the boughs of a tree;
Thy looks are so pleasing, thy charms so amazing,
  I fancy no other, my true-love, but thee.

Thus oft in the valley I think and I wonder
  Why cannot a maid with her lover agree?
Thy looks are so pleasing, thy charms so amazing,
  I pine for no other, my true-love, but thee.

I'd fly from thy frowns with a heart full of sorrow—
  Return, pretty damsel, and smile thou on me;
By ev'ry endeavor, I'll try thee forever;
  And languish until I am fancied by thee.

ON THE TRUTH OF THE SAVIOUR

E'en John the Baptist did not know
  Who Christ the Lord could be,
And bade his own disciples go,
  The strange event to see.

They said, Art thou the one of whom
    'Twas written long before?
Is there another still to come,
    Who will all things restore?

This is enough, without a name—
    Go, tell him what is done;
Behold the feeble, weak and lame,
    With strength rise up and run.

This is enough—the blind now see,
    The dumb Hosannas sing;
Devils far from his presence flee,
    As shades from morning's wing.

See the distress'd, all bathed in tears,
    Prostrate before him fall;
Immanuel speaks, and Lazarus hears—
    The dead obeys his call.

This is enough—the fig-tree dies,
    And withers at his frown;
Nature her God must recognize,
    And drop her flowery crown.

At his command the fish increase,
    And loaves of barley swell—
Ye hungry eat, and hold your peace,
    And find a remnant still.

At his command the water blushed,
    And all was turned to wine,
And in redundance flowed afresh,
    And owned its God divine.

Behold the storms at his rebuke,
    All calm upon the sea—

How can we for another look,
    When none can work as he?

This is enough—it must be God,
    From whom the plagues are driven;
At whose command the mountains nod
    And all the Host of Heaven!

———————

GEORGE MOSES HORTON, MYSELF

I feel myself in need
    Of the inspiring strains of ancient lore,
My heart to lift, my empty mind to feed,
    And all the world explore.

I know that I am old
    And never can recover what is past,
But for the future may some light unfold
    And soar from ages blast.

I feel resolved to try,
    My wish to prove, my calling to pursue,
Or mount up from the earth into the sky,
    To show what Heaven can do.

My genius from a boy,
    Has fluttered like a bird within my heart;
But could not thus confined her powers employ,
    Impatient to depart.

She like a restless bird,
    Would spread her wings, her power to be
        unfurl'd,
And let her songs be loudly heard,
    And dart from world to world.

DAVID WALKER

DAVID WALKER was the author of only one production, but in that one he made the boldest and most direct appeal for freedom of which we hear in the early years of the antislavery movement. He was born in Wilmington, N. C., September 28, 1785. While his mother was free, his father had been a slave, and he himself soon felt such detestation for the whole system of human bondage that he resolved not to live in the South. Having told his mother farewell, he turned his back upon the section, and after many trials he at length reached Boston, where he took up his permanent residence. He applied himself diligently and learned to read and write, hoping to contribute something to the cause of humanity. In 1827 he opened a clothing store on Brattle Street, and prospered. He joined a Methodist Church and in 1828 he married. His home had an air of hospitality and liberality and became a shelter for the poor and needy. He himself is described as being at this time six feet in height, slender, well proportioned, and dark, with loose hair. In 1829, from an over-flowing heart, came *Walker's Appeal, in Four Articles; together with a Preamble, to the Coloured Citizens of the World, but in Particular and very Expressly to Those of the United States of America.* The book created consternation among the slaveholders of the South. The governors of Virginia and North Carolina sent special messages to their legislatures about it, and the governor of Georgia wrote Harrison Gray Otis, mayor of Boston, to ask (one might almost say to demand) that it be suppressed. Otis replied that personally he did not approve of the pamphlet but that the author had not done anything that made him amenable to punishment and could not be forbidden in the lawful utterance of his thoughts. A reward of a thousand dollars was then offered for Walker's head, the amount to be ten times as much if he was taken alive. His wife and friends advised that he go to Canada, but he refused, saying, "I will stand my ground. Somebody must die in this cause. I may be doomed to the stake

and the fire, or to the scaffold tree, but it is not in me to falter if
I can promote the work of emancipation." Before the close of
1830 he died, and the belief was persistent that he met with foul
play.

Within hardly more than a year the *Appeal* was in the third
edition. In 1848 was printed an edition with a brief sketch of the
author's life by Henry Highland Garnet, which sketch is now the
chief source for information about Walker. Garnet was better
educated than Walker, and became a man of broader culture, but
in spirit he was the successor of the man whose book he admired.
In 1840 he delivered before the American Anti-Slavery Society
an address in which he clearly stated his position that the people
of color were entitled to all the rights and immunities of American citizens. In 1843 he read before a convention of Negro
men in Buffalo *An Address to the Slaves of the United States of
America.* To this objection was made, first, that it was warlike
and encouraged insurrection, and second, that if the convention
adopted it, those delegates who lived near the borders of the slave
states would not dare to return home; accordingly it was rejected,
though by a small majority. In 1848, however, in only slightly
modified form, it was appended to the new edition of the *Appeal.*
Garnet said to the slaves that it was sinful in the extreme to submit to the degradation visited upon them, he called attention to
the fact that they were three million strong, and urged them to
die as freemen rather than to live as slaves. He was original in
suggesting to them a general strike, urging that they cease to
labor for tyrants who would not remunerate them; and he directed attention to the example of such insurrectionists as Denmark Vesey, Nat Turner, and Joseph Cinque, hero of the *Amistad.*

In the *Appeal* as here given only about one-third of the complete work is presented, but the endeavor has been to make such
selection as would include all essential points made by the author.

WALKER'S APPEAL IN FOUR ARTICLES, TOGETHER WITH A
PREAMBLE TO THE COLOURED CITIZENS OF THE WORLD

Preamble

My dearly beloved Brethren and Fellow-Citizens:

Having travelled over a considerable portion of these
United States, and having, in the course of my travels, taken
the most accurate observations of things as they exist, the
result of my observations has warranted the full and un-
shaken conviction, that we (coloured people of these United
States) are the most degraded, wretched, and abject set of
beings that ever lived since the world began; and I pray God
that none like us ever may live again until time shall be no
more. They tell us of the Israelites in Egypt, the Helots in
Sparta, and of the Roman Slaves, which last were made up
from almost every nation under heaven, whose sufferings
under those ancient and heathen nations, were, in comparison with ours, under this enlightened and Christian nation,
no more than a cypher—or, in other words, those heathen
nations of antiquity, had but little more among them than
the name and form of slavery; while wretchedness and endless miseries were reserved, apparently in a phial, to be
poured out upon our fathers, ourselves and our children, by
Christian Americans.

These positions I shall endeavour, by the help of the
Lord, to demonstrate in the course of this *Appeal*, to the
satisfaction of the most incredulous mind—and may God
Almighty, who is the Father of our Lord Jesus Christ, open
your hearts to understand and believe the truth.

The *causes*, my brethren, which produce our wretchedness and miseries, are so very numerous and aggravating, that
I believe the pen only of a Josephus or a Plutarch, can well
enumerate and explain them. Upon subjects, then, of such
incomprehensible magnitude, so impenetrable, and so notori-

ous, I shall be obliged to omit a large class of, and content myself with giving you an exposition of a few of those, which do indeed rage to such an alarming pitch, that they cannot but be a perpetual source of terror and dismay to every reflecting mind.

⌐I am fully aware, in making this appeal to my much afflicted and suffering brethren, that I shall not only be assailed by those whose greatest earthly desires are to keep us in abject ignorance and wretchedness, and who are of the firm conviction that Heaven has designed us and our children to be slaves and *beasts of burden* to them and their children.⌐ I say, I do not only expect to be held up to the public as an ignorant, impudent and restless disturber of the public peace, by such avaricious creatures, as well as a mover of insubordination—and perhaps put in prison or to death, for giving a superficial exposition of our miseries, and exposing tyrants. But I am persuaded, that many of my brethren, particularly those who are ignorantly in league with slave-holders or tyrants, who acquire their daily bread by the blood and sweat of their more ignorant brethren—and not a few of those too, who are too ignorant to see an inch beyond their noses, will rise up and call me cursed—Yea, the jealous ones among us will perhaps use more abject subtlety, by affirming that this work is not worth perusing, that we are well situated, and there is no use in trying to better our condition, for we cannot. I will ask one question here.—Can our condition be any worse?—Can it be more mean and abject? If there are any changes, will they not be for the better, though they may appear for the worse at first? Can they get us any lower? Where can they get us? They are afraid to treat us worse, for they know well, the day they do it they are gone. But against all accusations which may or can be preferred against me, I appeal to Heaven for my motive in writing—who knows what my object is, if possible, to awaken in the breasts of my afflicted, degraded and slumbering brethren, a spirit of inquiry and investigation respecting our miseries and wretchedness in this *Republican Land of Liberty!!!!!*

The sources from which our miseries are derived, and on which I shall comment, I shall not combine in one, but shall put them under distinct heads and expose them in their turn; in doing which, keeping truth on my side, and not departing from the strictest rules of morality, I shall endeavor to penetrate, search out, and lay them open for your inspection. If you cannot or will not profit by them, I shall have done *my* duty to you, my country and my God. . . .

All persons who are acquainted with history, and particularly the Bible, who are not blinded by the God of this world, and are not actuated solely by avarice—who are able to lay aside prejudice long enough to view candidly and impartially things as they were, are, and probably will be—who are willing to admit that God made man to serve him *alone,* and that man should have no other Lord or Lords but Himself—that God Almighty is the *sole proprietor* or *master* of the whole human family, and will not on any consideration admit of a colleague, being unwilling to divide his glory with another—and who can dispense with prejudice long enough to admit that we are men, notwithstanding our improminent noses and woolly heads, and believe that we feel for our fathers, mothers, wives and children, as well as the whites do for theirs—I say, all who are permitted to see and believe these things, can easily recognize the judgments of God among the Spaniards. Though others may lay the cause of the fierceness with which they cut each other's throats, to some other circumstance, yet they who believe that God is a God of justice, will believe that Slavery *is the principal cause.* . . .

Article I

Our Wretchedness in Consequence of Slavery

My beloved brethren:—The Indians of North and of South America—the Greeks—the Irish, subjected under the king of Great Britain—the Jews, that ancient people of the Lord—the inhabitants of the islands of the sea—in fine, all the inhabitants of the earth, (except, however, the sons of Africa) are called *men,* and of course are, and ought to be free. But we, (coloured people) and our children are *brutes!!* and of course are and *ought to be* Slaves to the American people and their children forever!! to dig their mines and work their farms; and thus go on enriching them, from one generation to another with our *blood* and our tears!!!!

I promised in a preceding page to demonstrate to the satisfaction of the most incredulous, that we (coloured people of these United States of America) are the *most wretched, degraded* and *abject* set of beings that *ever lived* since the world began, and that the white Americans having reduced us to the wretched state of *slavery,* treat us in that condition *more cruel* (they being an enlightened and Christian people), than any heathen nation did any people whom it had reduced to our condition. These affirmations are so well confirmed in the minds of all unprejudiced men, who have taken the trouble to read histories, that they need no elucidation from me. But to put them beyond all doubt, I refer you in the first place to the children of Jacob, or of Israel in Egypt, under Pharaoh and his people. Some of my brethren do not know who Pharaoh and the Egyptians were—I know it to be a fact, that some of them take the Egyptians to have been a gang of *devils,* not knowing any better, and that they (Egyptians) having got possession of the Lord's people, treated them *nearly* as cruel as *Christian Americans* do us at the present day. For the information of such, I would only mention that the Egyptians were Africans or coloured people, such as we are—some of them yellow and others dark—a mixture of Ethiopians and the natives of Egypt—about the same as you see the coloured people of the United States at the present day. . . .

I saw a paragraph, a few years since, in a South Carolina paper, which, speaking of the barbarity of the Turks, said: "The Turks are the most barbarous people in the world—they treat the Greeks more like *brutes* than human beings." And in the same paper was an advertisement, which said: "Eight well built Virginia and Maryland *Negro fellows* and four *wenches* will positively be *sold* this day, to the highest bidder!" And what astonished me still more was, to see in this same *humane* paper!! the cuts of three men, with clubs and budgets on their backs, and an advertisement offering a considerable sum of money for their apprehension and delivery. I declare, it is really so amusing to hear the Southerners and Westerners of this country talk about *barbarity*, that it is positively enough to make a man *smile*.

The sufferings of the Helots among the Spartans, were somewhat severe, it is true, but to say that theirs were as severe as ours among the Americans, I do most strenuously deny—for instance, can any man show me an article on a page of ancient history which specifies, that, the Spartans chained, and hand-cuffed the Helots, and dragged them from their wives and children, children from their parents, mothers from their suckling babes, wives from their husbands, driving them from one end of the country to the other? Notice the Spartans were heathens, who lived long before our Divine Master made his appearance in the flesh. Can Christian Americans deny these barbarous cruelties? Have you not, Americans, having subjected us under you, added to these miseries, by insulting us in telling us to our face, because we are help-

less, that we are not of the human family? I ask you, O!
Americans, I ask you, in the name of the Lord, can you
deny these charges? . . .

The whites have always been an unjust, jealous, unmerciful, avaricious and blood-thirsty set of beings, always seeking
after power and authority.—We view them all over the confederacy of Greece, where they were first known to be any
thing, (in consequence of education) we see them there,
cutting each other's throats—trying to subject each other to
wretchedness and misery—to effect which, they used all kinds
of deceitful, unfair, and unmerciful means. We view them
next in Rome, where the spirit of tyranny and deceit raged
still higher. We view them in Gaul, Spain, and in Britain.—
In fine, we view them all over Europe, together with what
were scattered about in Asia and Africa, as heathens, and we
see them acting more like devils than accountable men. But
some may ask, did not the blacks of Africa, and the mulattoes
of Asia go on in the same way as did the whites of Europe. I
answer, no—they never were half so avaricious, deceitful and
unmerciful as the whites according to their knowledge. . . .

ARTICLE II

OUR WRETCHEDNESS IN CONSEQUENCE OF IGNORANCE

Ignorance, my brethren, is a mist, low down into the
very dark and almost impenetrable abyss in which, our fathers
for many centuries have been plunged. The Christians, and
enlightened of Europe, and some of Asia, seeing the ignorance and consequent degradation of our fathers, instead of
trying to enlighten them, by teaching them that religion and
light with which God had blessed them, they have plunged
them into wretchedness ten thousand times more intolerable,
than if they had left them entirely to the Lord, and to add
to their miseries, deep down into which they have plunged

them tell them, that they are an *inferior* and *distinct race* of beings. ...

Ignorance and treachery one against the other—a grovelling servile and abject submission to the lash of tyrants, we see plainly, my brethren, are not the natural elements of the blacks, as the Americans try to make us believe; but these are misfortunes which God has suffered our fathers to be enveloped in for many ages, no doubt in consequence of their disobedience to their Maker, and which do, indeed, reign at this time among us, almost to the destruction of all other principles: for I must truly say, that ignorance, the mother of treachery and deceit, gnaws into our very vitals. Ignorance, as it now exists among us, produces a state of things, O my Lord! too horrible to present to the world. Any man who is curious to see the full force of ignorance developed among the coloured people of the United States of America, has only to go into the southern and western states of this confederacy, where, if he is not a tyrant, but has the feeling of a human being, who can feel for a fellow creature, he may see enough to make his very heart bleed! He may see there a son take his mother, who bore almost the pains of death to give him birth, and by the command of a tyrant, strip her as naked as she came into the world, and apply the cowhide to her, until she falls a victim to death in the road! He may see a husband take his dear wife, not unfrequently in a pregnant state, and perhaps far advanced, and beat her for an unmerciful wretch until his infant falls a lifeless lump at her feet! Can the Americans escape God Almighty? If they do, can he be to us a God of Justice? God is just, and I know it—for he has convinced me to my satisfaction— I cannot doubt him. My observer may see fathers beating their sons, mothers their daughters, and children their parents, all to pacify the passions of unrelenting tyrants. He may also see them telling news and lies, making mischief

one upon another. These are some of the productions of
ignorance, which he will see practised among my dear
brethren, who are held in unjust slavery and wretchedness,
by avaricious and unmerciful tyrants to whom, and their
hellish deeds, I would suffer my life to be taken before I
would submit. And when my curious observer comes to take
notice of those who are said to be free, (which assertion I
deny) and who are making some frivolous pretentions to common sense, he will see that branch of ignorance among the
slaves assuming a more cunning and deceitful course of pro-
cedure. He may see some of my brethren in league with tyrants, selling their own brethren into *hell upon earth*, not dis-
similar to the exhibitions in Africa, but in a more secret, servile
and abject manner. O Heaven! I am full!! I can hardly move
my pen!!! and as I expect some will try to put me to death,
to strike terror into others, and to obliterate from their minds
the notion of freedom, so as to keep my brethren the more
secure in wretchedness, where they will be permitted to stay
but a short time (whether tyrants believe it or not)—I shall
give the world a development of facts, which are already witnessed in the courts of heaven. My observer may see some
of these ignorant and treacherous creatures (coloured people)
sneaking about in the large cities, endeavoring to find out all
strange coloured people, where they work, and where they
reside, asking them questions, and trying to ascertain whether
they are runaways or not, telling them, at the same time, that
they always have been, are, and always will be friends to their
brethren; and, perhaps, that they themselves are absconders,
and a thousand such treacherous lies to get the better information of the more ignorant!!! There have been and are at this
day in Boston, New-York, Philadelphia, and Baltimore,
coloured men, who are in league with tyrants, and who receive a great portion of their daily bread, of the moneys
which they acquire from the blood and tears of their more

miserable brethren, whom they scandalously delivered into the hands of our natural enemies!!!!!! ...

Men of colour, who are also of sense, for you particularly is my *Appeal* designed. Our more ignorant brethren are not able to penetrate its value. I call upon you therefore to cast your eyes upon the wretchedness of your brethren, and to do your utmost to enlighten them—*go to work and enlighten your brethren!*—Let the Lord see you doing what you can to rescue them and yourselves from degradation. There is a great work for you to do, as trifling as some of you may think of it. You have to prove to the Americans and the world, that we are *Men*, and not *brutes*, as we have been represented, and by millions treated. [Remember, to let the aim of your labours among your brethren, and particularly the youths, be the dissemination of education and religion.] It is lamentable, that many of our children go to school, from four until they are eight or ten, and sometimes fifteen years of age, and leave school knowing but a little more about the grammar of their language than a horse does about handling a musket—and not a few of them are really so ignorant that they are unable to answer a person correctly, general questions in geography, and to hear them read would only be to disgust a man who has a taste for reading; which, to do well, as trifling as it may appear to some (to the ignorant in particular) is a great part of learning. Some few of them, may make out to scribble tolerably well, over a half sheet of paper, which I believe has hitherto been a powerful obstacle in our way, to keep us from acquiring knowledge. [An ignorant father, who knows no more than what nature has taught him, together with what little he acquires by the senses of hearing and seeing, finding his son able to write a neat hand, sets it down for granted that he has as good learning as any body; the young, ignorant gump, hearing his father or mother, who perhaps may be ten times more ignorant, in point of literature, than himself, extolling his learning, struts about, in the full assurance, that his attainments in literature are sufficient to take him through the world when in fact, he has scarcely any learning at all!!

I must close this article by relating the very heart-rending fact, that I have examined school-boys, young men of colour, in different parts of Murray's English Grammar, and not more than one in thirty was able to give a correct answer to my interrogations. If any one contradicts me, let him step out of his door into the streets of Boston, New York, Philadelphia, or Baltimore (no use to mention any other, for the Christians are too charitable further south or west!)—I say, let him who disputes me step out of his door into the streets of either of those four cities, and promiscuously collect one hundred school-boys or young men of colour, *who have been to school*, and who are considered by the coloured people to have received an excellent education, because, perhaps, some of them can write a good hand, but who, notwithstanding their neat writing, may be almost as ignorant, in comparison as a horse.—And, I say it, he will hardly find (in this enlightened day, and in the midst of this *charitable* people) five in one hundred who are able to correct the false grammar of their language.—The cause of this almost universal ignorance among us, I appeal to our school-masters to declare. Here is a fact, which I this very minute take from the mouth of a young coloured man who has been to school in this state (Massachusetts) nearly nine years, and who knows grammar this day, *nearly* as well as he did the day he first entered the school-house, under a white master. This young man says: "My master would never allow me to study grammar." I asked him, why? "The school committee," said he "forbid the coloured children learning grammar—they would not allow any but the white children to study grammar." It is a notorious fact, that the major part of the white Americans, have, ever since we have been among them, tried to keep us

ignorant, and make us believe that God made us and our
children to be slaves on them and theirs. *O my God, have
mercy on Christian Americans!!!*

ARTICLE III

OUR WRETCHEDNESS IN CONSEQUENCE OF THE PREACHERS OF THE RELIGION OF JESUS CHRIST

Religion, my brethren, is a substance* of deep consideration among all nations of the earth. The Pagans have a kind,
as well as the Mahometans, the Jews and the Christians. But
pure and undefiled religion, such as was preached by Jesus
Christ and his apostles, is hard to be found in all the earth.
God, through his instrument Moses, handed a dispensation
of his divine will, to the children of Israel after they had
left Egypt for the land of Canaan or of Promise, who through
hypocrisy, oppression and unbelief, departed from the faith.—
He then by his apostles, handed a dispensation of his, together
with the will of Jesus Christ, to the Europeans in Europe,
who, in open violation of which, have made *merchandise* of
us, and it does appear as though they take this very dispensation to aid them in their *infernal* depredations upon us. Indeed, the way in which religion was and is conducted by the
Europeans and their descendants, one might believe it was
a plan fabricated by themselves and the *devils* to oppress us.
But hark! My master has taught me better than to believe
it—he has taught me that his gospel as it was preached by
himself and his apostles remains the same, nothwithstanding
Europe has tried to mingle blood and oppression with it.

It is well known to the Christian world, that Bartholo-
mew Las Casas, that very very notoriously avaricious Catholic
priest or preacher and adventurer with Columbus in his second voyage, proposed to his countrymen, the Spaniards in
Hispaniola, to import the Africans from the Portuguese set-

---

* Thus in all editions. Misprint for *subject?*

tlement in Africa, to dig up gold and silver, and work their
plantations for them, to effect which, he made a voyage thence
to Spain, and opened the subject to his master, Ferdinand,
then in declining health, who listened to the plan, but who
died soon after, and left it in the hand of his successor,
Charles V. This wretch, ("Las Casas, the Preacher,") succeeded so well in his plans of oppression, that in 1503, the first
blacks had been imported into the New World. Elated with
this success, and stimulated by sordid avarice only, he im-
portuned Charles V in 1511 to grant permission to a Flemish
merchant, to import 4000 blacks at one time. Thus we see,
through the instrumentality of a pretended preacher of the
gospel of Jesus Christ our common master, our wretchedness
first commenced in America—where it has been continued
from 1503 to this day 1829—a period of three hundred and
twenty-six years; but two hundred and nine, from 1620—
when twenty of our fathers were brought into Jamestown,
Virginia, by a Dutch man of war, and sold off like brutes to
the highest bidders; and there is not a doubt in my mind,
but that tyrants are in hope to perpetuate our miseries under
them and their children until the final consummation of all
things.—But if they do not get dreadfully deceived, it will
be because God has forgotten them. . . .

What the American preachers can think of us, I aver this
day before my God, I have never been able to define. They
have newspapers and monthly periodicals, which they receive
in continual succession, but on the pages of which, you will
scarcely ever find a paragraph respecting slavery, which is
ten thousand times more injurious to this country than all
the other evils put together; and which will be the final
overthrow of its government, unless something is very speedily done; for their cup is nearly full.—Perhaps they will
laugh at or make light of this; but I tell you Americans! that
unless you speedily alter your course, *you* and your Country

are gone!!!!! For God Almighty will tear up the very face
of the earth!!! Will not that very remarkable passage of
Scripture be fulfilled on Christian Americans? Hear it Americans!! "He that is unjust, let him be unjust still:—and he
which is filthy, let him be filthy still: and he that is righteous,
let him be righteous still: and he that is holy, let him be holy
still." [I hope that the Americans may hear, but I am afraid
that they have done us so much injury, and are so firm in
the belief that our Creator made us to be an inheritance to
them forever, that their hearts will be hardened, so that their
destruction may be sure. This language, perhaps, is too harsh
for the American's delicate ears. But O Americans! Americans!! I warn you in the name of the Lord (whether you
will hear, or forbear,) to repent and reform, or you are
ruined!!! Do you think that our blood is hiding from the
Lord, because you can hide it from the rest of the world, by
sending out missionaries, and by your charitable deeds to the
Greeks, Irish, etc.? Will he not publish your secret crimes
on the house top? Even here in Boston, pride and prejudice have got to such a pitch, that in the very houses erected
to the Lord, they have built little places for the reception of
coloured people, where they must sit during meeting, or keep
away from the house of God, and the preachers say nothing
about it—much less go into the hedges and highways seeking
the lost sheep of the house of Israel, and try to bring them
in to their Lord and Master. There are not a more wretched,
ignorant, miserable and abject set of beings in all the world
than the blacks in the southern and western sections of this
country, under tyrants and devils. The preachers of America can not see them, but they can send out missionaries to
convert the heathens, notwithstanding. . . . O Americans!
Americans!! I call God—I call angels—I call men, to witness, that your *destruction* is at hand, and will be speedily
consummated unless you *repent*.

ARTICLE IV
OUR WRETCHEDNESS IN CONSEQUENCE OF THE COLONIZING PLAN

My dearly beloved brethren:—This is a scheme on which so many able writers, together with that very judicious Baltimorean, William J. Watkins, in *Freedom's Journal*, have commented, that I feel my delicacy about touching it. But as I am compelled to do the will of my Master, I declare, I will give you my sentiments upon it.—Previous, however, to giving my sentiments, either for or against it, I shall give that of Mr. Henry Clay, together with that of Mr. Elias B. Caldwell, Esq., of the District of Columbia, as extracted from the *National Intelligence*, by Dr. Torrey, author of a series of "Essays on Morals, and the Diffusion of Useful Knowledge."

At a meeting which was convened in the District of Columbia, for the express purpose of agitating the subject of colonizing us in some part of the world, Mr. Clay was called to the chair, and having been seated a little while, he rose and spoke, in substance, as follows:—"That class of the mixt population of our country (coloured people) was peculiarly situated; they neither enjoyed the immunities of freemen, nor were they subjected to the incapacities of slaves, but partook, in some degree, of the qualities of both. From their condition, and the unconquerable prejudices resulting from their colour, they never could amalgamate with the free whites of this country. It was desirable, therefore, as it respected them, and the residue of the population of the country, to drain them off. Various schemes of colonization had been thought of, and a part of our continent, it was supposed by some, might furnish a suitable establishment for them. But, for his part, Mr. C. said, he had a decided preference for some part of the coast of Africa. There ample provision might be made for the colony itself, and it might be rendered instrumental to the introduction into that extensive quarter of the globe, of the arts, civilization, and Christianity." (Here I ask Mr. Clay, what kind of Christianity? Did he mean such as they have among the Americans—distinction, whip, blood and oppression? I pray the Lord Jesus Christ to forbid it.) "There," said he, "was a peculiar, a moral fitness, in restoring them to the land of their fathers, and if instead of the evils and sufferings which we had been the innocent cause of inflicting upon the inhabitants of Africa, we can transmit to her the blessings of our arts, or civilization and our religion, may we not hope, that America will extinguish a great portion of that moral debt which she has contracted to that unfortunate continent? Can there be a nobler cause than that which contemplates the spreading of the arts of civilized life, and the possible redemption from ignorance and barbarism, of a benighted quarter of the globe?"

Now I appeal and ask every citizen of these United States and of the world, both *white* and *black*, who has any knowledge of Mr. Clay's public labor for these States—I want you candidly to answer the Lord, who sees the secrets of our hearts.—Do you believe that Mr. Henry Clay, late Secretary of State, and now in Kentucky, is a friend to the blacks, further than his personal interests extends? Is it not his greatest object and glory upon earth to sink us into miseries and wretchedness by making slaves of us, to work his plantation to enrich him and his family? Does he care a pinch of snuff about Africa—whether it remains a land of Pagans and of blood, or of Christians, so long as he gets enough of her sons and daughters to dig up gold and silver for him? If he had no slaves, and could obtain them in no other way, if it were not repugnant to the laws of his country, which prohibits the importation of slaves (which act was, indeed, more through apprehension than through humanity) would he not try to import a few from Africa, to work his farm? Would he work in the hot sun to earn his bread, if he could make an African work for nothing, particularly if he could keep him in ignorance and make him believe that God made him for nothing else but to work for him? Is not Mr. Clay a white man, and too delicate to work in the hot sun!! Was he not made by his Creator to sit in the shade, and make the blacks work without remuneration for their services, to support him and his family!!! I have been for some time taking notice of this man's speeches and public writings, but never to my knowledge have I seen any thing in his writings which insisted on the emancipation of slavery, which has almost ruined his country. Thus we see the depravity of men's hearts, when in pursuit only of gain—particularly when they oppress their fellow creatures to obtain that gain—God suffers some to go on until they are lost forever. This same Mr. Clay, wants to know what he has done to merit the disapprobation of the American people. In a public speech delivered by him, he asked: "Did I involve my country in an unnecessary war?" to merit the censure of the Americans—"Did I bring obliquy upon the nation, or the people whom I represented?—Did I ever lose any opportunity to advance the fame, honor, and prosperity of this State and Union?" How astonishing it is, for a man who knows so much about God and his Ways, as Mr. Clay, to ask such frivolous questions? Does he believe that a man of his talents and standing in the midst of a people, will get along unnoticed by the penetrating and all-seeing eye of God, who is continually taking cognizance of the hearts of men? Is not God against him for advocating the murderous cause of slavery? If God is against him, what can the Americans, together with the whole world, do for him? Can they save him from the hand of the Lord Jesus Christ?

I shall now pass in review the speech of Mr. Elias B.

Caldwell, Esq., of the District of Columbia, extracted from the same page on which Mr. Clay's will be found. Mr. Caldwell, giving his opinion respecting us, at that ever memorable meeting, says: "The more you improve the condition of these people, the more you cultivate their minds, the more miserable you make them in their present state. You give them a higher relish for those privileges which they can never attain, and turn what we intend for a blessing into a curse." Let me ask this benevolent man, what he means by a blessing intended for us? Did he mean sinking us and our children into ignorance and wretchedness, to support him and his family? What he meant will appear evident and obvious to the most ignorant in the world. . . .

Here is a demonstrative proof of a plan got up by a gang of slave-holders to select the free people of colour from among the slaves, that our more miserable brethren may be the better secured in ignorance and wretchedness, to work their farms and dig their mines, and thus go on enriching the Christians with their blood and groans. | What our brethren could have been thinking about, who have left their native land and home and gone away to Africa, I am unable to say. This country is as much ours as it is the whites, whether they will admit it now or not, they will see and believe it bye and bye. They tell us about prejudice—what have we to do with it? Their prejudices will be obliged to fall like lightning to the ground, in succeeding generations; not, however, with the will and consent of all the whites, for some will be obliged to hold on to the old adage, viz.: the blacks are not men, but were made to be an inheritance to us and our children forever!!!!! I hope the residue of the coloured people, will stand still and see the salvation of God, and the miracle which he will work for our delivery from wretchedness under the Christians. . . .

Before I proceed further with this scheme, I shall give an

extract from the letter of that truly Reverend Divine (Bishop Allen,) of Philadelphia, respecting this trick. At the instance of the Editor of the *Freedom's Journal,* he says, "Dear Sir, I have been for several years trying to reconcile my mind to the Colonizing of Africans in Liberia, but there have always been, and there still remain great and insurmountable objections against the scheme. We are an unlettered people, brought up in ignorance, not one in a hundred can read or write, not one in a thousand has a liberal education; is there any fitness for such to be sent into a far country, among heathens, to convert or civilize them, when they themselves are neither civilized or christianized? See the great bulk of the poor, ignorant Africans in this country, exposed to every temptation before them: All for the want of their morals being refined by education and proper attendance paid unto them by their owners, or those who had the charge of them. It is said by the Southern slaveholders that the more ignorant they can bring up the Africans, the better slaves they make, ('go and come'.) Is there any fitness for such people to be colonized in a far country, to be their own rulers? Can we not discern the project of sending the free people of colour away from their country? Is it not for the interest of the slave-holders to select the free people of colour out of the different states, and send them to Liberia? Will it not make their slaves uneasy to see free men of colour enjoying liberty? It is against the law in some of the southern states, that a person of colour should receive an education, under a severe penalty. Colonizationists speak of America being first colonized, but is there any comparison between the two? America was colonized by as *wise, judicious* and *educated* men as the world afforded. William Penn did not want for learning, wisdom, or intelligence. If all the people in Europe and America were as ignorant, and in the same situation as our brethren, what would become of the world?

Where would be the principle or piety that would govern
the people? We were *stolen* from our mother country and
brought *here*. We have *tilled* the ground and made fortunes
for thousands, and still they are not weary of our services.
But they who stay to till the ground must be slaves. Is there
not land enough in America, or 'corn enough in Egypt?'
Why should they send us into a far country to die? See the
thousands of foreigners emigrating to America every year:
and if there be ground sufficient for them to cultivate, and
bread for them to eat, why would they wish to send the first
tillers of the land away? Africans have made fortunes for
thousands, who are yet unwilling to part with their services;
but the free must be sent away, and those who remain must
be *slaves*. I have no doubt that there are many good men
who do not see as I do, and who are for sending us to
Liberia; but they have not duly considered the subject—they
are not men of colour.—This land which we have watered
with our *tears* and *our blood*, is now our *mother country*,
and we are well satisfied to stay where wisdom abounds and
the gospel is free."

I have given you, my brethren, an extract verbatim, from
the letter of that godly man, as you may find it on the afore-
mentioned page of *Freedom's Journal*. I know that thousands, and perhaps millions of my brethren in these States,
have never heard of such a man as Bishop Allen—a man
whom God many years ago raised up among his ignorant
and degraded brethren, to preach Jesus Christ and him cruci-
fied to them—who notwithstanding, had to wrestle against
principalities and the powers of darkness to diffuse that
gospel with which he was endowed among his brethren—but
who having overcome the combined powers of devils and
wicked men, has under God planted a Church among us
which will be as durable as the foundation of the earth on
which it stands. Richard Allen! O my God!! The bare

recollection of the labours of this man, and his ministers among his deplorably wretched brethren, (rendered so by the whites) to bring them to a knowledge of the God of Heaven, fills my soul with all those very high emotions which would take the pen of an Addison to portray. It is impossible, my brethren, for me to say much in this work respecting that man of God. When the Lord shall raise up coloured historians in succeeding generations, to present the crimes of this nation, to the then gazing world, the Holy Ghost will make them do justice to the name of Bishop Allen of Philadelphia. Suffice it for me to say, that the name of this very man (Richard Allen) though now in obscurity and degradation, will notwithstanding, stand on the pages of history among the greatest divines who have lived since the apostolic age, and among the Africans, Bishop Allen's will be entirely pre-eminent. . . .

*   *   *   *   *   *   *

And now brethren, having concluded these four Articles, I submit them, together with my Preamble, dedicated to the Lord, for your inspection, in language so very simple, that the most ignorant, who can read at all, may easily understand —of which you may make the best you possibly can. . . . If any are anxious to ascertain who I am, know the world, that I am one of the oppressed, degraded and wretched sons of Africa, rendered so by the avaricious and unmerciful among the whites.—If any wish to plunge me into the wretched incapacity of a slave, or murder me for the truth, know ye, that I am in the hand of God, and at your disposal. I count my life not dear unto me, but I am ready to be offered at any moment. For what is the use of living, when in fact I am dead? But remember, Americans, that as miserable, wretched, degraded and abject as you have made us in the preceding, and in this generation, to support you and your families, some of you, (whites) on the continent of America, will yet curse the day that you ever were born. You want slaves, and want us for your slaves!!! My colour will yet root some of you out of the very face of the earth!!!!! You may doubt it if you please. I know that thousands will doubt—they think they have us so well secured in wretchedness to them and their children, that it is impossible for such things to occur. So did the antediluvians doubt Noah, until the day in which the flood came and swept them away. So did the Sodomites doubt, until Lot had got out of the city, and God rained down fire and brimstone from Heaven upon them, and burnt them up. So did the king of Egypt doubt the very existence of a God; he said, "Who is the Lord, that I should let Israel go?" Did he not find to his sorrow who the Lord was, when he and all his mighty men of war were smothered to death in the Red Sea? So did the Romans doubt, many of them were really so ignorant, that they thought the whole of mankind were made to be slaves to them; just as many of the Americans think now, of my colour. But they got dreadfuly deceived. When men got their eyes opened, they made the murderers scamper. The way in which they cut their tyrannical throats, was not much inferior to the way the Romans or murderers, served them, when they held them in wretchedness and degradation under their feet. So would Christian Americans doubt, if God should send an Angel from Heaven to preach their funeral sermon. The fact is, the Christians having a name to live, while they are dead, think that God will screen them on that ground.

See the hundreds and thousands of us that are thrown into the seas by Christians, and murdered by them in other ways. They cram us into their vessel holds in chains and in hand-cuffs—men, women and children, all together!! O! save us, we pray thee, thou God of Heaven and of earth, from the devouring hands of the white Christians!!!

Oh! thou Alpha and Omega!
The beginning and the end,
Enthron'd thou art, in Heaven above,
Surrounded by Angels there:

From whence thou seest the miseries
To which we are subject;
The whites have murder'd us, O God!
And kept us ignorant of thee.

Not satisfied with this, my Lord!
They throw us in the seas:
Be pleas'd, we pray, for Jesus' sake,
To save us from their grasp.

We believe that, for thy glory's sake.
Thou wilt deliver us;
But that thou may'st effect these things,
Thy glory must be sought.

In conclusion, I ask the candid and unprejudiced of the whole world, to search the pages of historians diligently, and see if the Antideluvians—the Sodomites—the Egyptians —the Babylonians—the Ninevites—the Carthaginians—the Persians—the Macedonians—the Greeks—the Romans—the Mohametans—the Jews—or devils, ever treated a set of human beings, as the white Christians of America do us, the blacks, or Africans. I also ask the attention of the world of mankind to the declaration of these very people of the United States. . . .

DANIEL A. PAYNE

DANIEL ALEXANDER PAYNE was a man whose labors for education and religion can only be described as prodigious. His life was one ceaseless round of activity. He was born of free parents, London and Martha Payne, in Charleston, S. C., February 24, 1811, but lost both parents before he was ten, being left to the care of a grand-aunt. When he was eight he began to attend a school conducted under the auspices of a society formed by a number of free colored men. After being hired for a few months to a shoe merchant, when he was thirteen he began to work under a relative at the carpenter's trade. At this he remained for four and a half years, and then for nine months he pursued that of a tailor. At eighteen he was converted, and he received great inspiration from the *Self-Interpreting Bible* of John Brown, of Haddington, Scotland, who became versed in Hebrew, Greek, and Latin almost wholly by his own efforts. Meanwhile he was making diligent advance in language and science. About the middle of 1829 he began to instruct three children in their home, but so many others came to him that he soon had to seek larger quarters. In 1834, however, there was enacted a law against the teaching of colored children; it took effect on April 1, 1835, and on May 9 Payne turned his face northward. The spiritual crisis through which he passed at this time is to be seen in his poem "The Mournful Lute, or the Preceptor's Farewell." He was leaving old moorings and launching forth into the unknown, but he was really going to greater opportunity. In New York he called on Peter Williams, rector of St. Philip's, and met young Alexander Crummell. He also met Lewis Tappan, who impressed him by his radiant countenance and who changed his idea that abolitionists were unprincipled agitators. Tappan asked him about slavery in the South and his opinion of immediate and unconditional emancipation. He said that he believed the slaves should be educated before emancipation, that they might know how to enjoy freedom when it came. Instantly Tappan replied: "Don't you know that men can't be educated in a state of slavery?" The lesson was one that the young student never forgot.

Having been advised that he might find his best field of service in the ministry, Payne entered the Lutheran Seminary at Gettysburg, Penn. There he worked very hard to support himself, and in 1837 he was licensed and in 1839 ordained as a Lutheran clergyman. The American Anti-Slavery Society offered him work, but he declined because, though strongly opposed to slavery, he did not want to be diverted from his work as a preacher; and he accepted a call to a Presbyterian church in East Troy, N. Y. There he injured his throat by his intense method of speaking, and for a year suffered the loss of his voice. In his illness he was visited by Gerrit Smith, who was attending an anti-slavery convention in the city. Before the close of 1840 he had recovered somewhat and opened a school in Philadelphia. Again he was successful, having by 1843 sixty pupils. In 1841, however, he had joined Bethel A. M. E. Church; in 1843 he was received by the Philadelphia Conference as a local preacher, and the next year fully accepted. At Bethel he aroused the opposition of many older members by his introduction of choral singing into the worship. His first appointment under the A. M. E. Church was to Israel Bethel in Washington. The congregation was poor and the church without equipment, so that the pastor availed himself of his knowledge of carpentry and helped to construct the pews. In 1844 he attended the General Conference of his church and as chairman of the Committee on Education secured the adoption of a course of study for young ministers, though not without opposition. The entire course of the action was significant, and it showed how Payne, with a slightly dogmatic air, sometimes failed at first to win support even for a good cause. On May 10, the fifth day of the meeting, he introduced a resolution for the appointment of a committee to draft a course of studies for the education of prospective preachers. He made in this connection no speech, as the need seemed obvious. When Bishop J. M. Brown put the question, however, it was overwhelmingly voted down, and the foes of progress were jubilant. The next day Rev. Abraham D. Lewis, described as "an aged father in Israel," made a powerful plea for light and learning, and then the resolution received general acceptance. In 1845 Payne was appointed to Bethel Church in Baltimore, and there he spent five years in a ministry rich in fruitage and also beset by storms. Once more it seemed necessary to conduct a school. At this time it was his habit to rise at five in the morning, take a walk, study from six to nine, be in school from nine to two, then to make five to ten pastoral visits, and to retire at ten o'clock. It was from Baltimore also that he sent forth a series of letters that denoted him more than ever as the opponent of ignorance in the pulpit. At the same time he discouraged in every way possible the use of "cornfield ditties" in worship and the actions of "praying and singing bands" reminiscent of old voodoo dances. Under the auspices of Bethel at the time were three societies—Bethel, Ebenezer, and Union Bethel; and Ebenezer was using property belonging to Bethel. Payne suggested the purchase of this. The Bethel trustees insisted on $4,000; but the pastor felt that such a nominal sum as $10 would be advisable, inasmuch as the congregation at Ebenezer was poor and struggling, and this point of view prevailed, though not without much opposition and strong feeling. In 1850 Payne was appointed by Bishop William Paul Quinn to the pastorate at Ebenezer. By this time, however, he was well known for his dignified manner, his refusal to cater to vulgarity, and his opposition to noisy modes of worship; and the congregation that he had befriended refused him. A controversy resulted from the fundamental question of polity thus raised, and the situation was not relieved until the appointee was commissioned to write a history of the denomination. In the conduct of this task he traveled East and West, visiting practically every A. M. E. church in the country, meanwhile supporting himself by lectures on education.

Already, in 1848, Payne had been asked by Bishop Quinn to consider candidacy for the bishopric, but had declined. In 1852, still over his protest, the General Conference elected him. "The announcement," he said, "fell like the weight of a mountain upon me. . . . I trembled from head to foot, and wept. I knew that I was unworthy of the office, because I had neither the physical strength, and the learning, nor the sanctity which make one fit for

such a high, holy, and responsible position." It happened moreover that at the time his home life was unsettled. His first wife,
Mrs. Julia A. Farris, whom he had married in 1847, had died
within a year, leaving a little daughter who died after a few
months; and it was not until 1854 that he married Mrs. Eliza
J. Clark, of Cincinnati. However, the election of Daniel A.
Payne as bishop proved to be the most important event in the history of the A. M. E. Church since the organization, and the
election of Richard Allen in 1816. There were two other bish-
ops at the time, but Payne especially traveled far and wide, from
New Orleans to Canada, consulting as to the welfare of congregations, visiting the homes of hundreds of fugitive Negroes,
and organizing historical and literary societies and mothers' clubs.
On the night of April 14, 1862, at the White House, he and
Carl Schurz together urged upon President Lincoln the signing
of the bill for emancipation in the District of Columbia. In 1863
he led in the purchase by his church of Wilberforce University, an
institution that had been established by the Methodist Episcopal
Church in 1856 for the education of colored youth; and he himself later served as president for sixteen years. It was characteristic that he required that all candidates for the ministry give themselves to a definite course of study and that they lead irreproach-
able lives. In 1865, thirty years after he left Charleston, to the
very day, he returned to the city, and on May 15 organized the
South Carolina Conference, from which in course of time the influence of the church extended into Georgia, Florida, and Ala-
bama. Payne made two trips to England; in 1881 he was a
delegate to the First Ecumenical Conference of the Methodist
Church and on September 17 presided over that body. He died
November 20, 1893. Those who knew him say that he was very
thin and not above the average in height, that his features were
sharp and his voice shrill, but that he had keen, penetrating eyes
and a forehead that indicated intellectual strength and refinement.

In his earlier years Payne seems to have written considerable
verse. He had not the imagination of the true poet, but with his
love of order and precision he had a sense of verification that
might have carried him far if he had been able to give himself

wholly to literary pursuits. A small volume, *Pleasures and Other Miscellaneous Poems,* was issued in Baltimore in 1850. In his *Recollections of Seventy Years,* a book of absorbing interest, Payne included "The Mournful Lute, or The Preceptor's Farewell," and while he was still a young minister and teacher there appeared in the *Liberator* for May 28, 1841, some lines under the heading, "An Original Poem composed for the Soirée of the Vigilant Committee of Philadephia, May 7, 1841." Included in *The Semi-Centenary and the Retrospection of the African Methodist Episcopal Church* (Baltimore, 1866), written by Payne in his capacity as historiographer, will be found "A Sacred Ode composed in the pulpit of Bethel Church" and a poem in praise of *The Christian Recorder.* See *Recollections of Seventy Years,* by Bishop Daniel Alexander Payne, with an Introduction by Rev. F. J. Grimké, Nashville, 1888; *The Life of Daniel Alexander Payne,* by Rev. C. S. Smith, with introduction by Bishop Abram Grant, and a poem "In Memoriam," by Bishop James A. Handy, Nashville, 1894; and the excellent sketch in *The Negro in American History,* by John W. Cromwell, Washington, 1914.

The Mournful Lute or the Preceptor's Farewell

Father and mother, authors of my birth,
Ye dwell in bliss; your son on sinful earth.
Hail, happy pair, who praise the Lamb above!
I strive to share your cup of perfect love.
Father, ere yet I knew thy manly form,
The ills of life were o'er, and hushed the storm;
Thy God called thee from earth to dwell on high;
In peace thou art, beyond the swelling sky.

O sainted parents, who my life have kept,
Preserved my sinful soul each night I slept;
Since God transported ye to realms of light,
And bade my youth in virtue take delight!

'Twas God.   'Tis he who still preserves my soul,
When foes unite, or waves of trouble roll,
Cared for my childhood, blessed my striving youth;
Me snatched from vice and led in paths of truth.

Delusive vice has spread her fictitious charms;
Threw out her purse, and wooed me to her arms.
I gazed, I trembled, grasped the motley toys;
But keen remorse sprung from her guilty joys!
My joyful sire, I blush to own my sin,
But can I hide when God surveys within?
Within my soul the Great Jehovah spies,
Nor word nor thought escapes his piercing eyes.

O sainted mother, high in glory thou,
If God permits, behold thy Daniel now!
Good Lord, give strength; my feeble mind sustain,
Nor let my sighs ascend to thee in vain.
Servants of God, extol the King of kings;
Let higher notes flow from your trembling strings;
He saves your son, puts all his foes to flight—
His human foes, or fiends of deepest night.

When Ignorance my mind in fetters bound,
He smote the fiend; then beams of light surround;
Broad beams of light described the way of truth,
And bade me lead therein benighted youth.
Oh, here's my bliss, that I the way have shown
To lovely youths which was before unknown;
From scientific shrines plucked golden fire,
And thrilled with notes divine the sacred lyre.

Did I conceive five rolling years ago,
The luscious fruits which Science can bestow?
Oh, bend in praise devout before his throne!
'Twas God that gave the boon, and God alone.

My sire, when on the bed of death you lay,
Did thy blest soul in fervent accents pray
That I should be what now I feel I am—
Favored of God, preserved from every harm?

Thou didst, my sire; thrice blessèd be thy name;
Come, Wisdom, clothe me in thy sacred flame;
Ye scientific truths, my mind control;
And thou, fair Virtue, guide my erring soul.
What's my ambition? What my great desire?
The youthful mind with knowledge to inspire.
Not worlds on worlds for this would I exchange,
Though cruel laws my noble scheme derange.

Soon from the land where first I drew my breath
I go a wanderer on the flying earth!
Where shall I go? O Thou my fortune guide,
Who led good Abram with his modest bride.
Him didst thou lead across the eastern wild,
Direct his steps and on his fortune smiled;
In foreign climes spread wide his fruitful boughs,
Made strong his bands and scattered all his foes.

Dost thou not roll the thunder 'cross the sky?
Arouse the storm, and bid the lightnings fly?
Bid teeming earth produce her pulpy grains,
By genial sunbeams or the fruitful rains?
Stop, falling tears; God lights the cheerful day,
Gives gloomy night, and leads the darksome way.
Frown, fortune, frown; my struggling breast shall bear
Thy worthless blows, and pointless arrows dare.

Oh, I had thought the moral plants would grow,
From all the care my talents can bestow,
Like trees of virtue lift their blooming heads
Where snowy clouds suspend their liquid beds!

Ye lads, whom I have taught with sacred zeal,
For your hard fate I pangs of sorrow feel;
Oh, who shall now your rising talents guide,
Where virtues reign and sacred truths preside?

Ye modest virgins, I have taught your minds
To fly from earth where sinful pleasure blinds,
The rugged hill of science to ascend,
Where sacred flames with human fires blend.
Who now shall call your willing, joyful feet
In "wisdom's institute" to learn and meet
Sweet piety and science, gods of light,
Whose precepts lead your erring minds aright?

Who shall for you Minerva's field explore,
Spread open wide fair Nature's roseate door?
Oh, who shall help your op'ning wings to fly
Where Virtue sits resplendent in the sky?
O God of mercy! whither shall I go?
Where turn my steps—to weal, or else to woe?
Speak. I the sacred mandate wait to hear,
Nor shall I ocean dread nor tempest fear.

Eternal Goodness, from thy shining seat
Let Mercy fly to guide my wandering feet.
On distant lands I will thy servant be,
To turn from vice the youthful mind to thee.
Just two revolving moons shall light the shores
When Carolina's laws shall shut the doors
Of this fine room, where Science holds his reign,
The humble tutor, hated Daniel Payne.

Oh, that my arms could reach yon burning sun,
And stop his motion till my work be done!
With these small fingers catch the flying moon—
Night should not triumph o'er the dazzling noon.

April should ne'er appear; but I would teach
Each yielding pupil till their minds could reach
The climax of proud science, and their plumes
Could soar where good John Locke or Newton blooms.

Ye blooming plants of moral culture fine,
The dews that wet ye be those dews divine.
The faithful gard'ner!   Ah, who shall he be?
The Father, Spirit, Son—the sacred three!
Before you nature spreads her blooming fields;
On verdant breast her fragrant produce yields.
Go seek her lilies, tulips, roseate sweets
When morning light her swelling bosom greets.

Each minute insect and each flying bird,
Each walking beast, whose tuneless notes are heard,
The scaly fish that lives not on the shore,
And man himself, the mighty being explore;
Aspiring mounts and hills, descending dales,
The floating air, when peace or storm prevails;
Oceans and seas, streams and expanding lakes,
When night leaps in, or sweet Aurora wakes.

The flying rays of light, the spangled sky,
On contemplation's wing mount ye on high.
Bright cherubim and flaming seraphim,
All things upon wide earth, th' eternal Him,
Children, all, all are yours!   Search, find them out.
Knowledge, where are thy bounds?   In depths without.
The heavens, within the heavens, nor time,
Nor vast eternity, the gods sublime,

Can in their sweeping compass e'er embrace!
He reigns o'er angels, guides the human race.
Seek not the joys which sinful earth can give;
They sparkle, perish, for a moment live.

Sweet innocents, behold each moving lip!
From cups of wisdom sacred sweets they sip.
What demon snatches from your hands those books,
And blasts your talents with his withering looks?

I weep.   Flow, then, ye sympathetic tears!
Each bitter stream the stamp of sorrow bears.
Oh, who those smiling infant cheeks can see
Destined to night, and not lament with me?
Could tears of blood revoke the fierce decree,
The statesman touch and make my pupils free,
I at their feet the crimson tide would pour
Till potent justice swayed the senate floor.

As when a deer does in the pasture graze,
The lion roars—she's filled with wild amaze,
Knows strength unequal for the dreadful fight,
And seeks sweet safety in her rapid flight—
So Payne prepares to leave his native home,
With pigmy purse on distant shores to roam.
Lo! in the skies my boundless storehouse is!
I go reclining on God's promises.

Pupils, attend my last departing sounds;
Ye are my hopes, and ye my mental crowns,
My monuments of intellectual might,
My robes of honor and my armor bright.
Like Solomon, entreat the throne of God;
Light shall descend in lucid columns broad,
And all that man has learned or man can know
In streams prolific shall your minds o'erflow.

Hate sin; love God; religion be your prize;
Her laws obeyed will surely make you wise,
Secure you from the ruin of the vain,
And save your souls from everlasting pain.

O fare you well for whom my bosom glows
With ardent love, which Christ my saviour knows!
'Twas for your good I labored night and day;
For you I wept, and now for you I pray.

Farewell! farewell! ye children of my love;
May joys abundant flow ye from above!
May peace celestial crown your useful days,
To bliss transported, sing eternal lays;
For sacred wisdom give a golden world,
And when foul vice his charming folds unfurl,
Oh spurn the monster, though his crystal eyes
Be like bright sunbeams streaming from the skies!
And I! Oh, whither shall your tutor fly?
Guide thou my feet, great Sovereign of the sky.
A useful life by sacred wisdom crowned,
Is all I ask, let weal or woe abound.

Charleston, S. C., February 2, 1835.

POEM COMPOSED FOR THE SOIRÉE OF THE VIGILANT COMMITTEE OF PHILADELPHIA
May 7, 1841

Rise, God of Freedom! From thy throne of light,
Stretch forth thine arm of uncreated might;
In dire confusion cause thy foes to fly,
Chased by the lightnings of thy frowning eye.
Long have they scorned and mocked thy regal crown,
Despised thy laws, and cast thine image down:
O hasten then, in thine appointed hour,
And crush to nought the proud oppressor's power.

Say, Righteous Sire, shall Afric ever mourn
Her weeping children from her bosom torn?
Chained, sold, and scattered far in Christian lands;

Scourged, beaten, murdered, too, by Christian hands!
Nor does she weep alone—her sons to thee
Stretch forth their hands imploring to be free;
Their bleeding hearts, by Sorrow's falchion riven,
Cry out for justice from the God of heaven.

From cotton fields, rice swamps, and verdant heath,
In howling tempests, gales, and zephyr's breath,
In smoky columns up to God arise
The groans of broken hearts, and dying agonies:
And pitying cherubs stoop them down to see
The scene of horror, crime and misery.
Hark! hark! they ask, whose arm will break their bonds,
Dry up their tears, and heal their gushing wounds.

Pride of the earth! shall Britain's voice command
That slaves breathe not upon her sacred land,
Whilst thou, before high heaven with brazen heart,
Sell men and women in thy brutish mart?
Make laws to crush the noble sons of earth,
And rank with chattels, minds of heavenly birth;
Shut from their eyes beams of ethereal light,
And doom their souls to shades of mental night?

Shame on thee! shame! land of the boasting free!
Go, shed thy tears—go, bend thy callous knee—
In dust and ashes hide thy guilty face,
And beg for pardon at the throne of grace!
Then o'er plantations, farms, and valleys green,
In town and country where the yoke is seen,
Let the loud trump of Freedom's jubilee
Bid tyrants die, and trembling slaves go free!

No captive's wail shall then ascend on high,
Nor clouds of vengeance veil thy sunny sky;
No husband then be sever'd from his wife,

Nor slavers cut the meanest cord of life;
No fugitive will seek our northern land,
Pursued by bloodhounds, or a viler band;
The "Vigilant Committees" then shall cease
Their toils of love—their wars be hushed in peace.

Then, O my country, shall thy honor glide,
Deep, broad, majestic, as the ocean's tide;
Thy starry banner then shall be unfurled
In spotless glory o'er the admiring world!
Truth then shall crown thy towering crest with light,
And Justice nerve thine arm with deathless might;
Then from our southern to our northern bound,
The songs of freemen ever shall resound.

Fly, glittering orbs! on rapid pinions fly,
With angel swiftness, through the blazing sky!
O usher in that morn of light and love,
When God, descending from the climes above,
With word omnific shall to all proclaim
The doom of slavery, sin, and every blame:
Bid Peace shed all her radiance o'er the globe,
With love divine all human hearts enrobe:
Say to all nations, "Hear my voice with glee—
Be free! be free! ye ransomed lands, be free!"

JOSIAH HENSON

WHEN UNCLE TOM's CABIN entered upon its successful career, there came forth several men who claimed to be the original of the central character. The best authenticated case was that of Josiah Henson. This man was born a slave in Charles County, Maryland, June 15, 1789. As a lad he saw his mother brutally assaulted and his father mutilated, and in course of time he himself was severely injured. It was the custom of the planters of the neighborhood to assemble on Saturday or Sunday to drink and gamble or to have horse-races and cock-fights all day. Perfectly aware that he would not be able to find his way home at night, each one told his personal servant to come for him; and it fell to Josiah thus to call for his master, Riley. On one occasion Riley got into a quarrel with Bryce Litton, overseer of his brother's plantation, and in a little while there was a general brawl. While the fight was at its height, Josiah went in, and, after considerable trouble, succeeded in getting his master out of the room. In the scuffle, however, Litton got a severe fall. About a week thereafter he waylaid Henson with three slaves to assist him, and while these men endeavored to seize and hold their powerful young opponent, he so beat Henson with a fence-rail as to break an arm and both shoulder-blades. The injuries did not receive proper attention and gave trouble throughout life. While still very young Henson became superintendent of the farm and succeeded in doubling the output for his harsh and incompetent master. At twenty-two he married a slave girl, who became the mother of several children. In 1825 he conducted to Kentucky for Riley a number of slaves, but, convinced at last of this man's baseness, and escaping only by an accident being sold into New Orleans, he decided to make his way from slavery, and on October 28, 1830, crossed into Canada. Thenceforth his rise was rapid. When eighteen years of age he had been deeply moved by a sermon that he heard, and he now became a Methodist preacher. In 1842 he endeavored to found a community and establish an industrial school near Dawn in Canada. The attempt was unsuccessful, but some black walnut boards that he exhibited at the World's Fair in England in 1851 were awarded a bronze medal. While he was still abroad as the representative of his Negro colony, he was accused of being an imposter, but no question seems to have been raised after he became known as the prototype of Uncle Tom. At the height of his career Henson was active in the work of the Underground Railroad, assisting more than a hundred slaves to escape from Kentucky to Canada. He made a second trip to England, and then, late in life, his first wife having died, he married a widow in Boston, with whom he made a third visit in 1876. He was received by Queen Victoria and greatly honored at a farewell meeting. He died in Dresden, Ontario, May 5, 1883. While he can not be said to have been a great character and perhaps exploited himself unduly, there was still something of the heroic about him, and some of the passages in his life story are of absorbing interest.

The Life of Josiah Henson, Formerly a Slave, Now an Inhabitant of Canada, as Narrated by Himself appeared in 1849 as a pamphlet of seventy-six pages, the work having been dictated to an editorial helper. It did not attract unusual attention, but Harriet Beecher Stowe read and was impressed by it, she talked with Henson, referred to him in *A Key to Uncle Tom's Cabin*, and herself wrote the introduction for the enlarged work, *Truth Stranger than Fiction: Father Henson's Story of His Own Life*, which was published in 1858. While Henson was on his last visit to England, in 1876, still another version of his story was published in London as *An Autobiography of Josiah Henson, (Mrs. Harriet Beecher Stowe's "Uncle Tom")*, the cover reading *Uncle Tom's Story of his Life*, and an enlarged edition of this was issued in 1878. All of the later accounts seem to have had extraordinary success. There is a sketch in the *Dictionary of American Biography*, and "The Story of Josiah Henson," by W. B. Hartgrove, is in the *Journal of Negro History*, III, 1-21 (January, 1918).

A Responsible Journey
(Chapter VI of *Truth Stranger than Fiction,* with a few slight
omissions, including two brief and irrelevant
paragraphs at the beginning)

After passing his youth in the manner I have mentioned
in a general way, and which I do not wish more particularly
to describe, my master, at the age of forty-five, or upwards,
married a young woman of eighteen, who had some little
property, and more thrift. Her economy was remarkable,
and was certainly no addition to the comfort of the establishment. She had a younger brother, Francis, to whom Riley
was appointed guardian, and who used to complain—not
without reason, I am confident—of the meanness of the provision made for the household; and he would often come to
me, with tears in his eyes, to tell me he could not get enough
to eat. I made him my friend for life, by sympathizing in his
emotions and satisfying his appetite, sharing with him the
food I took care to provide for my own family. He is still
living, and, I understand, one of the wealthiest men in
Washington City.

After a time, however, continual dissipation was more
than a match for domestic saving. My master fell into difficulty, and from difficulty into a lawsuit with a brother-in-law,
who charged him with dishonesty in the management of
property confided to him in trust.. The lawsuit was protracted
enough to cause his ruin of itself.

Harsh and tyrannical as my master had been, I really
pitied him in his present distress. At times he was dreadfully dejected, at others crazy with drink and rage. Day
after day he would ride over to Montgomery Court House
about his business, and every day his affairs grew more desperate. He would come into my cabin to tell me how things
were going, but spent the time chiefly in lamenting his mis-

fortunes and cursing his brother-in-law. I tried to comfort him as best I could. He had confidence in my fidelity and judgment, and partly through pride, partly through that divine spirit of love I had learned to worship in Jesus, I entered with interest into all his perplexities. The poor, drinking, furious, moaning creature was utterly incapable of managing his affairs. Shiftlessness, licentiousness, and drink had complicated them as much as actual dishonesty.

One night in the month of January, long after I had fallen asleep, he came into my cabin and waked me up. I thought it strange, but for a time he said nothing and sat moodily warming himself at the fire. Then he began to groan and wring his hands. "Sick, massa?" said I. He made no reply but kept on moaning. "Can't I help you any way, massa?" I spoke tenderly, for my heart was full of compassion at his wretched appearance. At last, collecting himself, he cried, "Oh, Sie! I'm ruined, ruined, ruined!" "How so, massa?" "They've got judgment against me, and in less than two weeks every nigger I've got will be put up and sold." Then he burst into a storm of curses at his brother-in-law. I sat silent, powerless to utter a word. Pity for him and terror at the anticipation of my own family's future fate filled my heart. "And now, Sie," he continued, "there's only one way I can save anything. You can do it; won't you, won't you?" In his distress he rose and actually threw his arms around me. Misery had leveled all distinctions. "If I can do it, massa, I will. What is it?" Without replying he went on, "Won't you, won't you? I raised you, Sie; I made you overseer; I know I've abused you, Sie, but I didn't mean it." Still he avoided telling me what he wanted. "Promise me you'll do it, boy." He seemed resolutely bent on having my promise first, well-knowing from past experience that what I agreed to do I spared no pains to accomplish. Solicited in this way, with urgency and tears, by the man whom I had so zealously served for over thirty years, and who now seemed absolutely dependent upon his slave,—impelled, too, by the fear which he skillfully awakened, that the sheriff would seize every one who belonged to him, and that all would be separated, or perhaps sold to go to Georgia, or Louisiana—an object of perpetual dread to the slave of the more northern States—I consented, and promised faithfully to do all I could to save him from the fate impending over him.

At last the proposition came. "I want you to run away, Sie, to your master Amos in Kentucky, and take all the servants along with you." I could not have been more startled had he asked me to go to the moon. Master Amos was his brother. "Kentucky, massa? Kentucky? I don't know the way." "O, it's easy enough for a smart fellow like you to find it. I'll give you a pass and tell you just what to do." Perceiving that I hesitated, he endeavored to frighten me by again referring to the terrors of being sold to Georgia.

For two or three hours he continued to urge the undertaking, appealing to my pride, my sympathies, and my fears, and at last, appalling as it seemed, I told him I would do my best. There were eighteen negroes, besides my wife, two children and myself, to transport nearly a thousand miles, through a country about which I knew nothing, and in midwinter—for it was the month of February, 1825. My master proposed to follow me in a few months and establish himself in Kentucky.

My mind once made up, I set earnestly about the needful preparations. They were few and easily made. A one-horse wagon, well stocked with oats, meal, bacon, for our own and the horse's support, was soon made ready. My pride was aroused in view of the importance of my responsibility, and heart and soul I became identified with my master's project of running off his negroes. The second night after the scheme was formed we were under way. Fortunately for the success of the undertaking, these people had long been under my direction, and were devotedly attached to me in return for the many alleviations I had afforded to their miserable condition, the comforts I had procured them, and the consideration I had always manifested for them. Under these circumstances no difficulty arose from want of submission to my authority. The dread of being separated and sold away down South, should they remain on the old estate, united them as one man, and kept them patient and alert.

We started from home about eleven o'clock at night, and till the following noon made no permanent halt. The men trudged on foot, the children were put into the wagon, and now and then my wife rode for a while. On we went through Alexandria, Culpepper, Fauquier, Harper's Ferry, Cumberland, over the mountains on the National Turnpike, to Wheeling. In all the taverns along the road were regular places for the droves of negroes continually passing along under the system of the internal slave trade. In these we lodged, and our lodging constituted our only expense, for our food we carried with us. To all who asked questions I showed my master's pass, authorizing me to conduct his negroes to Kentucky.

Arriving at Wheeling, in pursuance of the plan laid down by my master, I sold the horse and wagon, and purchased a large boat, called in that region a yawl. Our mode of locomotion was now decidedly more agreeable than tramping along day after day, at the rate we had kept up ever since leaving home. Very little labor at the oars was necessary. The tide floated us steadily along, and we had ample leisure to sleep and recruit our strength.

A new and unexpected trouble now assailed me. On passing along the Ohio shore, we were repeatedly told by persons conversing with us, that we were no longer slaves, but free men, if we chose to be so. At Cincinnati, especially, crowds of colored people gathered round us, and insisted on our remaining with them. They told us we were fools to think of going on and surrendering ourselves up to a new owner; that now we could be our own masters, and put ourselves out of all reach of pursuit. I saw the people under me were getting much excited. Divided counsels and signs of insubordination began to manifest themselves. I began, too, to feel my own resolution giving way. Freedom had ever been an object of my ambition, though no other means of obtaining it had occurred to me but purchasing myself. I had never dreamed of running away. I had a sentiment of honor on the subject. The duties of the slave to his master as appointed over him in the Lord, I had ever heard urged by ministers and religious men. It seemed like outright stealing. And now I felt the devil was getting the upper hand of me. Strange as all this may seem, I really felt it then. Entrancing as the idea was, that the coast was clear for a run for freedom, that I might liberate my companions, might carry off my wife and children, and some day own a house and land, and be no longer despised and abused—still my notions of right were against it. I had promised my master to take his property to Kentucky, and deposit it with his brother Amos. Pride, too, came in to confirm me. I had undertaken a great thing; my vanity had been flattered all along the road by hearing myself praised; I thought it would be a feather in my cap to carry it through thoroughly; and had often painted the scene in my imagination of the final surrender of my charge to master Amos, and the immense admiration and respect with which he would regard me.

Under the influence of these impressions, and seeing that the allurements of the crowd were producing a manifest effect, I sternly assumed the captain, and ordered the boat

to be pushed off into the stream. A shower of curses followed me from the shore; but the negroes under me,
accustomed to obey, and, alas! too degraded and ignorant
of the advantages of liberty to know what they were for-
feiting, offered no resistance to my command.

Often since that day has my soul been pierced with bitter
anguish at the thought of having been thus instrumental in
consigning to the infernal bondage of slavery so many of my
fellow-beings. I have wrestled in prayer with God for for-
giveness. Having experienced myself the sweetness of
liberty, and knowing too well the after misery of numbers
of many of them, my infatuation has seemed to me the un-
pardonable sin. But I console myself with the thought that
I acted according to my best light, though the light that
was in me was darkness. Those were my days of ignorance.
I knew not the glory of free manhood. I knew not that the
title-deed of the slave-owner is robbery and outrage.

What advantages I may have personally lost by thus
throwing away an opportunity of obtaining freedom, I know
not; but the perception of my own strength of character, the
feeling of integrity, the sentiment of high honor I thus
gained by obedience to what I believed right, these advantages
I do know and prize. He that is faithful over a little, will
alone be faithful over much. Before God, I tried to do my
best, and the error of judgment lies at the door of the degrading system under which I had been nurtured.

WILLIAM WELLS BROWN

IN HIS DAY William Wells Brown attempted more different things than any other writer connected with the Negro race, and he won success; but his importance is now almost wholly historical. He was born in Lexington, Ky., about 1815. His father was a slaveholder, and his mother, a mulatto, a slave. As a child he was taken to St. Louis and when ten years of age was hired to the captain of a steamboat on the Mississippi River. At twelve he was employed as office boy by Elijah P. Lovejoy, then editor of the *St. Louis Times*, but in little more than a year was again on a steamboat. In 1834, at Cincinnati, he escaped, and in making his way farther North was assisted by a Quaker, Wells Brown, whose name he adopted. Having found employment on a boat on Lake Erie, he later became a steward, and in this capacity helped many fugitives to get to Canada. The number thus assisted amounted each year to hardly less than sixty-five; and at Buffalo, where he made his home, Brown organized a vigilance committee to help any slave who might be making his way to freedom. Meanwhile he strove in every way to advance in education. In 1843 he was employed as an agent by the Western New York Anti-Slavery Society, in 1847 he transferred to the Massachusetts Anti-Slavery Society, and in 1849 went to England, with strong letters of introduction. He was received as a distinguished representative of the anti-slavery cause, and a speech that he made at the Peace Congress in Paris won the warm approval of Victor Hugo, the president. As the Fugitive Slave Law of 1850 made it dangerous for him to return, Brown remained in England for five years, until 1854, when he was formally manumitted. He supported himself by lectures and writing; and, having studied medicine, he settled in Cambridge, Mass., as a physician, later residing in Chelsea. Much of his time, however, was given to his books, and he was also interested in the temperance movement, woman suffrage, and prison reform. He died November 6, 1884.

[168]

Brown was a voluminous author. He contributed freely to the anti-slavery press, and was also the first American Negro to write a novel, a play, and a book of travel. He had, however, neither a sound education nor a sure sense of form, and he depended unduly on the sensational. In 1847 appeared in its first form *Narrative of William W. Brown*, and other editions followed rapidly. It was said that the first three editions, amounting to eight thousand copies, were sold in eight months. The book succeeded by its use of the concrete, many stories of slavery being included. The next year Brown edited *The Anti-Slavery Harp*, a small collection of song poems, including "Jefferson's Daughter," which was based on a statement that a daughter of Thomas Jefferson had been sold in New Orleans for $1,000—a theme that became the basis of the novel *Clotel*. *Three years in Europe* (London, 1852) was assisted to wide circulation by the excitement over *Uncle Tom's Cabin*. *Clotel, or The President's Daughter* (London, 1853) was the story of an efficient colored woman, represented as the housekeeper of Jefferson, who had two beautiful daughters. The young women at first lived in comfort, but later they were called to pass through many harrowing situations until at last the heroine, pursued by slave-catchers, drowned herself in the Potomac in sight of the Capitol. The scene shifts rapidly, and the crowded story includes several episodes that, like the Nat Turner insurrection, have no generic connection with the main theme. There were American editions in 1864 and 1867, but for these the title was *Clotelle: A Tale of the Southern States*, and any reference to Jefferson was deleted. *The Escape, or A Leap for Freedom* (Boston, 1858) was a drama in five acts. In this the language is stilted and there is an excess of moralizing, but occasionally there are flashes of genuine drama, as when a mistress reveals her jealousy of a favorite slave. One finds references to another novel and another play that Brown is said to have written, but neither of these works is now accessible. *The Black Man: His Antecedents, his Genius, and his Achievements* (New York and Boston, 1863) appeared just after the issuing of the Emancipation Proclamation and within a year was in the third edition. It was followed by the *The Negro in the Amer-*

ican Rebellion: His Heroism and his Fidelity (Boston, 1867). In
this work Brown showed that he had not the capacity for research
or the accuracy and perspective of the trained historian, but
by gossip and human interest stories he succeeded in producing a readable book.   Both works contributed to and were
superseded by *The Rising Son* (Boston, 1874).   This book was
not as scholarly as William C. Nell's *Colored Patriots of the American Revolution* (1855), to say nothing of George W. Williams'
History of the Negro Race in America (1883), but, like most of
Brown's efforts, it was a success, ten thousand copies being sold
within a year.   *My Southern Home, or The South and its People*
(Boston, 1880), is a series of narrative essays, sketchy, but often
bright, and sometimes valuable for the information they give.
None of the books of this author are of such sort that they can well
be represented by selections. The essay below is from the 1854 edition of *Autographs for Freedom*.

See *The Biography of an American Bondman, by his Daughter* (Josephine Brown), Boston, 1856; Memoir by William Farmer in *Three Years in Europe;* Memoir by Alonzo D. Moore in
The Rising Son; sketch in *Men of Mark*, by William J. Simmons,
Cleveland, 1887; *Boston Evening Transcript*, November 8,
1884; *The Negro Author*, by Vernon Loggins, New York, 1931,
pp. 156-173, 420-422; and sketch by Carter G. Woodson in
Dictionary of American Biography.

<hr />

Visit of a Fugitive Slave to the Grave
of Wilberforce

On a beautiful morning in the month of June, while
strolling about Trafalgar Square, I was attracted to the base
of the Nelson column, where a crowd was standing gazing
at the bas-relief representations of some of the great naval
exploits of the man whose statue stands on the top of the
pillar.   The death-wound which the hero received on board
the Victory, and his being carried from the ship's deck by
his companions, is executed with great skill.   Being no ad-

mi er of warlike heroes, I was on the point of turning away, when I perceived among the figures (which were as large as life) a fullblooded African, with as white a set of teeth as ever I had seen, and with all the other peculiarities of feature that distinguish that race from the rest of the human family, with musket in hand and a dejected countenance, which told that he had been in the heat of the battle, and shared with the other soldiers the pain in the loss of their commander. However, as soon as I saw my sable brother, I felt more at home, and remained longer than I intended. Here was the Negro, as black a man as was ever imported from the coast of Africa, represented in his proper place by the side of Lord Nelson, on one of England's proudest monuments. How different, thought I, was the position assigned to the colored man on similar monuments in the United States! Some years since, while standing under the shade of the monument erected to the memory of the brave Americans who fell at the storming of Fort Griswold, Connecticut, I felt a degree of pride as I beheld the names of two Africans who had fallen in the fight; yet I was grieved but not surprised to find their names colonized off, and a line drawn between them and the whites. This was in keeping with American historical injustice to its colored heroes.

The conspicuous place assigned to this representative of an injured race, by the side of one of England's greatest heroes, brought vividly before my eye the wrongs of Africa and the philanthropic man of Great Britain, who had labored so long and so successfully for the abolition of the slave trade, and the emancipation of the slaves of the West Indies; and I at once resolved to pay a visit to the grave of Wilberforce.

A half hour after, I entered Westminster Abbey, at Poets' Corner, and proceeded in search of the patriot's tomb. I had, however, gone but a few steps, when I found myself in front of the tablet erected to the memory of Granville

Sharpe, by the African Institution of London, in 1816; upon the marble was a long inscription, recapitulating many of the deeds of this benevolent man, and from which I copied the following:—"He aimed to rescue his native country from the guilt and inconsistency of employing the arm of freedom to rivet the fetters of bondage, and establish for the Negro race, in the person of Somerset, the long-disputed rights of human nature. Having in this glorious cause triumphed over the combined resistance of interest, prejudice, and pride, he took his post among the foremost of the honorable band associated to deliver Africa from the rapacity of Europe, by the abolition of the slave-trade; nor was death permitted to interrupt his career of usefulness, till he had witnessed that act of the British Parliament by which the abolition was decreed." After viewing minutely the profile of this able defender of the Negro's rights, which was finely chiseled on the tablet, I took a hasty glance at Shakespeare, on the one side, and Dryden on the other, and then passed on and was soon in the north aisle, looking upon the mementoes placed in honor of genius. There stood a grand and expressive monument to Sir Isaac Newton, which was in every way worthy of the great man to whose memory it was erected. A short distance from that was a statue to Addison, representing the great writer clad in his morning gown, looking as if he had just left the study, after finishing some chosen article for the *Spectator*. The stately monument to the Earl of Chatham is the most attractive in this part of the Abbey. Fox, Pitt, Grattan, and many others, are here represented by monuments. I had to stop at the splendid marble erected to the memory of Sir Foxwell Buxton, Bart. A long inscription enumerates his many good qualities, and concludes by saying:—"This monument is erected by his friends and fellow laborers, at home and abroad, assisted by the grateful contributions of many thousands of the African race." A few steps further and I was standing over the ashes of Wilberforce. In no other place so small do so many great men lie together. The following is the inscription on the monument erected to the memory of this devoted friend of the oppressed and degraded Negro race:—

"To the memory of WILLIAM WILBERFORCE, born in Hull, August 24, 1759, died in London, July 29, 1833. For nearly half a century a member of the House of Commons, and for six parliaments during that period, one of the two representatives for Yorkshire. In an age and country fertile with great and good men, he was among the foremost of those who fixed the character of their times; because to high and various talents, to warm benevolence, and to universal candor, he added the abiding eloquence, of a Christian life. Eminent as he was in every department of public labor, and a leader in every work of charity, whether to relieve the temporal or spiritual wants of his fellow men, his name will ever be specially identified with those exertions which, by the blessings of God, removed from England the guilt of the African slave-trade, and prepared the way for the abolition of slavery in every colony of the empire. In the prosecution of these objects, he relied not in vain on God but, in the progress, he was called to endure great obloquy and great opposition. He outlived, however, all enmity, and, in the evening of his days, withdrew from public life and public observation, to the bosom of his family. Yet he died not unnoticed or forgotten by his country; the Peers and Commons of England, with the Lord Chancellor and the Speaker at their head, in solemn procession from their respective houses, carried him to his fitting place among the mighty dead around, here to repose, till, through the merits of Jesus Christ his only Redeemer and Savior, whom in his life and in his writings he had desire to glorify, he shall rise in the resurrection of the just."

The monument is a fine one; his figure is seated on a pedestal, very ingeniously done, and truly expressive of his age, and the pleasure he seemed to derive from his own thoughts.   Either the orator or the poet have said or sung the praises of most of the great men who lie buried in Westminster Abbey, in enchanting strains.   The statues of heroes, princes, and statesmen are there to proclaim their power, worth or brilliant genius, to posterity.   But as time shall step between them and the future, none will be sought after with more enthusiasm or greater pleasure than that of Wilberforce.   No man's philosophy was ever moulded in a nobler cast than his; it was founded in the school of Christianity, which was, that all men are by nature equal, that they are wisely and justly endowed by their Creator with certain rights which are irrefragable, and no matter how human pride and avarice may depress and debase, still God is the author of good to man, and of evil, man is the artificer to himself and to his species.   Unlike Plato and Socrates, his mind was free from that gloom that surrounded theirs.   Let the name, the worth, the zeal, and other excellent qualifications of this noble man, ever live in our hearts, let his deeds ever be the theme of our praise, and let us teach our children to honor and love the name of William Wilberforce.

FREDERICK DOUGLASS

FREDERICK DOUGLASS has a place not only in the literature of the Negro but in the oratory of the world. His career was a romance of progress from the lowly estate of a slave to an exalted place in the life of his people and the nation. He was born at Tuckahoe, Talbot County, Maryland, probably in February, 1817. His father was an unknown white man, and his mother, Harriet Bailey, a slave. In his early years he was taken to Baltimore as a servant, but he learned his letters and thenceforth was eager for a education. When about thirteen years of age he got hold of a book of speeches called *The Columbian Orator*, and stirring appeals for liberty awoke in him something that he never lost. At sixteen he was sent to work on a farm. The lash was freely applied to the slaves; but one day the stalwart youth resisted the attempt to whip him, and nevermore was he thus corrected. In 1836 he planned with some others to escape, but the plot was divulged and he was thrown into jail. His master then arranged for his return to Baltimore, where he learned the trade of a calker and eventually was permitted to hire his time. In September, 1838, he made his escape to New York, being then twenty-one years of age. The events of his life at this time he himself has told in the selections below. Having conferred with David Ruggles, an alert and helpful Negro, and having married Anna Murray, who had come from Baltimore, he went to New Bedford, Mass., with a letter of introduction to Nathan Johnson, another Negro of public spirit. This man was helpful in innumerable ways, and from a reading of *The Lady of the Lake* suggested instead of *Bailey* the name *Douglas*, though as used later this was spelled with the *s* doubled. For the next three years the young man from Maryland worked around the docks of the city. In 1841, at an anti-slavery convention in Nantucket, an abolitionist who had heard him speak to the Negro people asked him to address the meeting. He was hesitant and stammering, but exhibited such intelligence and showed himself the possessor of such a remarkable voice that he was made an agent of the organization. For the next four years, under the tutelage of Garrison, he lectured extensively in the North and East, and very soon the impression he made was such that some people doubted that he had ever been a slave. Notable at this time was his effort against a new constitution in Rhode Island designed to disfranchise the Negro.

In 1845 Douglass went to England. There he remained for two years, meeting distinguished liberals, speaking often to large audiences, and growing rapidly in intellectual stature. As Dr. DuBois has said, "he began to conceive emancipation not simply as physical freedom, but as social equality and economic and spiritual opportunity." English friends raised £150 to enable him regularly to purchase his freedom; and on his return to the United States in 1847 he began to issue in Rochester a weekly paper, *The North Star*. After 1850 the name was *Frederick Douglass' Paper*; in 1860 this was merged with *Douglass' Monthly*, a small magazine begun two years before primarily for circulation in England, and as a monthly it appeared for three years more. The establishment of this periodical by Douglass signalized a break with his old friend and tutor, Garrison, who was aloof from politics, and henceforth he stood with Gerrit Smith and the Liberty Party—in general with those who sought to do away with slavery by constitutional means. He was friendly with John Brown, so much so that the Governor of Virginia sought to have him arrested after the raid; but he went abroad again and for six months lectured in England and Scotland. He was often in conference with President Lincoln and assisted with enlistments for the 54th and 55th Massachusetts regiments of Negro men, his own sons being among the first recruits. After the war Douglass spoke strongly for the suffrage and civil rights; from 1869 to 1872 he conducted in Washington another weekly, *The New National Era;* and later he was United States marshal, recorder of deeds in the District of Columbia, and minister to Hayti. In 1884, his first wife having died, he married Helen Pitts, a white woman, and thereby provoked much criticism in view of his life work. He died February 20, 1895.

Douglass was essentially an orator, not a logician or debater, and he was at his best in exposing the woes of slavery and in denouncing those who upheld the system. He was not a man of great faith; and sometimes, as in his attitude toward the exodus of 1879, which he opposed, he did not fully fathom the deeper yearning of his people. After all, it was not the work of his later years that made him great, but that of his young manhood, when he had a story to tell, and when no one could fail to be moved by his message. In him the cause of freedom found a voice, a voice that spoke for thousands; and greater even than anything he might say was himself—the supreme exhibit from the house of bondage. Charles W. Chesnutt in his brief biography has given us an admirable description. He tells us that "Douglass possessed, in large measure, the physical equipment most impressive in an orator. He was a man of magnificent figure, tall, strong, his head crowned with a mass of hair which made a striking element of his appearance. He had deep-set and flashing eyes, a firm, well-moulded chin, a countenance somewhat severe in repose, but capable of a wide range of expression. His voice was rich and melodious, and of carrying power." To this it may be added that he was distinctly dignified and majestic; he had irony, but he could not be witty and he had no humor. Perhaps the greatest of all his speeches was that which he delivered at Rochester, July 5, 1852, an extract from which is given below. With withering scorn he queried, "What to the slave is the 4th of July?" Of abiding significance was the address, "What the Black Man Wants," delivered in a time of hesitation, in the year of the close of the war, to the Massachusetts Anti-Slavery Society. Only less effective than such efforts as these were the commemorative addresses on Garrison and John Brown. Douglass insisted that the black man be treated simply like any other American. He asked not alms but opportunity, not sympathy but justice; and though he faced a hostile audience, though he might even be attacked, he never quailed, and he gave to the Western world a new sense of the Negro's possibilities.

In one way Frederick Douglass was fundamentally different from such a leader as Richard Allen. When Allen and his friends found that in a white church they were not treated with courtesy,

they said, We shall have our own church, we shall have our own
bishop; we shall build up our own enterprises in any line whatsoever; and even today the A. M. E. Church is the greatest single
effort of the race in organization.   As early as 1848, however, in
a speech at Rochester, Douglass said: "I am well aware of the
anti-Christian prejudices which have excluded many colored persons from white churches, and the consequent necessity for erecting their own places of worship.   But such a necessity does not
now exist to the extent of former years.   There are societies where
color is not regarded as a test of membership, and such places I
deem more appropriate for colored persons than exclusive or
isolated organizations."   There is more difference between these
positions than can be accounted for by the mere lapse of forty years
between the height of the work of Allen and that of Douglass.
Allen certainly did not sanction segregation under the law, and no
man worked harder than he to relieve his people from proscription.
Douglass, moreover, who did not formally approve organizations
that made distinction of race, again and again presided over
gatherings of Negro men.   In the last analysis, however, it was
Allen who was foremost in laying the basis of distinctively Negro
enterprise, and Douglass who felt that the solution of the whole
matter was for the race to lose itself in the general body politic.

In 1845 appeared in Boston the first edition of the *Narrative
of the Life of Frederick Douglass,* with introductions by Garrison
and Phillips.   The little book was hailed by the abolitionists as a
life story of the highest importance, and in the flood of slave
narratives then appearing it immediately took precedence.   A much
larger work, *My Bondage and My Freedom,* was published in
1855, and this time the introduction was by a member of the
author's own race, James McCune Smith.   In 1881 appeared the
third form of the autobiography, *Life and Times of Frederick
Douglass,* with an introduction by George L. Ruffin.   This was
enlarged in 1892.   Our selections are from the second of these
works.   Closing his introduction Smith said:

"It is not without a feeling of pride, dear reader, that I present
you with this book.   The son of a self-emancipated bond-woman,
I feel joy in introducing to you my brother, who has rent his own

bonds, and who, in his every relation—as a public man, as a husband, and as a father—is such as does honor to the land which
gave him birth. I shall place this book in the hands of the only
child spared me, bidding him to strive and emulate its noble
example. You may do likewise. It is an American book, for
Americans, in the fullest sense of the idea. It shows that the
worst of our institutions, in its worst aspect, cannot keep down
energy, truthfulness, and earnest struggle for the right. It proves
the justice and practicability of Immediate Emancipation. It shows
that any man in our land, 'no matter in what battle his liberty may
have been cloven down, . . . no matter what complexion an
Indian or an African sun may have burned upon him,' not only
may 'stand forth redeemed and disenthralled,' but may also stand
up a candidate for the highest suffrage of a great people—the
tribute of their honest, hearty admiration."

Aside from works of Douglass mentioned, see especially *Fred-
erick Douglass, the Colored Orator* (in American Reformers
Series), by Frederick May Holland, New York, 1891; *In
Memoriam: Frederick Douglass,* edited by Helen Pitts Douglass,
Philadelphia, 1897; *Frederick Douglass, a Biography* (in Beacon
Biographies), by Charles W. Chesnutt, Boston, 1899; *Frederick
Douglass* (in American Crisis Biographies), by Booker T. Washington, Philadelphia, 1906; *The Evening Star,* Washington, Feb-
bruary 21, 1895; the sections in *The Negro in American History,*
by John W. Cromwell, Washington, 1914, *Men of Maryland,*
by George P. Bragg, Baltimore, 1925, and *The Negro Author,*
by Vernon Loggins, New York, 1931; also the sketch by
W. E. B. DuBois in the *Dictionary of American Biography.*

SELECTIONS FROM "MY BONDAGE AND MY FREEDOM"
CHAPTER XXII
Liberty Attained

There is no necessity for any extended notice of the incidents of this part of my life. There is nothing very striking
or peculiar about my career as a freeman, when viewed apart

from my life as a slave. The relation subsisting between my early experience and that which I am now about to narrate, is, perhaps, my best apology for adding another chapter to this book.

Disappearing from the kind reader, in a flying cloud or balloon, (pardon the figure,) driven by the wind, and knowing not where I should land—whether in slavery or in freedom—it is proper that I should remove, at once, all anxiety, by frankly making known where I alighted. The flight was a bold and perilous one; but here I am, in the great city of New York, safe and sound, without loss of blood or bone. In less than a week after leaving Baltimore, I was walking amid the hurrying throng, and gazing upon the dazzling wonders of Broadway. The dreams of my childhood and the purposes of my manhood were now fulfilled. A free state around me, and a free earth under my feet! What a moment was this to me! A whole year was pressed into a single day. A new world burst upon my agitated vision. I have often been asked, by kind friends to whom I have told my story, how I felt when first I found myself beyond the limits of slavery; and I must say here, as I have often said to them, there is scarcely anything about which I could not give a more satisfactory answer. It was a moment of joyous excitement, which no words can describe. In a letter to a friend, written soon after reaching New York, I said I felt as one might be supposed to feel on escaping from a den of hungry lions. But, in a moment like that, sensations are too intense and too rapid for words. Anguish and grief, like darkness and rain, may be described, but joy and gladness, like the rainbow of promise, defy alike the pen and pencil.

For ten or fifteen years I had been dragging a heavy chain, with a huge block attached to it, cumbering my every motion. I had felt myself doomed to drag this chain and this block through life. All efforts, before, to separate myself from the hateful encumbrance, had only seemed to rivet me the more firmly to it. Baffled and discouraged at times, I had asked myself the question, May not this, after all, be God's work? May He not, for wise ends, have doomed me to this lot? A contest had been going on in my mind for years, between the clear consciousness of right and the plausible errors of superstition; between the wisdom of manly courage, and the foolish weakness of timidity. The contest was now ended; the chain was severed; God and right stood vindicated. *I was a freeman,* and the voice of peace and joy thrilled my heart.

Free and joyous, however, as I was, joy was not the only sensation I experienced. It was like the quick blaze, beautiful at first, but which subsiding, leaves the building charred and desolate. I was soon taught that I was still in an enemy's land. A sense of loneliness and insecurity oppressed me sadly. I had been but a few hours in New York, before I was met in the streets by a fugitive slave, well known to me, and the information I got from him respecting New York, did nothing to lessen my apprehension of danger. The fugitive in question was "Allender's Jake," in Baltimore; but, said he, "I am William Dixon, in New York!" I knew Jake well, and knew when Tolly Allender and Mr. Price (for the latter employed Master Hugh as his foreman, in his shipyard on Fell's Point) made an attempt to recapture Jake, and failed. Jake told me all about his circumstances, and how narrowly he escaped being taken back to slavery; that the city was now full of southerners, returning from the springs; that the black people in New York were not to be trusted; that there were hired men on the lookout for fugitives from slavery, and who, for a few dollars, would betray me into the hands of the slave-catchers; that I must trust no man with my secret; that I must not think of going either on the wharves to work, or to a boarding-house to board; and, worse still, this same Jake told me it was not in his power to help me. He seemed, even while cautioning me, to be fearing lest, after all, I might be a party to a second attempt to recapture him. Under the inspiration of this thought, I must suppose it was, he gave signs of a wish to get rid of me, and soon left me—his whitewash brush in hand—as he said, for his work. He was soon lost to sight among the throng, and I was alone again, an easy prey to the kidnappers, if any should happen to be on my track.

New York, seventeen years ago, was less a place of safety for a runaway slave than now, and all know how unsafe it now is, under the new fugitive slave bill. I was much troubled. I had very little money—enough to buy me a few loaves of bread, but not enough to pay board, outside a lumber yard. I saw the wisdom of keeping away from the ship yards, for if Master Hugh pursued me, he would naturally expect to find me looking for work among the calkers. For a time, every door seemed closed against me. A sense of my loneliness and helplessness crept over me, and covered me with something bordering on despair. In the midst of thousands of my fellow-men, and yet a perfect stranger! In the midst of human brothers, and yet more fearful of them than of hungry wolves! I was without home, without friends, without work, without money, and without any definite knowledge of which way to go, or where to look for succor.

Some apology can easily be made for the few slaves who have, after making good their escape, turned back to slavery, preferring the actual rule of their masters, to the life of loneliness, apprehension, hunger, and anxiety, which meets them on their first arrival in a free state. It is difficult for a freeman to enter into the feelings of such fugitives. He cannot see things in the same light with the slave, because he does not, and cannot, look from the same point from which the slave does. "Why do you tremble?" he says to the slave; "you are in a free state;" but the difficulty is in realizing that he is in a free state, the slave might reply. A freeman cannot understand why the slave-master's shadow is bigger to the slave, than the might and majesty of a free state; but when he reflects that the slave knows more about the slavery of his master than he does of the might and majesty of the free state, he has the explanation. The slave has been all his life learning the power of his master—being trained to dread his approach—and only a few hours learning the power of the state. The master is to him a stern and flinty reality, but the state is little more than a dream. He has been accustomed to regard every white man as the friend of his master, and every colored man as more or less under the control of his master's friends—the white people. It takes stout nerves to stand up, in such circumstances. A man, homeless, shelterless, breadless, friendless, and moneyless, is not in a condition to assume a very proud or joyous tone; and in just this condition was I, while wandering about the streets of New York city, and lodging, at least one night, among the barrels on one of its wharves. I was not only free from slavery, but I was free from home as well. The reader will easily see that I had something more than the simple fact of being free to think of, in this extremity.

I kept my secret as long as I could, and at last was forced to go in search of an honest man—a man sufficiently *human* not to betray me into the hands of slave-catchers. I was not a bad reader of the human face, nor long in selecting the right man, when once compelled to disclose the facts of my condition to some one.

I found my man in the person of one who said his name was Stewart. He was a sailor, warm-hearted and generous, and he listened to my story with a brother's interest. I told him I was running for my freedom—knew not where to go

—money almost gone—was hungry—thought it unsafe to
go to the shipyards for work, and needed a friend. Stewart
promptly put me in the way of getting out of my trouble.
He took me to his house, and went in search of the late
David Ruggles, who was then secretary of the New York
Vigilance Committee, and a very active man in all anti-
slavery works.   Once in the hands of Mr. Ruggles, I was
comparatively safe.   I was hidden with Mr. Ruggles several
days.   In the meantime, my intended wife, Anna, came on
from Baltimore—to whom I had written, informing her of
my safe arrival at New York—and, in the presence of Mrs.
Mitchell and Mr. Ruggles, we were married, by Rev. James
W. C. Pennington.

Mr. Ruggles was the first officer on the underground
railroad with whom I met after reaching the north, and indeed, the first of whom I ever heard anything.   Learning
that I was a calker by trade, he promptly decided that New
Bedford was the proper place to send me.   "Many ships,"
said he, "are there fitted out for the whaling business, and you
may there find work at your trade, and make a good living."
Thus, in one fortnight after my flight from Maryland, I was
safe in New Bedford, regularly entered upon the exercise of
the rights, responsibilities, and duties of a freeman.

I may mention a little circumstance which annoyed me
on reaching New Bedford.   I had not a cent of money, and
lacked two dollars toward paying our fare from Newport,
and our baggage—not very costly—was taken by the stage
driver, and held until I could raise the money to redeem it.
This difficulty was soon surmounted. Mr. Nathan Johnson,
to whom we had a line from Mr. Ruggles, not only received
us kindly and hospitably, but, on being informed about our
baggage, promptly loaned me two dollars with which to
redeem my little property.   I shall ever be deeply grateful,
both to Mr. and Mrs. Nathan Johnson, for the lively interest

they were pleased to take in me, in this hour of my extremest need. They not only gave myself and wife bread and shelter, but taught us how to begin to secure those benefits for ourselves. Long may they live, and may blessings attend them in this life and in that which is to come!

Once initiated into the new life of freedom, and assured by Mr. Johnson that New Bedford was a safe place, the comparatively unimportant matter, as to what should be my name, came up for consideration. It was necessary to have a name in my new relations. The name given me by my beloved mother was no less pretentious than "Frederick Augustus Washington Bailey." I had, however, before leaving Maryland, dispensed with the *Augustus Washington*, and retained the name *Frederick Bailey*. Between Baltimore and New Bedford, however, I had several different names, the better to avoid being overhauled by the hunters, who I had good reason to believe would be put on my track. Among honest men an honest man may well be content with one name, and to acknowledge it at all times and in all places; but towards fugitives, Americans are not honest. When I arrived at New Bedford, my name was Johnson; and finding that the Johnson family in New Bedford were already quite numerous—sufficiently so to produce some confusion in attempts to distinguish one from another—there was the more reason for making another change in my name. In fact, "Johnson" had been assumed by nearly every slave who had arrived in New Bedford from Maryland, and this, much to the annoyance of the original "Johnsons" (of whom there were many) in that place. Mine host, unwilling to have another of his own name added to the community in this unauthorized way, after I spent a night and a day at his house, gave me my present name. He had been reading *The Lady of the Lake*, and was pleased to regard me as a suitable person to wear this, one of Scotland's many famous names.

Considering the noble hospitality and manly character of Nathan Johnson, I have felt that he, better than I, illustrated the virtues of the great Scottish chief. Sure I am, that had any slave-catcher entered his domicile, with a view to molest any one of his household, he would have shown himself like him of the "stalwart hand."

The reader will be amused at my ignorance, when I tell the notions I had of the state of northern wealth, enterprise, and civilization. Of wealth and refinement, I supposed the North had none. My *Columbian Orator,* which was almost my only book, had not done much to enlighten me concerning northern society. The impressions I had received were all wide of the truth. New Bedford, especially, took me by surprise, in the solid wealth and grandeur there exhibited. I had formed my notions respecting the social condition of the free states, by what I had seen and known of free, white, non-slave-holding people in the slave states. Regarding slavery as the basis of wealth, I fancied that no people could become very wealthy without slavery. A free white man, holding no slaves, in the country, I had known to be the most ignorant and poverty-stricken of men, and the laughing stock even of slaves themselves—called generally by them, in derision, *"poor white trash."* Like the non-slaveholders at the south, in holding no slaves, I supposed the northern people like them, also, in poverty and degradation. Judge, then, of my amazement and joy, when I found—as I did find—the very laboring population of New Bedford living in better houses, more elegantly furnished—surrounded by more comfort and refinement—than a majority of the slaveholders on the Eastern Shore of Maryland. There was my friend, Mr. Johnson, himself a colored man, (who at the south would have been regarded as a proper marketable commodity,) who lived in a better house—dined at a richer board—was owner of more books—the reader of more newspapers—was more conversant with the political and social condition of this nation and the world—than nine-tenths of all the slaveholders of Talbot County, Maryland. Yet Mr. Johnson was a working man, and his hands were hardened by honest toil. Here, then, was something for observation and study. Whence the difference? The explanation was soon furnished, in the superiority of mind over simple brute force. Many pages might be given to the contrast, and in explanation of its causes. But an incident or two will suffice to show the reader as to how the mystery gradually vanished before me.

My first afternoon, on reaching New Bedford, was spent in visiting the wharves and viewing the shipping. The sight of the broad brim and the plain, Quaker dress, which met me at every turn, greatly increased my sense of freedom and security. "I am among the Quakers," thought I, "and am safe." Lying at the wharves and riding in the stream, were full-rigged ships of finest model, ready to start on whaling voyages. Upon the right and the left, I was walled in by large granite-fronted warehouses, crowded with the good things of this world. On the wharves, I saw industry without bustle, labor without noise, and heavy toil without the whip. There was no loud singing, as in southern ports, where ships are loading or unloading—no loud cursing or swearing—but everything went on as smoothly as the works of a well adjusted machine. How different was all this from the noisily fierce and clumsily absurd manner of labor-life in Baltimore and St. Michael's! One of the first incidents which illustrated the superior mental character of northern labor over that of the south, was the manner of unloading a ship's cargo of oil. In a southern port, twenty or thirty hands would have been employed to do what five or six did here, with the aid of a single ox attached to the end of a fall. Main strength, unassisted by skill, is slavery's method of labor. An old ox, worth eighty dollars, was doing, in New Bedford, what would have required fifteen thousand dollars' worth of human bones and muscles to have performed in a southern port. I found that everything was done here with a scrupulous regard to economy, both in regard to men and things, time and strength. The maid servant, instead of spending at least a tenth part of her time in bringing and carrying water, as in Baltimore, had the pump at her elbow. The wood was dry, and snugly piled away for winter. Woodhouses, indoor pumps, sinks, drains, self-shutting gates, washing machines, pounding barrels, were all new things, and told me that I was among a thoughtful and sensible people. To the ship-repairing dock I went, and saw the same wise prudence. The carpenters struck where they aimed, and the calkers wasted no blows in idle flourishes of the mallet. I learned that men went from New Bedford to Baltimore, and bought old ships, and brought them here to repair, and made them better and more valuable than they ever were before. Men talked here of going whaling on a four *years'* voyage with more coolness than sailors where I came from talked of going on a four *months'* voyage.

I now find that I could have landed in no part of the United States where I should have found a more striking and gratifying contrast to the condition of the free people of color in Baltimore, than I found here in New Bedford. No colored man is really free in a slaveholding state. He wears the badge of bondage while nominally free, and is often subjected to hardships to which the slave is a stranger; but here in New Bedford, it was my good fortune to see a pretty near approach to freedom on the part of the colored people. I was taken all aback when Mr. Johnson—who lost no time in making me acquainted with the fact—told me that there was nothing in the constitution of Massachusetts to prevent a colored man from holding any office in the state. There, in New Bedford, the black man's children—although anti-slavery was then far from popular—went to school side by side with the white children, and apparently without objection from any quarter. To make me at home, Mr. Johnson assured me that no slaveholder could take a slave from New Bedford; that there were men there who would lay down their lives before such an outrage could be perpetrated. The colored people themselves were of the best metal, and would fight for liberty to the death.

Soon after my arrival in New Bedford, I was told the following story, which was said to illustrate the spirit of the colored people in that goodly town: A colored man and a fugitive slave happened to have a little quarrel, and the former was heard to threaten the latter with informing his master of his whereabouts. As soon as this threat became known, a notice was read from the desk of what was then the only colored church in the place, stating that business of importance was to be then and there transacted. Special measures had been taken to secure the attendance of the would-be Judas, and had proved successful. Accordingly, at the hour appointed, the people came, and the betrayer, also. All the usual formalities of public meetings were scrupulously gone through, even to the offering of prayer for Divine direction in the duties of the occasion. The president himself performed this part of the ceremony, and I was told that he was unusually fervent. Yet at the close of his prayer, the old man (one of the numerous family of Johnsons) rose from his knees, deliberately surveyed his audience, and then said in a tone of solemn resolution, *"Well, friends, we have got him here, and I would now recommend that you young men should just take him outside the door and kill him."* With this, a large body of the congregation, who well understood the business they had come there to transact, made a rush at the villain, and doubtless would have killed him, had he not availed himself of an open sash, and made good his escape.

He has never shown his head in New Bedford since that time. This little incident is perfectly characteristic of the spirit of the colored people in New Bedford. A slave could not be taken from that town seventeen years ago, any more than he could be so taken away now. The reason is, that the colored people in that city are educated up to the point of fighting for their freedom, as well as speaking for it.

Once assured of my safety in New Bedford, I put on the habiliments of a common laborer, and went on the wharf in search of work. I had no notion of living on the honest and generous sympathy of my colored brother, Johnson, or that of the abolitionists. My cry was like that of Hood's laborer, "Oh! only give me work." Happily for me, I was not long in searching. I found employment, the third day after my arrival in New Bedford, in stowing a sloop with a load of oil for the New York market. It was new, hard, and dirty work, even for a calker, but I went at it with a glad heart and a willing hand. I was now my own master— a tremendous fact—and the rapturous excitement with which I seized the job, may not easily be understood, except by some one with an experience something like mine. The thoughts—"I can work! I can work for a living; I am not afraid of work; I have no Master Hugh to rob me of my earnings"—placed me in a state of independence, beyond seeking friendship or support of any man. That day's work I considered the real starting point of something like a new existence. Having finished this job and got my pay for the same, I went next in pursuit of a job at calking. It so happened that Mr. Rodney French, late mayor of the city of New Bedford, had a ship fitting out for sea, and to which there was a large job of calking and coppering to be done. I applied to that noble-hearted man for employment, and he promptly told me to go to work; but going on the float-stage for the purpose, I was informed that every white man would leave the ship if I struck a blow upon her. "Well, well," thought I, "this is a hardship, but yet not a very serious one for me." The difference between the wages of a calker and that of a common day laborer, was an hundred per cent. in favor of the former; but then I was free, and free to work, though not at my trade. I now prepared myself to do anything which came to hand in the way of turning an honest penny; sawed wood—dug cellars—shoveled coal—swept chimneys with Uncle Lucas Debuty—rolled oil casks on the wharves—helped to load and unload vessels—worked in Ricketson's candle works—in Richmond's brass foundry, and elsewhere; and thus supported myself and family for three years.

The first winter was unusually severe, in consequence of the high prices of food; but even during that winter we probably suffered less than many who had been free all their lives. During the hardest of the winter, I hired out for nine dollars a month; and out of this rented two rooms for nine dollars per quarter, and supplied my wife—who was unable to work—with food and some necessary articles of furniture. We were closely pinched to bring our wants within our means; but the jail stood over the way, and I had a wholesome dread of the consequences of running in debt. This winter passed, and I was up with the times—got plenty of work—got well paid for it—and felt that I had not done a foolish thing to leave Master Hugh and Master Thomas. I was now living in a new world, and was wide awake to its advantages. I early began to attend the meetings of the colored people of New Bedford, and to take part in them. I was somewhat amazed to see colored men drawing up resolutions and offering them for consideration. Several colored young men of New Bedford, at that period, gave promise of great usefulness. They were educated, and possessed what seemed to me, at that time, very superior talents. Some of them have been

cut down by death, and others have removed to different parts
of the world, and some remain there now, and justify, in
their present activities, my early impressions of them.

Among my first concerns on reaching New Bedford, was
to become united with the church, for I had never given up,
in reality, my religious faith. I had become lukewarm and
in a backslidden state, but I was still convinced that it was
my duty to join the Methodist church. I was not then aware
of the powerful influence of that religious body in favor
of the enslavement of my race, nor did I see how the northern churches could be responsible for the conduct of the
southern churches; neither did I fully understand how it
could be my duty to remain separate from the church, because bad men were connected with it. The slaveholding
church, with its Coveys, Weedens, Aulds, and Hopkinses, I
could see through at once. But I could not see how Elm
Street Church, in New Bedford, could be regarded as sanc-
tioning the Christianity of these characters in the church
at St. Michael's. I therefore resolved to join the Methodist
church in New Bedford, and to enjoy the spiritual advantage
of public worship. The minister of the Elm Street Methodist
Church, was the Rev. Mr. Bonney; and although I was not
allowed a seat in the body of the house, and was proscribed
on account of my color, regarding this proscription simply
as an accommodation of the unconverted congregation who
had not yet been won to Christ and his brotherhood, I was
willing thus to be proscribed, lest sinners should be driven
away from the saving power of the gospel. Once converted,
I thought that they would be sure to treat me as a man and a
brother. "Surely," thought I, "these Christian people have
none of this feeling against color. They, at least, have re-
nounced this unholy feeling." Judge, then, dear reader, of
my astonishment and mortification, when I found, as soon as
I did find, all my charitable assumptions at fault.

An opportunity was soon afforded me for ascertaining the exact position of Elm Street Church on that subject. I had a chance of seeing the religious part of the congregation by themselves; and although they disowned, in effect, their black brothers and sisters, before the world, I did not think that·where none but the saints were assembled, and no offense could be given to the wicked, and the gospel could not be "blamed," they would certainly recognize us as children of the same Father, and heirs of the same salvation, on equal terms with themselves.

The occasion to which I refer, was the sacrament of the Lord's Supper, that most sacred and most solemn of all the ordinances of the Christian church. Mr. Bonney had preached a very solemn and searching discourse, which really proved him to be acquainted with the inmost secrets of the human heart. At the close of his discourse, the congregation was dismissed, and the church remained to partake of the sacrament. I remained to see, as I thought, this holy sacrament celebrated in the spirit of its great Founder.

There were only about a half dozen colored members attached to the Elm Street Church, at this time. After the congregation was dismissed, these descended from the gallery, and took a seat against the wall most distant from the altar. Brother Bonney was very animated, and sung very sweetly, "Salvation 'tis a joyful sound," and soon began to administer the sacrament. I was anxious to observe the bearing of the colored members, and the result was most humiliating. During the whole ceremony, they looked like sheep without a shepherd. The white members went forward to the altar by the bench full; and when it was evident that all the whites had been served with the bread and wine, Brother Bonney—pious Brother Bonney—after a long pause, as if inquiring whether all the white members had been served, and fully assuring himself on that important point, then raised his voice to an unnatural pitch, and looking to the corner where his black sheep seemed penned, beckoned with his hand, exclaiming, "Come forward, colored friends!— come forward! You, too, have an interest in the blood of Christ. God is no respecter of persons. Come forward and take this holy sacrament to your comfort." The colored members—poor, slavish souls—went forward, as invited. I went *out,* and have never been in that church since, although I honestly went there with a view to joining that body. I found it impossible to respect the religious profession of any who were under the dominion of this wicked prejudice, and I could not, therefore, feel that in joining them, I was joining a Christian church at all. I tried other churches in New Bedford, with the same result, and, finally, I attached myself to a small body of colored Methodists, known as the Zion Methodists. Favored with the affection and confidence of the members of this humble communion, I was soon made a class-leader and a local preacher among them. Many seasons of peace and joy I experienced among them, the remembrance of which is still precious, although I could not see it to be my duty to remain with that body, when I found that it consented to the same spirit which held my brethren in chains.

In four or five months after reaching New Bedford, there came a young man to me, with a copy of the *Liberator,* the paper edited by William Lloyd Garrison, and published by Isaac Knapp, and asked me to subscribe for it. I told him I had just escaped from slavery, and was of course very poor, and remarked further, that I was unable to pay for it then; the agent, however, very willingly took me as a subscriber, and appeared to be much pleased with securing my name to his list. From this time I was brought in contact with the mind of William Lloyd Garrison. His paper took its place with me next to the Bible.

The *Liberator* was a paper after my own heart. It detested slavery—exposed hypocrisy and wickedness in high places—made no truce with the traffickers in the bodies and souls of men; it preached human brotherhood, denounced oppression, and, with all the solemnity of God's word, demanded the complete emancipation of my race. I not only liked— I *loved* this paper, and its editor. He seemed a match for all the opponents of emancipation, whether they spoke in the name of the law, or the gospel. His words were few, full of holy fire, and straight to the point. Learning to love him, through his paper, I was prepared to be pleased with his presence. Something of a hero worshiper, by nature, here was one, on first sight, to excite my love and reverence.

Seventeen years ago, few men possessed a more heavenly countenance than William Lloyd Garrison, and few men evinced a more genuine or a more exalted piety. The Bible was his text book—held sacred as the word of the Eternal Father—sinless perfection—complete submission to insults and injuries—literal obedience to the injunction, if smitten on one side to turn the other also. Not only was Sunday a Sabbath, but all other days were Sabbaths, and to be kept holy. All sectarianism false and mischievous—the regenerated, throughout the world, members of one body, and the *Head* Christ Jesus. Prejudice against color was rebellion against God. Of all men beneath the sky, the slaves, because most neglected and despised, were nearest and dearest to his great heart. Those ministers who defended slavery from the Bible, were of their "father the devil;" and those churches which fellowshipped slaveholders as Christians, were synagogues of Satan, and our nation was a nation of liars. Never loud or noisy—calm and serene as a summer sky, and as pure. "You are the man, the Moses, raised up by God, to deliver his modern Israel from bondage," was the spontaneous feeling of my heart, as I sat away back in the hall and listened to his mighty words; mighty in truth—mighty in their simple earnestness.

I had not long been a reader of the *Liberator*, and listener to its editor, before I got a clear apprehension of the principles of the anti-slavery movement. I had already the spirit of the movement and only needed to understand its principles and measures. These I got from the *Liberator*, and from those who believed in that paper. My acquaintance with the movement increased my hope for the ultimate freedom of my race, and I united with it from a sense of delight, as well as duty.

Every week the *Liberator* came, and every week I made myself master of its contents. All the anti-slavery meetings held in New Bedford I promptly attended, my heart burning at every true utterance against the slave system, and every rebuke of its friends and supporters. Thus passed the first three years of my residence in New Bedford. I had not then dreamed of the possibility of my becoming a public advocate of the cause so deeply imbedded in my heart. It was enough for me to listen—to receive and applaud the great words of others, and only whisper in private, among the white laborers on the wharves, and elsewhere, the truths which burned in my breast.

Chapter XXIII

Introduced to the Abolitionists

In the summer of 1841, a grand anti-slavery convention was held in Nantucket, under the auspices of Mr. Garrison and his friends. Until now, I had taken no holiday since my escape from slavery. Having worked very hard that spring and summer, in Richmond's brass foundry—sometimes working all night as well as all day—and needing a day or two of rest, I attended this convention, never supposing that I should take part in the proceedings. Indeed, I was not aware that anyone connected with the convention even so much as knew my name. I was, however, quite mistaken. Mr. William C. Coffin, a prominent abolitionist in those days of trial, had heard me speaking to my colored friends, in the little schoolhouse on Second Street, New Bedford, where we worshipped. He sought me out in the crowd, and invited me to say a few words to the convention. Thus sought out, and thus invited, I was induced to speak out the feelings inspired by the occasion, and the fresh recollection of the scenes through which I had passed as a slave. My speech on this occasion is about the only one I ever made, of which I do not remember a single connected sentence. It was with the utmost difficulty that I could stand erect, or that I could command and articulate two words without hesitation and stammering. I trembled in every limb. I am not sure that my embarrassment was not the most effective part of my speech, if speech it could be called. At any rate, this is about the only part of my performance that I now distinctly remember. But excited and convulsed as I was, the audience, though remarkably quiet before, became as much excited as myself. Mr. Garrison followed me, taking me as his text; and now, whether I had made an eloquent speech in behalf of freedom or not, his was one never to be forgotten by those who heard it. Those who had heard Mr. Garrison oftenest, and had known him longest were astonished. It was an effort of unequaled power, sweeping down, like a very tornado, every opposing barrier, whether of sentiment or opinion. For a moment, he possessed that almost fabulous inspiration, often referred to but seldom attained, in which a public meeting is transformed, as it were, into a single individuality—the orator wielding a thousand heads and hearts at once, and by the simple majesty of his all controlling thought, converting his hearers into the express image of his own soul. That night there were at least one thousand Garrisonians in Nantucket!

At the close of this great meeting, I was duly waited on by Mr. John A. Collins—then the general agent of the Massachusetts Anti-slavery Society—and urgently solicited by him to become an agent of that society, and to publicly advocate its anti-slavery principles. I was reluctant to take the proffered position. I had not been quite three years from slavery—was honestly distrustful of my ability—wished to be excused; publicity exposed me to discovery and arrest by my master; and other objections came up, but Mr. Collins was not to be put off, and I finally consented to go out for three months, for I supposed that I should have got to the end of my story and my usefulness, in that length of time.

Here opened upon me a new life—a life for which I had no preparation. I was a "graduate from the peculiar institution," Mr. Collins used to say, when introducing me, "*with my diploma written on my back!*" The three years of my freedom had been spent in the hard school of adversity. My hands had been furnished by nature with something like a solid leather coating, and I had bravely marked out for myself a life of rough labor, suited to the hardness of my hands, as a means of supporting myself and rearing my children.

Now what shall I say of this fourteen years' experience as a public advocate of the cause of my enslaved brothers and sisters? The time is but a speck, yet large enough to justify a pause for retrospection—and a pause it must only be.

Young, ardent, and hopeful, I entered upon this new life in the full gush of unsuspecting enthusiasm. The cause was good; the men engaged in it were good; the means to attain its triumph, good; Heaven's blessing must attend all, and freedom must soon be given to the pining millions under a ruthless bondage. My whole heart went with the holy cause, and my most fervent prayer to the Almight Disposer of the hearts of men, were continually offered for its early triumph. "Who or what," thought I, "can withstand a cause so good, so holy, so indescribably glorious?   The God of Israel is with us.   The might of the Eternal is on our side.   Now let but the truth be spoken, and a nation shall start forth at the sound!"   In this enthusiastic spirit, I dropped into the ranks of freedom's friends, and went forth to the battle.   For a time I was made to forget that my skin was dark and my hair crisped.   For a time I regretted that I could not have shared the hardships and dangers endured by the earlier workers for the slaves' release.   I soon, however, found that my enthusiasm had been extravagant; that hardships and dangers were not yet passed; and that the life now before me, had shadows as well as sunbeams.

Among the first duties assigned me, on entering the ranks, was to travel, in company with Mr. George Foster, to secure subscribers to the *Anti-Slavery Standard* and the *Liberator*. With him I traveled and lectured through the eastern counties of Massachusetts.   Much interest was awakened—large meetings assembled.   Many came, no doubt, from curiosity to hear what a Negro could say in his own cause.   I was generally introduced as a *"chattel"*—a *"thing"*—a piece of southern *"property"*—the chairman assuring the audience that *it* could speak.   Fugitive slaves at that time were not so plentiful as now; and as a fugitive slave lecturer, I had the advantage of being a *"brand new fact"*—the first one out. Up to that time, a colored man was deemed a fool who confessed himself a runaway slave, not only because of the danger to which he exposed himself of being retaken, but because it was a confession of a very *low* origin!   Some of my colored friends in New Bedford thought very badly of my wisdom for thus exposing and degrading myself.   The only precaution I took, at the beginning, to prevent Master Thomas from knowing where I was, and what I was about, was the withholding my former name, my master's name, and the name of the state and county from which I came.   During the first three or four months, my speeches were almost exclusively made up of narrations of my own personal experience as a slave. "Let us have the facts," said the people. So also said Friend George Foster, who always wished to pin me down to my simple narrative. "Give us the facts," said Collins, "we will take care of the philosophy." Just here arose some embarrassment. It was impossible for me to repeat the same old story month after month, and to keep up my interest in it. It was new to the people, it is true, but it was an old story to me; and to go through with it night after night, was a task altogether too mechanical for my nature. "Tell your story, Frederick," would whisper my then revered friend, William Lloyd Garrison, as I stepped upon the platform. I could not always obey, for I was now reading and thinking. New views of the subject were presented to my mind. It did not entirely satisfy me to *narrate* wrongs; I felt like *denouncing* them. I could not always curb my moral indignation for the perpetrators of slaveholding villainy, long enough for a circumstantial statement of the facts which I felt almost everybody must know. Besides, I was growing and needed room. "People won't believe you ever was a slave, Frederick, if you keep on this way," said Friend Foster. "Be yourself," said Collins, "and tell your story." It was said to me, "Better have a *little* of the plantation manner of speech than not; 'tis not best that you seem too learned." These excellent friends were actuated by the best of motives, and were not altogether wrong in their advice; and still I must speak just the word that seemed to *me* the word to be spoken *by* me.

At last the apprehended trouble came. People doubted if I had ever been a slave. They said I did not talk like a slave, look like a slave, nor act like a slave, and that they believed I had never been south of Mason and Dixon's line. "He don't tell us where he came from—what his master's name was—how he got away—nor the story of his experience. Besides, he is educated, and is, in this, a contradiction of all the facts we have concerning the ignorance of the slaves." Thus, I was in a pretty fair way to be denounced as an imposter. The committee of the Massachusetts Anti-slavery Society knew all the facts in my case, and agreed with me in the prudence of keeping them private. They, therefore, never doubted my being a genuine fugitive; but going down the aisles of the churches in which I spoke, and hearing the free spoken Yankees saying repeatedly, *"He's never been a slave, I'll warrant ye,"* I resolved to dispel all doubt, at no distant day, by such a revelation of facts as could not be made by any other than a genuine fugitive.

In a little less than four years, therefore, after becoming a public lecturer, I was induced to write out the leading facts connected with my experience in slavery, giving names of persons, places, and dates—thus putting it in the power of any who doubted, to ascertain the truth or falsehood of my story of being a fugitive slave. This statement soon became known in Maryland, and I had reason to believe that an effort would be made to recapture me.

It is not probable that any open attempt to secure me as a slave could have succeeded, further than the obtainment, by my master, of the money value of my bones and sinews. Fortunately for me, in the four years of my labors in the abolition cause, I had gained many friends, who would have suffered themselves to be taxed to almost any extent to save me from slavery. It was felt that I had committed a double offense of running away, and exposing the secrets and crimes of slavery and slaveholders. There was a double motive for seeking my re-enslavement—avarice and vengeance; and while, as I have said, there was little probability of successful recapture, if attempted openly, I was constantly in danger of being spirited away, at a moment when my friends could render me no assistance. In traveling about from place to place—often alone—I was much exposed to this sort of attack. Any one cherishing the design to betray me, could easily do so, by simply tracing my whereabouts through the anti-slavery journals, for my meetings and movements were promptly made known in advance. My true friends, Mr. Garrison and Mr. Phillips, had no faith in the power of Massachusetts to protect me in my right to liberty. Public sentiment and the law, in their opinion, would hand me over to the tormentors. Mr. Phillips, especially, considered me in danger, and said, when I showed him the manuscript of my story, if in my place, he would throw it into the fire. Thus, the reader will observe, the settling of one difficulty only opened the way for another; and that though I had reached a free state, and had attained a position for public usefulness, I was still tormented with the liability of losing my liberty.

American Slavery

Fellow-citizens: Pardon me, allow me to ask, why am I called upon to speak here to-day? What have I, or those I represent, to do with your national independence? Are the great principles of political freedom and of natural justice, embodied in that Declaration of Independence, extended to us? and am I, therefore, called upon to bring our humble offering to the national altar, and to confess the benefits and express devout gratitude for the blessings resulting from your independence to us?

Would God, both for your sakes and ours, that an affirmative answer could be truthfully returned to these questions! Then would my task be light, and my burden easy and delightful. For *who* is there so cold that a nation's sympathy could not warm him? Who so obdurate and dead to the claims of gratitude, that would not thankfully acknowledge such prideless benefits? Who so stolid and selfish, that would not give his voice to swell the hallelujahs of a nation's jubilee, when the chains of servitude had been torn from his limbs? I am not that man. In a case like that, the dumb might eloquently speak, and the "lame man leap as an hart."

But such is not the state of the case. I say it with a sad sense of the disparity between us. I am not included within the pale of this glorious anniversary! Your high independence only reveals the immeasurable distance between us. The blessings in which you, this day, rejoice, are not enjoyed in common. The rich inheritance of justice, liberty, prosperity and independence, bequeathed by your fathers, is shared by you, not by me. The sunlight that brought light and healing to you, has brought stripes and death to me. This Fourth of July is *yours*, not *mine*. *You* may rejoice, *I* must mourn. To drag a man in fetters into the grand illuminated temple of liberty, and call upon him to join you in joyous anthems, were inhuman mockery and sacrilegious irony. Do you mean, citizens, to mock me, by asking me to speak to-day? If so, there is a parallel to your conduct. And let me warn you that it is dangerous to copy the example of a nation whose crimes, towering up to heaven, were thrown down by the breath of the Almight, burying that nation in irrevocable ruin! I can to-day take up the plaintive lament of a peeled and woe-smitten people!

"By the waters of Babylon, there we sat down. Yea! we wept when we remembered Zion. We hanged our harps upon the willows in the midst thereof. For there, they that carried us away captive, required of us a song; and they who wasted us required of us mirth, saying, Sing us one of the songs of Zion. How can we sing the Lord's song in a strange land? If I forget thee, O Jerusalem, let my right hand forget her cunning. If I do not remember thee, let my tongue cleave to the roof of my mouth."

Fellow-citizens, above your national tumultuous joy, I hear the mournful wail of millions whose chains, heavy and grievous yesterday, are, to-day, rendered more intolerable by the jubilee shouts that reach them. If I do forget, if I do not faithfully remember those bleeding children to sorrow this day, "may my right hand forget her cunning, and may my tongue cleave to the roof of my mouth." To forget them, to pass lightly over their wrongs, and to chime in with the popular theme, would be treason most scandalous and shocking, and would make me a reproach before God and the world. My subject, then, fellow-citizens, is *American Slavery*. I shall see this day and its popular characteristics from the slave's point of view. Standing there identified with the American bondman, making his wrongs mine, I do not hesitate to declare, with all my soul, that the character and conduct of this nation never looked blacker to me than on this 4th of July! Whether we turn to the declarations of the past, or to the professions of the present, the conduct of the nation seems equally hideous and revolting. America is false to the past, false to the present, and solemnly binds herself to be false to the future. Standing with God and the crushed and bleeding slave on this occasion, I will in the name of humanity which is outraged, in the name of liberty which is fettered, in the name of the Constitution and the Bible which are disregarded and trampled upon, dare to call in question and to denounce, with all the emphasis I can command, everything that serves to perpetuate slavery—the great sin and shame of America! "I will not equivocate; I will not excuse"; I will use the severest language I can command; and yet not one word shall escape me that any man, whose judgment is not blinded by prejudice, or who is not at heart a slaveholder, shall not confess to be right and just.

But I fancy I hear some one of my audience say, "It is just in this circumstance that you and your brother abolition-

ists fail to make a favorable impression on the public mind.
Would you argue more and denounce less, would you per-
suade more and rebuke less, your cause would be much more
like to succeed." But, I submit, where all is plain there is
nothing to be argued. What point in the anti-slavery creed
would you have me argue? On what branch of the subject
do the people of this country need light? Must I undertake
to prove that the slave is a man? That point is conceded
already. Nobody doubts it. The slaveholders themselves
acknowledge it in the enactment of laws for their government. They acknowledge it when they punish disobedience
on the part of the slave. There are seventy-two crimes in
the state of Virginia which, if committed by a black man (no
matter how ignorant he be), subject him to the punishment
of death, while only two of the same crimes will subject a
white man to the like punishment. What is this but acknowl-
edgment that the slave is a moral, intellectual, and responsible
being? The manhood of the slave is conceded. It is admitted
in the fact that Southern statute books are covered with enactments forbidding, under severe fines and penalties, the teaching of the slave to read or to write. When you can point to
any such laws in reference to the beasts of the field, then I
may consent to argue the manhood of the slave. When the
dogs in your streets, when the fowls of the air, when the
cattle on your hills, when the fish of the sea, and the reptiles
that crawl, shall be unable to distinguish the slave from a
brute, *then* will I argue with you that the slave is a man.

For the present, it is enough to affirm the equal manhood
of the Negro race. Is it not astonishing that, while we are
ploughing, planting, and reaping, using all kinds of mechanical tools, erecting houses, constructing bridges, building ships,
working in metals of brass, iron, copper, silver and gold; that,
while we are reading, writing and ciphering, acting as clerks,
merchants and secretaries, having among us lawyers, doctors,

ministers, poets, authors, editors, orators and teachers; that, while we are engaged in all manner of enterprises common to other men, digging gold in California, capturing the whale in the Pacific, feeding sheep and cattle on the hill-side, living, moving, acting, thinking, planning, living in families as husbands, wives and children, and, above all, confessing and worshipping the Christian's God, and looking hopefully for life and immortality beyond the grave, we are called upon to prove that we are men!

Would you have me argue that man is entitled to liberty? that he is the rightful owner of his own body? You have already declared it. Must I argue the wrongfulness of slavery? Is that a question for Republicans? Is it to be settled by the rules of logic and argumentation, as a matter beset with great difficulty, involving a doubtful application of the principle of justice, heard to be understood? How should I look to-day, in the presence of Americans, dividing and subdividing a discourse, to show that men have a natural right to freedom? speaking of it relatively and positively, negatively and affirmatively? To do so, would be to make myself ridivulous, and to offer an insult to your understanding. There is not a man beneath the canopy of heaven that does not know that slavery is wrong *for him*.

What, am I to argue that it is wrong to make men brutes, to rob them of their liberty, to work them without wages, to keep them ignorant of their relations to their fellow men, to beat them with sticks, to flay their flesh with the lash, to load their limbs with irons, to hunt them with dogs, to sell them at auction, to sunder their families, to knock out their teeth, to burn their flesh, to starve them into obedience and submission to their masters? Must I argue that a system thus marked with blood, and stained with pollution, is *wrong?* No! I will not. I have better employment for my time and strength than such arguments would imply.

What, then, remains to be argued? Is it that slavery is not divine; that God did not establish it; that our doctors of divinity are mistaken? There is blasphemy in the thought. That which is inhuman cannot be divine. *Who* can reason on such a proposition? They that can, may; I cannot. The time for such argument is passed.

At a time like this, scorching irony, not convincing argument is needed. O! had I the ability, and could I reach the nation's ear, I would, to-day, pour out a fiery stream of biting ridicule, blasting reproach, withering sarcasm, and stern rebuke. For it is not light that is needed, but fire; it is not the gentle shower, but thunder. We need the storm, the whirlwind, and the earthquake. The feeling of the nation must be quickened; the conscience of the nation must be roused; the propriety of the nation must be startled; the hypocrisy of the nation must be exposed; and its crimes against God and man must be proclaimed and denounced.

What, to the American slave, is your 4th of July? I answer; a day that reveals to him, more than all other days in the year, the gross injustice and cruelty to which he is the constant victim. To him, your celebration is a sham; your boasted liberty, an unholy license; your national greatness, swelling vanity; your sounds of rejoicing are empty and heartless; your denunciation of tyrants, brass fronted impudence; your shouts of liberty and equality, hollow mockery; your prayers and hymns, your sermons and thanksgivings, with all your religious parade and solemnity, are, to him, mere bombast, fraud, deception, impiety, and hypocrisy—a thin veil to cover up crimes which would disgrace a nation of savages. There is not a nation on the earth guilty of practises more shocking and bloody than are the people of the United States, at this very hour.

Go where you may, search where you will, roam through all the monarchies and despotisms of the Old World, travel through South America, search out every abuse, and when you have found the last, lay your facts by the side of the everyday practises of this nation, and you will say with me, that, for revolting barbarity and shameless hypocrisy, America reigns without a rival.

WHAT THE BLACK MAN WANTS

(Delivered at the Annual Meeting of the Massachusetts Anti-Slavery Society in Boston, 1865)

MR. PRESIDENT: I came here, as I come always to the meetings in New England, as a listener, and not as a speaker; and one of the reasons why I have not been more frequently to the meetings of this society, has been because of the disposition on the part of some of my friends to call me out upon the platform, even when they knew that there was some difference of opinion and of feeling between those who rightfully belong to this platform and myself; and for fear of being misconstrued, as desiring to interrupt or disturb the proceedings of these meetings, I have usually kept away, and have thus been deprived of that educating influence, which I am always free to confess is of the highest order, descending from this platform. I have felt, since I have lived out West, that in going there I parted from a great deal that was valuable; and I feel, every time I come to these meetings, that I have lost a great deal by making my home west of Boston, west of Massachusetts; for, if anywhere in the country there is to be found the highest sense of justice, or the truest demands for my race, I look for it in the East, I look for it here. The ablest discussions of the whole question of our rights occur here, and to be deprived of the privilege of listening to those discussions is a great deprivation.

I do not know, from what has been said, that there is any difference of opinion as to the duty of Abolitionists at the present moment. How can we get up any difference at this point, or at any point, where we are so united, so agreed? I went especially, however, with that word of Mr. Phillips, which is the criticism of General Banks and General Banks's policy.* I hold that that policy is our chief danger at the present moment; that it practically enslaves the Negro, and makes the proclamation of 1863 a mockery and delusion. What is freedom? It is the right to choose one's own employment. Certainly it means that, if it means anything; and when any individual or combination of individuals undertakes to decide for any man when he shall work, where he shall work, at what he shall work, and for what he shall work, he or they practically reduce him to slavery. He is a slave. That I understand General Banks to do—to determine for the so-called freedman when, and where, at what, and for how much he shall work, when he shall be punished, and by whom punished. It is absolute slavery. It defeats the beneficent intentions of the government, if it has beneficent intentions, in regard to the freedom of our people.

I have had but one idea for the last three years to present to the American people, and the phraseology in which I clothe it is the old abolition phraseology. I am for the "immediate, unconditional, and universal" enfranchisement of the black man, in every state in the Union. Without this, his liberty is a mockery; without this, you might as well almost retain the old name of slavery for his condition; for, in fact, if he is not the slave of the individual master, he is the slave

* Nathaniel P. Banks (1816-1894), congressman, governor of Massachusetts, and Union soldier, was in the spring of 1863 in charge of the operations against Port Hudson, a village in Louisiana overlooking the Mississippi where the Confederates had erected powerful batteries. On May 25 and 27 he made costly attempts to capture the place by assault, calling into action Negro troops, who he said showed the utmost daring and determination. In 1864, because of his lack of success in leading an expedition up the Red River, he was relieved of his command and led to resign, though later he was vindicated by Grant. His policy as to the Negro at the close of the war is explained by Douglass in the speech.

of society, and holds his liberty as a privilege, not as a right. He is at the mercy of the mob, and has no means of protecting himself.

It may be objected, however, that this pressing of the Negro's right to suffrage is premature. Let us have slavery abolished, it may be said, let us have labor organized, and then, in the natural course of events, the right of suffrage will be extended to the Negro. I do not agree with this. The constitution of the human mind is such, that if it once disregards the conviction forced upon it by a revelation of truth, it requires the exercise of a higher power to produce the same conviction afterward. The American people are now in tears. The Shenandoah has run blood, the best blood of the North. All around Richmond, the blood of New England and of the North has been shed, of your sons, your brothers, and your fathers. We all feel, in the existence of this rebellion, that judgments terrible, widespread, far-reaching, overwhelming, are abroad in the land; and we feel, in view of these judgments, just now, a disposition to learn righteousness. This is the hour. Our streets are in mourning, tears are falling at every fireside, and under the chastisement of this rebellion we have almost come up to the point of conceding this great, this all-important right of suffrage. I fear that if we fail to do it now, if Abolitionists fail to press it now, we may not see, for centuries to come, the same disposition that exists at this moment. Hence, I say, now is the time to press this right.

It may be asked, "Why do you want it? Some men have got along very well without it. Women have not this right." Shall we justify one wrong by another? That is a sufficient answer. Shall we at this moment justify the deprivation of the Negro of the right to vote, because some one else is deprived of that privilege? I hold that women, as well as men, have the right to vote, and my heart and my voice go with the movement to extend suffrage to woman; but that question rests upon another basis than that on which our right rests. We may be asked, I say, why we want it. I will tell you why we want it. We want it because it is our right, first of all. No class of men can, without insulting their own nature, be content with any deprivations of their rights. We want it, again, as a means for educating our race. Men are so constituted that they derive their conviction of their own possibilities largely from the estimate formed of them by others. If nothing is expected of a people, that people will find it difficult to contradict that expectation. By depriving us of suffrage, you affirm our incapacity to form an intelligent judgment respecting public men and public measures; you declare before the world that we are unfit to exercise the elective franchise, and by this means lead us to undervalue ourselves, to put a low estimate upon ourselves, and to feel that we have no possibilities like other men. Again, I want the elective franchise, for one, as a colored man, because ours is a peculiar government, based upon a peculiar idea, and that idea is universal suffrage. If I were in a monarchical government, or an autocratic or aristocratic government, where the few bore rule and the many were subject, there would be no special stigma resting upon me, because I did not exercise the elective franchise. It would do me no great violence. Mingling with the mass, I should partake of the strength of the mass, and I should have the same incentives to endeavor with the mass of my fellow men; it would be no particular burden, no particular deprivation; but here, where universal suffrage is the rule, where that is the fundamental idea of the government, to rule us out is to make us an exception, to brand us with the stigma of inferiority, and to invite to our heads the missiles of those about us; therefore, I want the franchise for the black man.

There are, however, other reasons, not derived from any

consideration merely of our rights, but arising out of the condition of the South, and of the country; considerations which have already been referred to by Mr. Phillips; considerations which must arrest the attention of statesmen. I believe that when the tall heads of this rebellion shall have been swept down, when the Davises and Toombses and Stephenses and others who are leading in this rebellion shall have been blotted out, there will be this rank undergrowth of treason, to which reference has been made, growing up there, and interfering with, and thwarting the quiet operation of the federal government in those States. You will see those traitors handing down, from sire to son, the same malignant spirit which they have manifested, and which they are now exhibiting, with malicious hearts, broad blades, and bloody hands in the field, against our sons and brothers. That spirit will still remain; and whoever sees the federal government extended over those southern States will see that government in a strange land, and not only in a strange land, but in an enemy's land. A postmaster of the United States in the South will find himself surrounded by a hostile spirit; a United States marshal or a United States judge will be surrounded there by a hostile element. That enmity will not die out in a year, will not die out in an age. The federal government will be looked upon in those States precisely as the governments of Austria and France are looked upon in Italy at the present moment. They will endeavor to circumvent, they will endeavor to destroy, the peaceful operation of this government. Now, where will you find the strength to counterbalance this spirit, if you do not find it in the Negroes of the South? They are your friends. They were your friends even when the government did not regard them as such. They comprehended the genius of this war before you did. It is a significant fact, it is a marvelous fact, it seems almost to imply a direct interposition of Providence, that this

war, which began in the interest of slavery on both sides, bids
fair to end in the interest of liberty on both sides. It was
begun, I say, in the interest of slavery on both sides. The
South was fighting to take slavery out of the Union, and the
North fighting to keep it in the Union; the South fighting to
get it beyond the limits of the United States constitution, and
the North fighting to retain it within those limits; the South
fighting for new guarantees, and the North fighting for the
old guarantees; both despising the Negro, both insulting the
Negro. Yet, the Negro, apparently endowed with wisdom
from on high, saw more clearly the end from the beginning
than we did. When Seward said the status of no man in the
country would be changed by the war, the Negro did not
believe him. When our generals sent their underlings in
shoulder-straps to hunt the flying Negro back from our lines
into the jaws of slavery, from which he had escaped, the
Negroes thought that a mistake had been made, and that the
intentions of the government had not been rightly understood by our officers in shoulder-straps, and they continued
to come into our lines, treading their way through bogs and
fens, over briers and thorns, fording streams, swimming
rivers, bringing us tidings as to the safe path to march, and
pointing out the dangers that threatened us. They are our
only friends in the South, and we should be true to them in
this their trial hour, and see to it that they have the elective
franchise.

*   *   *   *   *   *   *

I ask my friends who are apologizing for not insisting
upon this right, where can the black man look in this country
for the assertion of this right, if he may not look to the
Massachusetts Anti-Slavery Society? Where under the whole
heavens can he look for sympathy in asserting this right, if
he may not look to this platform? Have you lifted us up to a
certain height to see that we are men, and then are any dis-

posed to leave us there, without seeing that we are put in possession of all our rights? We look naturally to this platform for the assertion of all our rights, and for this one especially. I understand the anti-slavery societies of this country to be based on two principles—first, the freedom of the blacks of this country; and, second, the elevation of them. Let me not be misunderstood here. I am not asking for sympathy at the hands of Abolitionists, sympathy at the hands of any. I think the American people are disposed often to be generous rather than just. I look over this country at the present time, and I see educational societies, sanitary commissions, freedmen's associations and the like,—all very good: but in regard to the colored people there is always more that is benevolent, I perceive, than just, manifested towards us. What I ask for the Negro is not benevolence, not pity, not sympathy, but simple justice. The American people have always been anxious to know what they shall do with us. General Banks was distressed with solicitude as to what he should do with the Negro. Everybody has asked the question, and they learned to ask it early of the Abolitionists, "What shall we do with the Negro?" I have had but one answer from the beginning. Do nothing with us! Your doing with us has already played the mischief with us. Do nothing with us! If the apples will not remain on the tree of their own strength, if they are worm-eaten at the core, if they are early ripe and disposed to fall, let them fall! I am not for tying or fastening them on the tree in any way, except by nature's plan, and if they will not stay there, let them fall. And if the Negro can not stand on his own legs, let him fall also. All I ask is, give him a chance to stand on his own legs! Let him alone! If you see him on his way to school, let him alone,—don't disturb him. If you see him going to the dinner table at a hotel, let him go! If you see him going to the ballot-box, let him alone,—don't disturb him! If you see him going into a workshop, just let him alone,—your interference is doing him a positive injury. General Banks's "preparation" is of a piece with this attempt to prop up the Negro. Let him fall if he can not stand alone! If the Negro can not live by the line of eternal justice, so beautifully pictured to you in the illustration used by Mr. Phillips, the fault will not be yours; it will be his who made the Negro, and established that line for his government. Let him live or die by that. If you will only untie his hands, and give him a chance, I think he will live. He will work as readily for himself as the white man. A great many delusions have been swept away by this war. One was that the Negro would not work; he has proved his ability to work. Another was that the Negro would not fight, that he possessed only the most sheepish attributes of humanity, was a perfect lamb or an "Uncle Tom," disposed to take off his coat whenever required, fold his hands, and be whipped by anybody who wanted to whip him. But the war has proved that there is a great deal of human nature in the Negro, and that "he will fight," as Mr. Quincy, our president, said in earlier days than these, "when there is a reasonable probability of his whipping anybody."

MARTIN ROBISON DELANY

MARTIN ROBISON DELANY was born in Charles Town, Va. (now in W. Va.) May 6, 1812, the son of free Negroes, Samuel and Pati Delany. Because of persecution his parents were forced to remove to Chambersburgh, Penn., in 1822, and now for the first time he had opportunity to go to school. In 1831 he went to Pittsburgh. He soon became concerned about the social and political welfare of his people, and especially did he receive training and inspiration in the Theban Literary Society, an organization of young Negro men of which he was a leading spirit. He began the study of medicine, and in 1843 started the publication of a newspaper, *The Mystery*. On March 15, 1843, he married Katherine A. Richards. Of the eleven children born of the marriage seven grew up, and something of the father's interests may be seen from the Christian names that they received— Toussaint L'Ouverture, Charles Lennox Remond, Alexandre Dumas, Saint Cyprian, Faustin Soulouque, Rameses Placido, and Ethiopia Halle Amelia.

From 1847 to 1849 Delany was associated with Frederick Douglass on *The North Star*, issued at Rochester, N. Y., and in July, 1848, he was attacked by a mob in northern Ohio. In 1849 he entered the Harvard Medical School, later lectured in the West, and he rendered valiant service in connection with the cholera epidemic in Pittsburgh in 1854. Two years later he removed to Chatham, Ontario, where he engaged in the practice of medicine. Meanwhile, in 1852, in Philadelphia, he had published his best book, *The Condition, Elevation, Emigration, and Destiny of the Colored People of the United States, Politically Considered.* About this time such enactments as the Fugitive Slave Law and the Kansas-Nebraska Bill had forced thoughtful Negro men to reconsider the whole matter of colonization; and, after a series of conventions, in calling which he himself had played a leading part, Delany was chosen "chief commissioner" of a party to explore the Valley of the Niger "for the purpose of science and for general

information," his organization making it clear that his going in
no way committed it to actual colonization. He sailed in May,
1859; the next year he visited Liverpool and London; and in
1861 he issued his Official Report of the *Niger Valley Exploring
Party*.

While in London Delany figured in an incident that received
wide publicity in the American press. It was on July 16, 1860,
that he attended the International Statistical Congress, having been
given a royal commission on the basis of individual claim. It was
a time of tense feeling in America, as the country was drifting into
Civil War; and there were present distinguished people from all
over the world. Prince Albert presided, and by him sat on one
side Lord Brougham, the first vice-president, and on the other
George M. Dallas, the American minister. Henry Brougham
had had a distinguished career in statesmanship. Eccentric as he
was at times, he was a man of amazing capacity for work, and in
Parliament in the earlier years of the century he had been equalled
only by Wilberforce in his opposition to slavery. The presence of
Delany in London and at the Congress had elicited his kindly interest. Preliminaries being over and the address of the Prince
concluded, Brougham made some remarks referring to the visitors
present and, turning to Dallas, called attention to the fact that
there was a Negro among the delegates. Delany, not knowing
just what the effect of this might be on the assemblage, rose and
said, "I rise, your Royal Highness, to thank his lordship, the
unflinching friend of the Negro, for the remarks he has made in
reference to myself, and to assure your Royal Highness and his
lordship that *I am a man*." This statement was received with
great applause. The American delegates, however, led by Judge
A. B. Longstreet, of Georgia, took great umbrage at the incident,
and withdrew, all expect Dr. Jarvis, of Boston, who was a state,
not a national, delegate. Their feeling was shown in the word
of Longstreet to Howell Cobb, Secretary of the Treasury, who
was also from Georgia: "I regarded this an ill-timed assault upon
our country, a wanton indignity offered to our minister, and a
pointed insult offered to me. I immediately withdrew from the
body. The propriety of my course is respectfully submitted to my

government." The next day in opening the meeting Brougham said that he had made reference to the presence of the Negro member only because he regarded it as "one of the most gratifying as well as extraordinary facts of the age." Frederick Douglass wrote as to the incident: "Never was there a more telling rebuke administered to the pride, prejudice, and hypocrisy of a nation." Of Brougham he said: "There was, doubtless, something of his sarcastic temper shown in the manner of his announcement of Delany; but we doubt not there was the same philanthropic motive at the bottom of his action which has distinguished him through life."

Before leaving London Delany read before the Royal Geographical Society, by special request, a paper on his researches in Africa. Back in the United States he assisted in recruiting Negro soldiers for the Civil War and for some time served as an examining surgeon in Chicago. On February 8, 1865, he received his commission as major, and on April 5 was ordered to Charleston. For three years he served in the Freedmen's Bureau, for some years also he was a custom-house inspector, and for four years a trial justice in the city. In the troublous era of Reconstruction Delany stood for good government, and in 1874 was nominated for lieutenant-governor of South Carolina on the Independent Republican ticket, but was defeated. In 1879 he published *Principia of Ethnology: the Origin of Races and Color;* and four years later he was the subject of a full-length biography, *Life and Public Services of Martin R. Delany,* by a woman of the race, Frances E. Rollin Whipper, who wrote under the name Frank A. Rollin. He died in Xenia, Ohio, January 24, 1885. He was an eager, restless character, frequently changing his work and his abode, but he was also a man ever awake to the best interest of his people and one of high personal integrity.

Delany was not a man of genuine literary gifts; nevertheless he tried his hand at many things. In the *Anglo-African* in 1859 appeared serially several chapters of a novel, *Blake, or The Huts of America,* obviously influenced by *Uncle Tom's Cabin;* but the work never appeared in book form. Less pretentious, hastily done, but much more significant was *The Condition, Elevation, Emigra-*

tion, and Destiny of the Colored People of the United States, Politically Considered. The chief purpose of the little book seems to have been to encourage emigration to Central America or the West Indies. It was attacked by the abolitionists as yielding to the idea of colonization that they had opposed and as impeding immediate emancipation. The author, whose own ideas had yet not fully crystallized, realizing the force of the objection, with his usual honesty ordered that the sale be stopped. For us to-day the work is a mine of information about the social and economic status of the Negro ten years before the Civil War. In his preface Delany said that he wrote the book within a month while detained in New York in such time as he had after attending to other business in the day and lecturing on physiology sometimes in the evening. His object was to place before the American public and especially the Negro people, certain great truths which had sometimes been overlooked. There were, he said in the United States a great many colored people who had independence of spirit and who desired to think for themselves, but who labored under the handicap that no opinion must be expressed unless it emanated from some old, orthodox, stereotyped doctrine. "The colored people of to-day," he informed his hearers, "are not the colored people of a quarter of a century ago, and require very different means and measures to satisfy their wants and demands, and to effect their advancement." In the body of the work he opposed the American Colonization Society as the agency of slaveholders, and then he considered the claims of the Negro citizen upon the United States. He reviewed the work of the Negro in the wars in which the country had engaged, and devoted several chapters to the achievements of representative men and women. He then took up again the whole question of colonization, opposing Liberia, and considering in turn the Canadas, Central America, South America, and the West Indies. Throughout the book he is very practical and he has his facts well in hand. He is especially effective when advocating practical education along industrial lines, and he laid down quite clearly the principle on which Booker T. Washington began to work thirty years later.

THE CONDITION, ELEVATION, EMIGRATION, AND DESTINY OF
THE COLORED PEOPLE OF THE UNITED STATES,
POLITICALLY CONSIDERED
(Selections)

The United States, untrue to her trust and unfaithful to her professed principles of republican equality, has also pursued a policy of political degradation to a large portion of her native born countrymen, and that class is the Colored People. Denied an equality not only of political but of natural rights, in common with the rest of our fellow citizens, there is no species of degradation to which we are not subject.

    *   *   *   *   *   *   *

It was expected that Anti-Slavery, according to its professions, would extend to colored persons, as far as in the power of its adherents, those advantages nowhere else to be obtained among white men; that colored boys would get situations in their shops and stores, and every other advantage tending to elevate them as far as possible, would be extended to them. . . . But in all this we were doomed to disappointment, sad, sad disappointment. Instead of realizing what we had hoped for, we find ourselves occupying the very same position in relation to our Anti-Slavery friends, as we do in relation to the pro-slavery part of the community—a mere secondary, underling position, in all our relations to them, and anything more than this is not a matter-of-course affair—it comes not by established anti-slavery custom or right, but, like that which emanates from the pro-slavery portion of the community, by mere sufferance.

It is true that the *Liberator* office, in Boston, has got Elijah Smith, a colored youth, at the cases—the *Standard*, in New York, a young colored man, and the *Freeman*, in Philadelphia, William Still, another, in the publication office, as "packing clerk"; yet these are but three out of the hosts that fill these offices in their various departments, all occupying places that could have been, and as we once thought, would have been, easily enough, occupied by colored men. . . .

And if it be urged that colored men are incapable as yet to fill these positions, all we have to say is, that the cause has fallen far short; almost equivalent to a failure, of a tithe, of what it promised to do in half the period of its existence, to this time, if it have not as yet, now a period of twenty years, raised up colored men enough, to fill the offices within its patronage. We think it not unkind to say, if it had been half as faithful to itself, as it should have been—its professed principles we mean, it could have reared and tutored from childhood colored men enough by this time, for its own especial purpose. These we know could have been easily obtained, because colored people in general are favorable to the anti-slavery cause, and wherever there is an adverse mani-festation, it arises from sheer ignorance; and we have now but comparatively few such among us.

*   *   *   *   *   *   *

When we speak of colonization, we wish distinctly to be understood as speaking of the American Colonization Society—or that which is under its influence—commenced in Rich-mond, Va., in 1817, under the influence of Mr. Henry Clay of Kentucky, Judge Bushrod Washington of Virginia, and other Southern slaveholders, having for their express object, as their speeches and doings all justify us in asserting in good faith, the removal of the free colored people from the land of their birth, for the security of the slaves, as property to the slave propagandists.

The scheme had no sooner been propagated than the old and leading colored men of Philadelphia, Pa., with Richard Allen, James Forten, and others at their head, true to their trust and the cause of their brethren, summoned the colored people together, and then and there, in language and with voices pointed and loud, protested against the scheme as an outrage, having no other object in view, than the benefit of the slave-holding interests of the country, and that as freemen they would never prove recreant to the cause of their brethren in bondage, by leading them without hope of redemption from their chains. This determination of the colored patriots of Philadelphia was published in full, authentically, and circulated throughout the length and breadth of the country by the papers of the day. The colored people everywhere received the news, and at once endorsed with heart and soul, the doings of the Anti-Colonization Meeting of colored freemen. From that time forth the colored people generally have had no sympathy with the colonization scheme, nor confidence in its leaders, looking upon them all as arrant hypocrites, seeking every opportunity to deceive them. In a word, the monster was crippled in its infancy, and has never as yet recovered from the stroke.

*   *   *   *   *   *   *

The colored races are highly susceptible of religion; it is a constituent principle of their nature, and an excellent trait in their character. But unfortunately for them, they carry it too far. Their hope is largely developed, and, consequently, they usually stand still—hope in God, and really expect Him to do that for them, which it is necessary they should do themselves. This is their great mistake, and arises from a misconception of the character and ways of Deity.

*   *   *   *   *   *   *

Moral theories have long been resorted to by us, as a means of effecting the redemption of our brethren in bonds, and the elevation of the free colored people in this country. Experience has taught us that speculations are not enough; that the *practical* application of principles adduced, the thing carried out, is the only true and proper course to pursue.

We have speculated and moralized much about equality—

claiming to be as good as our neighbors, and everybody else— all of which may do very well in ethics, but not in politics. We live in society among men, conducted by men, governed by rules and regulations. However arbitrary, there are certain policies that regulate all well organized institutions and corporate bodies. . . . Society regulates itself, being governed by mind, which, like water, finds its own level. . . . By the regulations of society, there is no equality of persons where there is not an equality of attainments.

We will suppose a case for argument: In this city reside two colored families, of three sons and three daughters each. At the head of each family there is an old father and mother. The opportunities of these families may or may not be the same for educational advantages; be that as it may, the children of the one go to school, and become qualified for the duties of life. One daughter becomes a school teacher, another a mantua-maker, and a third a fancy shopkeeper; while one son becomes a farmer, another a merchant, and a third a mechanic. All enter into the business with fine prospects, marry respectably, and settle down in domestic comfort; while the six sons and daughters of the other family grow up without educational and business qualifications, and the highest aim they have is to apply to the sons and daughters of the first named family, to hire for domestics! Would there be an equality here between the children of these two families? Certainly not. This, then, is precisely the position of the colored people generally in the United States, compared with the whites. What is necessary to be done, in order to attain an equality, is to change the condition, and the person is at once changed. If, as before stated, a knowledge of all the various business enterprises, trades, professions and sciences is necessary for the elevation of the white, a knowledge of them also is necessary for the elevation of the colored man; and he can not be elevated without them.

White men are producers; we are consumers. They build houses, and we rent them. They raise produce, and we consume it. They manufacture clothes and wares, and we garnish ourselves with them. They build coaches, vessels, cars, hotels, saloons, and other vehicles and places of accommodation, and we deliberately wait until they have got them in readiness, then walk in, and contend with as much assurance for a "right," as though the whole thing was bought by, paid for, and belonged to us.

*   *   *   *   *   *   *

It ever has been denied that the United States recognized or knew any difference between the people. This is not true. . . . By the provisions of this bill* the colored people of the United States are positively degraded beneath the level of the whites—are made liable at any time, in any place, and under all circumstances, to be arrested, and, upon the claim of any white person, without the privilege even of making a defence, sent into endless bondage. Let no visionary nonsense about *habeas corpus*, or a fair trial, deceive us; there are no such rights granted in this bill, and, except where the commissioner is too ignorant to understand when reading it, or too stupid to enforce it when he does understand, there is no earthly chance—no hope under heaven for the colored person who is brought before one of these officers of the law. Any leniency that may be expected must proceed from the whims or caprice of the magistrate—in fact, it is optional with them; and *our* rights and liberty entirely at their disposal.

We are slaves in the midst of freedom, waiting patiently, and unconcernedly—indifferently, and stupidly, for masters to come and lay claim to us, trusting to their generosity, whether or not they will own us and carry us into endless bondage.

The slave is more secure than we; he knows who holds

* That of September 18, 1850, establishing the Fugitive Slave Law.

the heel upon his bosom—we know not the wretch who may grasp us by the throat. His master may be a man of some conscientious scruples; ours may be unmerciful. Good or bad, mild or harsh, easy or hard, lenient or severe, saint or Satan—whenever that master demands any one of us, even our affectionate wives and darling little children, *we must go into slavery*—there is no alternative. The *will* of the man who sits in judgment on our liberty, is the law. To him is given *all power* to say whether or not we have a right to enjoy freedom. This is the power over the slave in the South that is now extended to the North. The will of the man who sits in judgment over us is the law; because it is explicitly provided that the *decision* of the commissioner shall be final, from which there can be no appeal. . . .

What can we do? What shall we do? This is the great and important question:—Shall we submit to be dragged like brutes before heartless men, and sent into degradation and bondage? Shall we fly, or shall we resist?

This important inquiry we shall answer, and find a remedy in when treating of the emigration of the colored people.

*   *   *   *   *   *   *

That there have been people in all ages under certain circumstances, that may be benefited by emigration, will be admitted; and that there are circumstances under which emigration is absolutely necessary to their political elevation, can not be disputed.

This we see in the Exodus of the Jews from Egypt to the land of Judea; in the expedition of Dido and her followers from Tyre to Mauritania; and, not to dwell upon hundreds of modern European examples, also in the ever memorable emigration of the Puritans, in 1620, from Great Britain, the land of their birth to the wilderness of the New World, at which may be fixed the beginning of emigration to this continent as a permanent residence.

This may be acknowledged; but to advocate the emigration of the colored people of the United States from their native homes, is a new feature in our history, and at first view may be considered objectionable, as pernicious to our interests. This objection is at once removed, when reflecting on our condition as incontrovertibly shown in a foregoing part of this work. And we shall proceed at once to give the advantages to be derived from emigration, to us as a people, in preference to any other policy that we may adopt. This granted, the question will then be, Where shall we go? This we conceive to be all-important, of paramount consideration, and shall endeavor to show the most advantageous locality; and premise the recommendation with the strictest advice against any countenance whatever to the emigration scheme of the so-called Republic of Liberia.

*   *   *   *   *   *   *

Let our young men and women prepare themselves for usefulness and business; that the men may enter into merchandise, trading, and other things of importance; the young women may become teachers of various kinds, and otherwise fill places of usefulness. Parents must turn their attention more to the education of their children. We mean, to educate them for useful practical building purposes. Educate them for the store and the counting house—to do everyday practical business. Consult the children's propensities, and direct their education according to their inclinations. It may be that there is too great a desire on the part of parents to give their children a professional education, before the body of the people are ready for it. A people must be a business people, and have more to depend upon than mere help in people's houses and hotels, before they are either able to support, or capable of properly appreciating the services of professional men among them. This has been one of our great mistakes—we have gone in advance of ourselves.

We have commenced at the superstructure of the building instead of the foundation—at the top instead of the bottom. We should first be mechanics and common tradesmen, and professions as a matter of course would grow out of the wealth made thereby. Young men and women must now prepare for usefulness—the day of our elevation is at hand —all the world now gazes at us—and Central and South America, and the West Indies, bid us come and be men and women, protected, secure, beloved and Free.

JAMES M. WHITFIELD

COMPARATIVELY few facts are known about James M. Whitfield, but those few are sufficient to give him definite place in the agitation in the decade before the Civil War. He was born in Boston, but as a young man removed to Buffalo, where he worked as a barber. Delany in his book published in 1852 referred to the humble position of the poet, with the added remark, "for which we think he is somewhat reprehensible." Already, however, Whitfield was contributing his verses to different papers, and in 1853 published a little book, *America, and Other Poems*. This was dedicated to Delany, and the next year Whitfield attended the National Emigration Convention of Colored Men that Delany had called in Cleveland. Douglass pronounced the call "unwise, unfortunate, and premature," and his position led him into a wordy discussion in the press with Whitfield. In spite of opposition the convention met and considered places that might be most favorable for emigration. Either in this or in the succeeding conventions Bishop James Theodore Holly was commissioned to Hayti, Delany was sent to Africa, and Whitfield was thought of in connection with Central America. However, the plan for a colony in this last place came to naught when the leading spirit died in San Francisco on his way thither. Eager and earnest, he soon burned out. Like other poets of the period, he was much influenced by Byron, in both temper and form; but he was stronger than Reason and Vashon. In fact, the vigorous movement in some of his pieces leaves one speculating as to what he might not have done if he had had more systematic training.

AMERICA

America, it is to thee,
Thou boasted land of liberty,—
It is to thee I raise my song,
Thou land of blood, and crime, and wrong.

It is to thee, my native land,
From which has issued many a band
To tear the black man from his soil,
And force him here to delve and toil;
Chained on your blood-bemoistened sod,
Cringing beneath a tyrant's rod,
Stripped of those rights which Nature's God
    Bequeathed to all the human race,
Bound to a petty tyrant's nod,
    Because he wears a paler face.
Was it for this that freedom's fires
Were kindled by your patriot sires?
Was it for this they shed their blood,
On hill and plain, on field and flood?
Was it for this that wealth and life
Were staked upon that desperate strife,
Which drenched this land for seven long years
With blood of men, and women's tears?
When black and white fought side by side,
    Upon the well-contested field,—
Turned back the fierce opposing tide,
    And made the proud invader yield—
When, wounded, side by side they lay,
    And heard with joy the proud hurrah
From their victorious comrades say
    That they had waged successful war,
The thought ne'er entered in their brains
That they endured those toils and pains,
To forge fresh fetters, heavier chains
For their own children, in whose veins
Should flow that patriotic blood,
So freely shed on field and flood.
Oh, no; they fought, as they believed,
    For the inherent rights of man;

But mark, how they have been deceived
    By slavery's accursed plan.
They never thought, when thus they shed
    Their heart's best blood, in freedom's cause,
That their own sons would live in dread,
    Under unjust, oppressive laws:
That those who quietly enjoyed
    The rights for which they fought and fell,
Could be the framers of a code,
    That would disgrace the fiends of hell!
Could they have looked, with prophet's ken,
    Down to the present evil time,
    Seen free-born men, uncharged with crime,
Consigned unto a slaver's pen,—
Or thrust into a prison cell,
With thieves and murderers to dwell—
While that same flag whose stripes and stars
Had been their guide through freedom's wars
As proudly waved above the pen
Of dealers in the souls of men!
Or could the shades of all the dead,
    Who fell beneath that starry flag,
Visit the scenes where they once bled,
    On hill and plain, on vale and crag,
By peaceful brook, or ocean's strand,
    By inland lake, or dark green wood,
Where'er the soil of this wide land
    Was moistened by their patriot blood,—
And then survey the country o'er,
    From north to south, from east to west,
And hear the agonizing cry
Ascending up to God on high,
From western wilds to ocean's shore,
    The fervent prayer of the oppressed;

The cry of helpless infancy
 Torn from the parent's fond caress
By some base tool of tyranny,
 And doomed to woe and wretchedness;
The indignant wail of fiery youth,
 Its noble aspirations crushed,
Its generous zeal, its love of truth,
 Trampled by tyrants in the dust;
The aerial piles which fancy reared,
 And hopes too bright to be enjoyed,
Have passed and left his young heart seared,
 And all its dreams of bliss destroyed.
The shriek of virgin purity,
 Doomed to some libertine's embrace,
Should rouse the strongest sympathy
 Of each one of the human race;
And weak old age, oppressed with care,
 As he reviews the scene of strife,
Puts up to God a fervent prayer,
 To close his dark and troubled life,
The cry of fathers, mothers, wives,
 Severed from all their hearts hold dear,
And doomed to spend their wretched lives
 In gloom, and doubt, and hate, and fear;
And manhood, too, with soul of fire,
And arm of strength, and smothered ire,
Stands pondering with brow of gloom,
Upon his dark unhappy doom,
Whether to plunge in battle's strife,
And buy his freedom with his life,
And with stout heart and weapon strong,
Pay back the tyrant wrong for wrong
Or wait the promised time of God,
 When his Almighty ire shall wake,

And smite the oppressor in his wrath,
And hurl red ruin in his path,
And with the terrors of his rod,
    Cause adamantine hearts to quake.
Here Christian writhes in bondage still,
    Beneath his brother Christian's rod,
And pastors trample down at will,
    The image of the living God.
While prayers go up in lofty strains,
    And pealing hymns ascend to heaven,
The captive, toiling in his chains,
    With tortured limbs and bosom riven,
Raises his fettered hand on high,
    And in the accents of despair,
To him who rules both earth and sky,
    Puts up a sad, a fervent prayer,
To free him from the awful blast
    Of slavery's bitter galling shame—
Although his portion should be cast
    With demons in eternal flame!
Almighty God! 'tis this they call
    The land of liberty and law;
Part of its sons in baser thrall
    Than Babylon or Egypt saw—
Worse scenes of rapine, lust and shame,
    Than Babylonian ever knew,
Are perpetrated in the name
    Of God, the holy, just, and true;
And darker doom than Egypt felt,
May yet repay this nation's guilt.
Almighty God! thy aid impart,
And fire anew each faltering heart,
And strengthen every patriot's hand,
Who aims to save our native land.

We do not come before thy throne,
    With carnal weapons drenched in gore,
Although our blood has freely flown,
    In adding to the tyrant's store.
Father! before thy throne we come,
    Not in the panoply of war,
With pealing trump, and rolling drum,
    And cannon booming loud and far;
Striving in blood to wash out blood,
    Through wrong to seek redress for wrong;
For while thou'rt holy, just and good,
    The battle is not to the strong;
But in the sacred name of peace,
    Of justice, virtue, love and truth,
We pray, and never mean to cease,
    Till weak old age and fiery youth
In freedom's cause their voices raise,
And burst the bonds of every slave;
Till, north and south, and east and west,
The wrongs we bear shall be redressed.

How Long?

How long, O gracious God! how long,
    Shall power lord it over right?
The feeble, trampled by the strong,
    Remain in slavery's gloomy night?
In every region of the earth,
    Oppression rules with iron power;
And every man of sterling worth,
    Whose soul disdains to cringe or cower
Beneath a haughty tyrant's nod,
And, supplicating, kiss the rod
That, wielded by oppression's might,

Smites to the earth his dearest right,—
The right to speak, and think, and feel,
    And spread his uttered thoughts abroad,
To labor for the common weal,
    Responsible to none but God,—
Is threatened with the dungeon's gloom,
The felon's cell, the traitor's doom,
And treacherous politicians league
    With hireling priests, to crush and ban
All who expose their vile intrigue,
    And vindicate the rights of man.
How long shall Afric' raise to thee
    Her fettered hand, O Lord! in vain,
And plead in fearful agony
    For vengeance for her children slain?
I see the Gambia's swelling flood,
    And Niger's darkly rolling wave,
Bear on their bosoms, stained with blood,
    The bound and lacerated slave;
While numerous tribes spread near and far,
Fierce, devastating, barbarous war,
Earth's fairest scenes in ruin laid,
To furnish victims for that trade,
Which breeds on earth such deeds of shame,
As fiends might blush to hear or name.
I see where Danube's waters roll,
    And where the Magyar vainly strove,
With valiant arm and faithful soul,
    In battle for the land he loved,—
A perjured tyrant's legions tread
The ground where Freedom's heroes bled,
And still the voice of those who feel
Their country's wrongs, with Austrian steel.
I see the "Rugged Russian Bear"

Lead forth his slavish hordes, to war
Upon the right of every State
Its own affairs to regulate;
To help each despot bind the chain
Upon the people's rights again,
And crush beneath his ponderous paw
All constitutions, rights, and law.
I see in France,—O burning shame!—
The shadow of a mighty name,
Wielding the power her patriot bands
Had boldly wrenched from kingly hands,
With more despotic pride of sway
Than ever monarch dared display.
The Fisher, too, whose world-wide nets
    Are spread to snare the souls of men,
By foreign tyrants' bayonets
    Established on his throne again,
Blesses the swords still reeking red
    With the best blood his country bore,
And prays for blessings on the head
    Of him who wades through Roman gore.
The same unholy sacrifice
Where'er I turn bursts on mine eyes,
Of princely pomp, and priestly pride,
    The people trampled in the dust,
Their dearest, holiest rights denied,
    Their hopes destroyed, their spirit crushed:
But when I turn the land to view,
    Which claims, par excellence, to be
The refuge of the brave and true,
    The strongest bulwark of the free,
The grand asylum for the poor
    And trodden down of every land,
Where they may rest in peace, secure,

Nor fear the oppressor's iron hand,—
Worse scenes of rapine, lust, and shame,
Than e'er disgraced the Russian name,
Worse than the Austrian ever saw,
Are sanctioned here as righteous law.
Here might the Austrian butcher* make
 Progress in shameful cruelty,
Where women-whippers proudly take
 The meed and praise of chivalry.
Here might the cunning Jesuit learn,
 Though skilled in subtle sophistry,
And trained to persevere in stern
 Unsympathizing cruelty,
And call that good, which, right or wrong,
Will tend to make his order strong:
He here might learn from those who stand
 High in the gospel ministry,
The very magnates of the land
 In evangelic piety,
That conscience must not only bend
 To everything the church decrees,
But it must also condescend,
 When drunken politicians please
To place their own inhuman acts
 Above the "higher law" of God,
And on the hunted victim's tracks
 Cheer the malignant fiends of blood,
To help the man-thief bind the chain
 Upon his Christian brother's limb,
And bear to slavery's hell again
 The bound and suffering child of Him
Who died upon the cross, to save
Alike, the master and the slave.

* Haynau.

While all the oppressed from every land
Are welcomed here with open hand,
And fulsome praises rend the heaven
For those who have the fetters riven
Of European tyranny,
And bravely struck for liberty;
And while from thirty thousand fanes
　　Mock prayers go up, and hymns are sung,
Three million drag their clanking chains,
　　"Unwept, unhonored, and unsung:"
Doomed to a state of slavery,
　　Compared with which the darkest night
Of European tyranny,
　　Seems brilliant as the noonday light.
While politicians void of shame,
　　Cry this is law and liberty,
The clergy lend the awful name
　　And sanction of the Deity,
To help sustain the monstrous wrong,
And crush the weak beneath the strong.
Lord, thou hast said the tyrant's ear
　　Shall not be always closed to thee,
But that thou wilt in wrath appear,
　　And set the trembling captive free.
And even now dark omens rise
　　To those who either see or hear,
And gather o'er the darkening skies
　　The threatening signs of fate and fear;
Not like the plagues which Egypt saw,
　　When rising in an evil hour,
A rebel 'gainst the "higher law,"
　　And glorying in her mighty power,—
Saw blasting fire, and blighting hail,
Sweep o'er her rich and fertile vale,

And heard on every rising gale
Ascend the bitter mourning wail;
And blighted herd, and blasted plain,
Through all the land the first-born slain,
Her priests and magi made to cower
In witness of a higher power,
And darkness like a sable pall
    Shrouding the land in deepest gloom,
Sent sadly through the minds of all,
    Forebodings of approaching doom.
What though no real shower of fire
    Spreads o'er this land its withering blight,
Denouncing wide Jehovah's ire,
    Like that which palsied Egypt's might;
And though no literal darkness spreads
    Upon the land its sable gloom,
And seems to fling around our heads
    The awful terrors of the tomb?
Yet to the eye of him who reads
    The fate of nations past and gone,
And marks with care the wrongful deeds
    By which their power was overthrown,—
Worse plagues than Egypt ever felt
    Are seen wide-spreading through the land,
Announcing that the heinous guilt
    On which the nation proudly stands,
Has risen to Jehovah's throne,
    And kindled his Almighty ire,
And broadcast through the land has sown
    The seeds of a devouring fire;
Blasting with foul pestiferous breath
    The fountain springs of mortal life,
And planting deep the seeds of death,
    And future germs of deadly strife;

And moral darkness spreads its gloom
    Over the land in every part,
And buries in a living tomb
    Each generous prompting of the heart.
Vice in its darkest, deadliest stains,
    Here walks with brazen front abroad,
And foul corruption proudly reigns
    Triumphant in the church of God,
And sinks so low the Christian name
In foul degrading vice and shame,
That Moslem, Heathen, Atheist, Jew,
    And men of every faith and creed,
To their professions far more true,
    More liberal both in word and deed,
May well reject with loathing scorn
    The doctrines taught by those who sell
Their brethren in the Savior born,
    Down into slavery's hateful hell;
And with the price of Christian blood
Build temples to the Christian's God,
And offer up as sacrifice,
    And incense to the God of heaven,
The mourning wail, and bitter cries,
    Of mothers from their children riven;
Of virgin purity profaned
    To sate some brutal ruffian's lust,
Millions of godlike minds ordained
    To grovel ever in the dust,
Shut out by Christian power and might
From every ray of Christian light.
How long, O Lord! shall such vile deeds
    Be acted in thy holy name,
And senseless bigots o'er their creeds
    Fill the whole world with war and flame?

How long shall ruthless tyrants claim
    Thy sanction to their bloody laws,
And throw the mantle of thy name
    Around their foul, unhallowed cause?
How long shall all the people bow
    As vassals of the favored few,
And shame the pride of manhood's brow,—
    Give what to God alone is due,
Homage to wealth and rank and power,
Vain shadows of a passing hour?
Oh, for a pen of living fire,
    A tongue of flame, an arm of steel!
To rouse the people's slumbering ire,
    And teach the tyrants' hearts to feel.
O Lord! in vengeance now appear.
    And guide the battles for the right,
The spirits of the fainting cheer,
    And nerve the patriot's arm with might;
Till slavery's banished from the world,
And tyrants from their power hurled;
And all mankind, from bondage free,
Exult in glorious liberty.

PRAYER OF THE OPPRESSED

O great Jehovah! God of love,
    Thou monarch of the earth and sky,
Canst thou from thy great throne above
    Look down with an unpitying eye?—

See Afric's sons and daughters toil,
    Day after day, year after year,
Upon this blood-bemoistened soil,
    And to their cries turn a deaf ear?

Canst thou the white oppressor bless
　　With verdant hills and fruitful plains,
Regardless of the slave's distress,
　　Unmindful of the black man's chains?

How long, O Lord! ere thou wilt speak
　　In thy Almighty thundering voice,
To bid the oppressor's fetters break,
　　And Ethiopia's sons rejoice?

How long shall Slavery's iron grip,
　　And Prejudice's guilty hand,
Send forth, like bloodhounds from the slip,
　　Foul persecutions o'er the land?

How long shall puny mortals dare
　　To violate thy just decree,
And force their fellow-men to wear
　　The galling chain on land and sea?

Hasten, O Lord! the glorious time
　　When everywhere beneath the skies,
From every land and every clime,
　　Paeans to Liberty shall rise!

When the bright sun of liberty
　　Shall shine o'er each despotic land,
And all mankind, from bondage free,
　　Adore the wonders of thy hand.

The Misanthropist

In vain thou bid'st me strike the lyre,
　　And sing a song of mirth and glee,
Or kindling with poetic fire,
　　Attempt some higher minstrelsy;

In vain, in vain! for every thought
    That issues from this throbbing brain,
Is from its first conception fraught
With gloom and darkness, woe and pain.
From earliest youth my path has been
    Cast in life's darkest, deepest shade,
Where no bright ray did intervene,
    Nor e'er a passing sunbeam strayed;
But all was dark and cheerless night,
    Without one ray of hopeful light.
From childhood, then, through many a shock,
    I've battled with the ills of life,
Till, like a rude and rugged rock,
    My heart grew callous in the strife.
When other children passed the hours
    In mirth, and play, and childish glee,
Or gathering the summer flowers
    By gentle brook, or flowery lea,
I sought the wild and rugged glen
    Where Nature, in her sternest mood,
Far from the busy haunts of men,
    Frowned in the darksome solitude.
There have I mused till gloomy night,
    Like the death-angel's brooding wing,
Would shut out everything from sight,
    And o'er the scene her mantle fling;
And seeking then my lonely bed
    To pass the night in sweet repose,
Around my fevered, burning head,
    Dark visions of the night arose;
And the stern scenes which day had viewed
    In sterner aspects rose before me,
And specters of still sterner mood
    Wayed their menacing fingers o'er me.

When the dark storm-fiend soared abroad,
  And swept to earth the waving grain,
On whirlwind through the forest rode,
  And stirred to foam the heaving main,
I loved to mark the lightning's flash,
  And listen to the ocean's roar,
Or hear the pealing thunder's crash,
  And see the mountain torrents pour
Down precipices dark and steep,
  Still bearing, in their headlong course
To meet th' embrace of ocean deep,
  Mementoes of the tempest's force;
For fire and tempest, flood and storm,
  Wakened deep echoes in my soul,
And made the quickening life-blood warm
  With impulse that knew no control;
And the fierce lightning's lurid flash
  Rending the somber clouds asunder,
Followed by the terrific crash
  Which marks the hoarsely rattling thunder,
Seemed like the gleams of lurid light
  Which flashed across my seething brain,
Succeeded by a darker night,
  With wilder horrors in its train.
And I have stood on ocean's shore
  And viewed its dreary waters roll,
Till the dull music of its roar
  Called forth responses in my soul;
And I have felt that there was traced
  An image of my inmost soul,
In that dark, dreary, boundless waste,
  Whose sluggish waters aimless roll—
Save when aroused by storms' wild force
  It lifts on high its angry wave,

And thousands driven from their course
    Find in its depths a nameless grave.
Whene'er I turned in gentler mood
    To scan the old historic page,
It was not where the wise and good,
    The Bard, the Statesman, or the Sage,
Had drawn in lines of living light,
Lessons of virtue, truth and right;
But that which told of secret league,
    Where deep conspiracies were rife,
And where, through foul and dark intrigue,
    Were sowed the seeds of deadly strife;
Where hostile armies met to seal
    Their country's doom, for woe or weal;
Where the grim-visaged death-fiend drank
    His full supply of human gore,
And poured through every hostile rank
    The tide of battle's awful roar;
For then my spirit seemed to soar
    Away to where such scenes were rife,
And high above the battle's roar
    Sit as spectator of the strife—
And in those scenes of war and woe,
A fierce and fitful pleasure know.
There was a time when I possessed
    High notions of Religion's claim,
Nor deemed its practise, at the best,
    Was but a false and empty name;
But when I saw the graceless deeds
    Which marked its strongest votaries' path,
How senseless bigots, o'er their creeds,
    Blazing with wild fanatic wrath,
Let loose the deadly tide of war,
Spread devastation near and far,

Through scenes of rapine, blood and shame,
Of cities sacked, and towns on flame,
Caused unbelievers' hearts to feel
The arguments of fire and steel
By which they sought t' enforce the word,
    And make rebellious hearts approve
Those arguments of fire and sword
    As mandates of the God of love—
How could I think that such a faith,
    Whose path was marked by fire and blood,
That sowed the seeds of war and death,
    Had issued from a holy God?
There was a time that I did love,
    Such love as those alone can know,
Whose blood like burning lava moves,
    Whose passions like the lightning glow;
And when that ardent, truthful love,
    Was blighted in its opening bloom,
And all around, below, above,
    Seemed like the darkness of the tomb,
'Twas then my stern and callous heart,
Riven in its most vital part
Seemed like some gnarled and knotted oak,
That, shivered by the lightning's stroke,
Stands in the lonely wanderer's path,
A ghastly monument of wrath.
Then how can I attune the lyre
    To strains of love or joyous glee?
Break forth in patriotic fire,
    Or soar on higher minstrelsy,
To sing the praise of virtue bright,
Condemn the wrong, and laud the right;
When neither vice nor guilt can fling
    A darker shadow o'er my breast,

Nor even Virtue's self can bring,
    Unto my moody spirit, rest.
It may not be, it cannot be!
    Let others strike the sounding string,
And in rich strains of harmony,
    Songs of poetic beauty sing;
But mine must still the portion be,
    However dark and drear the doom,
To live estranged from sympathy,
    Buried in doubt, despair and gloom;
To bare my breast to every blow,
To know no friend, and fear no foe,
Each generous impulse trod to dust,
Each noble aspiration crushed,
Each feeling struck with withering blight,
With no regard for wrong or right,
No fear of hell, no hope of heaven,
Die all unwept and unforgiven,
Content to know and dare the worst
Which mankind's hate, and heaven's curse,
Can heap upon my living head,
Or cast around my memory dead;
And let them on my tombstone trace,
Here lies the Pariah of his race.

———

LINES ON THE DEATH OF JOHN QUINCY ADAMS*

The great, the good, the just, the true,
    Has yielded up his latest breath;
The noblest man our country knew,
    Bows to the ghastly monster, Death;

---

* In June, 1839, the Spanish schooner, *L'Amistad,* sailed from Havana for Puerto Principe, Cuba, having on board fifty-three Negroes recently from Africa. On the night of June 30 the Negroes, under the lead of Joseph Cinque, an African prince, revolted and took possession of the vessel; and they commanded their

The son of one whose deathless name
  Stands first on history's brightest page;
The highest on the list of fame
  As statesman, patriot, and sage.

In early youth he learned to prize
  The freedom which his father won;
The mantle of the patriot sire
  Descended on his mightier son.
Science her deepest hidden lore
  Beneath his potent touch revealed;
Philosophy's abundant store,
  Alike his mighty mind could wield.

The brilliant page of poetry
  Received additions from his pen,
Of holy truth and purity,
  And thoughts which rouse the souls of men,
Eloquence did his heart inspire,
  And from his lips in glory blazed,
Till nations caught the glowing fire,
  And senates trembled as they praised.

While all the recreant of the land
  To slavery's idol bowed the knee—
A fawning, sycophantic band,
  Fit tools of petty tyranny—
He stood amid the recreant throng,

---

owners, the two white men whose lives they had spared, to steer them back to
Africa. These men made a pretense of so doing, but really steered north. After
some weeks of wandering the vessel was captured off Long Island by the United
States brig *Washington*, and taken into the harbor of New London, Connecticut.
The Spanish minister Calderon demanded that the Negroes be surrendered as
"property rescued from pirates," but the suggestion met with violent opposition
from the anti-slavery element. The case finally reached the United States Supreme
Court, before which John Quincy Adams, former President, appeared in behalf of
the Negroes. Judgment was in his favor. The argument which he advanced on
this occasion covers in print 135 octavo pages.

The chosen champion of the free,
And battled fearlessly and long
    For justice, right, and liberty.

What though grim Death has sealed his doom
    Who faithful proved to God and us;
And slavery, o'er the patriot's tomb
    Exulting pours its deadliest curse?
Among the virtuous and free
    His memory will ever live;
Champion of right and liberty,
    The blessings, truth and virtue give.

The North Star*

Star of the North! whose steadfast ray
    Pierces the sable pall of night,
Forever pointing out the way
    That leads to freedom's hallowed light:
The fugitive lifts up his eye
To where thy rays illume the sky.

That steady, calm, unchanging light,
    Through dreary wilds and trackless dells,
Directs his weary steps aright
    To the bright land where freedom dwells;
And spreads, with sympathizing breast,
Her aegis over the oppressed;

Though other stars may round thee burn,
    With larger disk and brighter ray,
And fiery comets round thee turn,
    While millions mark their blazing way;
And the pale moon and planets bright
Reflect on us their silvery light.

* Written for *The North Star*, a newspaper edited by Frederick Douglass.

Not like that moon, now dark, now bright,
　　In phase and place forever changing;
Or planets with reflected light,
　　Or comets through the heavens ranging;
They all seem varying in our view,
While thou art ever fixed and true.

So may that other bright North Star,
　　Beaming with truth and freedom's light,
Pierce with its cheering ray afar,
　　The shades of slavery's gloomy night;
And may it never cease to be
The guard of truth and liberty.

CHARLES L. REASON

CHARLES L. REASON was born in New York City August 18, 1818. He had good advantages in his youth, and his industry and ambition were seen in the fact that he was willing to pay for special instruction in mathematics. As the choice of the vestry of St. Philip's Church he pursued for some time studies preparatory to entering the Theological Seminary of the Protestant Episcopal Church; but the bishop of the diocese interposed and forbade his entrance except as a listener. This condition Reason refused to accept, and as the vestry was unwilling to support him in any remonstrance, he resigned. In 1849 he became teacher of languages and mathematics at the New York Central College, McGrawville, Cortlandt County, N. Y., an institution founded by the abolitionists to sustain "the doctrine of the unity, common origin, equality, and brotherhood of the human race." In 1852 he accepted the principalship of the Institute for Colored Youth in Philadelphia, which had been founded by the bequest of a Quaker, Richard Humphreys, who at his death in 1832 left $10,000 "for the education of the descendants of the African race." As the time was one of great agitation, nothing was done immediately to carry out the terms of the will; but in 1839 a board was appointed, a tract of land purchased, and a beginning made in instruction in simple industries. In 1842 the institution was incorporated, and soon came a bequest of $18,000 from another Quaker, Jonathan Zane. The work was still not well organized, however, when Reason took charge, and he did much for the upbuilding of the school on the academic side. After three years there he entered upon his long career as a teacher in New York, being first connected with schools 6 and 3 and then principal of 80. There he was serving as late as June, 1892. He was thrice married, his last wife being Mrs. Clorice Estève. He died in or about 1898.

All accounts agree that Reason was a man of culture, slight of figure and of polished manner, with handsome and pleasant countenance and clearcut features. He frequently wrote resolutions in gatherings of Negro men, but was in no sense a politician and never an office-seeker.   Bishop Daniel A. Payne spoke of seeing him in New York, mentioned a second marriage, and then continued as follows: "The Professor is more of a meditative than a public character.   Too upright to be a politician, but not lacking in the spirit of a patriot, he has made himself known and felt rather by his pen than by his tongue, because he is no windy rhetorician. . . . When I was in New York soliciting funds to put a medium-sized museum in Wilberforce University, the names of at least half a dozen men of color were given.   They were reported to be worth from $10,000 to $100,000.   He was the only one who was a practical friend of education.   He gave me twenty-five dollars, and his noble wife also gave me twenty-five. . . . I have visited many schoolrooms in the United States and in foreign lands, and closely watched the methods of many teachers; but I have seldom met his equal, never his superior."   See *Recollections of Seventy Years*, by Daniel A. Payne, Nashville, 1888, pp. 46-48, and *Men of Mark*, by William J. Simmons, Cleveland, 1887, pp. 1105-1108.   For the facts about the service as teacher in New York the editor is indebted to Mr. Joseph B. Curran, of the Record Division of the Board of Education.

Reason was a man of fine feeling, but his muse found it impossible to take wing and soar.   His verse has no technical excellence and seldom rises above the commonplace.   No collection of his poems was made, but here and there separate pieces are to be found.   An ode entitled "Freedom," in rather grandiloquent vein, was printed with *A Eulogy on the Life and Character of Thomas Clarkson*, by Rev. Alexander Crummell, New York, 1847. "Hope and Confidence," a poem of romantic temper with some very faulty lines, is in *Autographs for Freedom* for 1854.   "The Spirit Voice, or Liberty Call to the Disfranchised" and "Silent Thoughts" are included in the sketch in *Men of Mark*.

FREEDOM

"Sans Toi l'univers est un temple
Qui n'a plus ni parfums, ni chants."
—Lamartine.

O Freedom! Freedom! O! how oft
    Thy loving children call on Thee!
In wailings loud, and breathings soft,
    Beseeching God, Thy face to see.

With agonizing hearts we kneel,
    While 'round us howls the oppressor's cry,—
And suppliant pray, that we may feel
    The ennob'ling glances of Thine eye.

We think of Thee as once we saw
    Thee, jewel'd by Thy Father's hand,
Afar beside dark Egypt's shore,
    Exulting with Thy ransom'd band.

We hear, as then, the thrilling song,
    That hail'd Thy passage through the sea,—
While distant echoes still prolong
    The cymbal'd anthem, sung to Thee.

And wafted yet, upon the gales
    Borne pure and fresh from sunny skies,
Come startling words; that 'long the vales
    Where Pelion and Ossa rise,

Were shouted by Thine own clear voice!
    And Grecian hearts leap'd at the call:
E'en as now Patriot souls rejoice,
    To see invading tyrants fall.

We view Thy stately form, loom o'er
    The topmost of the seven hills!

While 'round Thee glittering eagles soar—
　　The symbol'd rise of freeborn wills.

Down in the plains, we still behold
　　The circled forums built to Thee;—
Hear Tully's strains, and Brutus bold,
　　Call on his country to be free.

When from those groves of citron bloom,
　　And classic Helle's vine clad shore,—
Through countries hung in castled gloom,
　　Attending winds Thy chariot bore,—

We followed Thee o'er all the fields
　　Of Europe, crimson-dyed with blood;
Where broken spears, and buried shields,
　　Now mark the spots where Thou hast stood.

At Morgarten, through drifting snows,
　　That seem'd to guard the Switzer's home!—
And where the walls of Sempach rose,
　　We saw the mail-clad Austrians come.

Three times we saw Thee bear the shock
　　Of stalwart knight, and plunging steed;—
And crush their front, as does the rock
　　The waves, that 'gainst its bosom speed.

Yet, vainly striving, Thou, to part
　　That brist'ling sea of pikes had'st tried,
Till Underwalden's patriot heart
　　Bore down the foe, and glorious died.

Yes!   Victory, as Arnold fell
　　Her white plume waved from every peak,—
And ringing loud, the voice of Tell
　　Still greater triumphs bade thee seek.

With trophies from Thy conflicts deck'd,
  (Allied by God to injured men,)
We saw Thy struggle at Utrecht,
  At Zealand, Brabant, and Lutzen.

Where'er the sunbeams flash'd, Thy shield
  Lit up oppression's funeral pile;
And though o'erwhelm'd on Calsgrave field,
  And banished from Thy sea-girt isle;

Yet cheering on Thy gallant Poles,
  From Slavon bondage to be free,
We see Thy hurried pace, as rolls
  The alarm of danger o'er the sea.

Above the heaving mountain crest,
  As to the isles of thought and song
Thou bad'st adieu,—from out the west,
  Were heard deep mutterings of wrong.

On many a frozen battle ground,
  Opposing swords were gleaming bright;
While 'long the skies, the thundering sound
  Of cannon woke the silent night.

Exulting in their mission high,
  Columbia's sons had pledged Thy cause—
Thy first endeavor,—"to untie
  The cords of caste and slavish laws."

Long years roll'd by, and still went on
  The strife of man, 'gainst regal power;
Till, falsely, in Thy strength, was won,
  Thy since, polluted, blood-stained dower.

We mourn for this! yet joyfully
  O Freedom! we loud praises give,

That on Thine altar in the sea,
    For us Thy holy fires live.

Oh! grant unto our parent home,
    Thy constant presence and Thy shield!
That when again rude hirelings come,
    Though scarr'd from every battle field,

The spirit of the patriot true,
    Toussaint, the "man of men," may ring
The shrill war cry the welkin through,
    And plain to mount the echo sing.

But not 'mid trick'ling blood and smoke,
    The wailings of the dying foe,
The bayonet thrust—the sabre stroke,—
    Canst Thou alone great victories show.

Along thy pathway, glory shines:
    And grateful wreaths before Thee fall:—
More worth than all Golconda's mines,
    Or power, that twines in Coronal.

Thine is the mission, to subdue
    The soul, encased in triple steel;
And so the world with love imbue,
    That tyrants shall before Thee kneel.

When from the slave's crush'd, aching heart,
    The cry went up to Sabaoth's God,—
And man with his immortal part,
    Alike, were thrust beneath the sod,

We saw Thee wield conviction's strength,
    And heard thy blows fall thick and fast;
While loud and clear through all the length
    Of Britain, blew Thy trumpet blast.

Thou wast the answer!   *Clarkson! thou*
    The mighty soul that woke to life!
That took the consecrated vow,
    To conquer—perish in the strife.

Well hast thou fought, great pioneer!
    The snows of age upon thy head,
Were Freedom's wreaths; by far, more dear,
    Than finest sculpture o'er the dead.

We leave thee to thy long repose!
    Thou hast the blessings of the slave:
We pray that at the world's dread close,
    Thou rise *a freeman* from the grave.

What more can we O Freedom! speak
    In praise of Thee? our hearts grow faint!
Where else shall we Thy triumphs seek?
    What fairer pictures can we paint?

We stand upon the shaking ground
    Of tyranny! we call it home:
The earth is strewn with Christians bound,—
    We've cried to Thee—Thou dost not come.

We know Thou hast Thy chosen few,—
    The men of heart, who live by right,—
Who steadily their way pursue,
    Though round them pall the shades of night.

We hold them dear: defamed, beset,
    They fight the civil war of man:
The fiercest struggle that has yet
    Been waged against oppression's ban.

We give them thanks: the bondman's prayer
    As holy incense soars on high,

That nought to Thee their love impair,
   'Til shall be gained the victory.

But, O! Great Spirit! see'st Thou
   Thy spotless ermine men defile?
God's civil rulers cringing bow
   To hate, and fraud, and customs vile!

The *church*, to her great charge untrue,
   Keeps Christian guard, o'er slavery's den!
Her coward laymen, wrong pursue,
   Her recreant priesthood, say—amen.

O! purify each holy court!
   The ministry of law and light!
That man, no longer, may be bought
   To trample down his brother's right.

We lift imploring hands to Thee!
   We cry for those in prison bound!
O! in thy strength, come! Liberty!
   And 'stablish right the wide world round.

We pray to see Thee, face to face:
   To feel our souls grow strong and wide;
So ever shall our injured race,
   By Thy firm principles abide.

The Spirit Voice
Or, Liberty Call to the Disfranchised
(State of New York)

Come! rouse ye brothers, rouse! a peal now breaks
From lowest island to our gallant lakes:
'Tis summoning you, who long in bonds have lain,
To stand up manful on the battle plain,
Each as a warrior, with his armor bright,

Prepared to battle in a bloodless fight.
Hark! How each breeze that blows o'er Hudson's tide
Is calling loudly on your birth-right pride
And each near cliff, whose peak fierce storms has stood,
Shouts back responsive to the calling flood.
List! from those heights that once with freedom rung,
And those broad fields, where Earth has oft-times sung,
A voice goes up, invoking men to prove
How dear is freedom, and how strong their love.
From every obscure vale and swelling hill
The spirit tones are mounting; louder still
From out the din where noble cities rise
On Mohawk's banks, the peal ascends the skies.
Responding sweet with morning's opening praise,
The sounds commingle, far, to where the rays
Of light departing, sink to partial sleep,
'Mid caverned gems in Erie's bosomed deep.
Nor yet less heard, from inland slopes it swells,
In chiming music, with the village bells,
And mixes loud e'en with the ocean's waves,
Like shrill-voiced echo in the mountain caves.
'Tis calling you, who now too long have been
Sore victims suffering under legal sin,
To vow, no more to sleep, till raised and freed
From partial bondage, to a life indeed.
Behold ye now! here consecrate from toil
And love, your homes abide on holy soil.
To these, as sacred temples, fond you cling:
For, thence alone, life's narrow comforts spring,
'Tis here the twilight of existence broke,
The first warm throbbings of your hearts awoke.
Here first o'er you, fond mothers watch'd and pray'd,
Here friendship rose and holy vows were made.
On yon familiar height or gentle stream,

You first did mark the pleasant moonlight gleam.
Here, happy, laugh'd o'er life in cradled bloom
And here, first pensive, wept at age's tomb,
Yes; many a sire, with burnt and furrowed brow
Here died, in hope that you in freedom now
Would feel the boasted pledge your country gave,
That her defender should not be her slave.
And wherefore, round your homes has not been thrown
That guardian shield, which strangers call their own?
Why, now, do ye, as your poor fathers did,
Bow down in silence to what tyrants bid?
And sweat and bleed from early morn till eve,
To earn a dower less than beggars leave?
Why are ye pleased to delve at mammon's nod?
To buy that manhood which is yours from God,
Free choice to say who worthy is to lead
Your country's cause, to give your heart-felt meed
Of praise to him that, barring custom's rule,
Would nobly dare attack the cringing tool
That with a selfish aim and ruthless hand,
Would tear in twain love's strong and holy band:
Why can ye not, as men who know and feel
What most is needed for your nation's weal,
Stand in her forums, and with burning words
Urge on the time, when to the bleeding herds,
Whose minds are buried now in polar night,
Hope shall descend; when freedom's mellow light
Shall break, and usher in the endless day,
That from Orleans to Pass'maquoddy Bay,
Despots no more may earthly homage claim,
Nor slaves exist, to soil Columbia's name.
Then, up! awake! nor let dull slumber waste
Your soul's devotion! life doth bid you haste;
The captive in his hut, with watchful ear,

Awaits the sweet triumphant songs to hear,
That shall proclaim the glorious jubilee
When crippled thousands shall in truth be free.
Come! rouse ye brothers, rouse! nor let the voice
That shouting, calls you onward to rejoice,
Be heard in vain! but with ennobled souls,
Let all whom now an unjust law controls,
Press on in strength of mind, in purpose bent,
To live by right; to swell the free tones sent
On Southern airs, from this, your native State,
A glorious promise for the captive's fate.
Then up! and vow no more to sleep, till freed
From partial bondage to a life indeed.

New York, July 20, 1841.

GEORGE B. VASHON

About the middle of the last century George Boyer Vashon was prominent, first as teacher, then as lawyer and man of letters. He was enrolled in Oberlin College from 1840 to 1844, and then spent a year in the theological seminary. He received the A.B. degree in 1844, and the A.M. was conferred on him in 1849. For some time he was one of the three Negro professors (the other two being Charles L. Reason and William G. Allen) employed at New York Central College, McGrawville, N. Y., an institution established by the abolitionists. Becoming interested in the law, he had as preceptor Judge Walter Forward, later Secretary of the Treasury of the United States, and in 1847 was admitted to the bar in New York City. Soon after that event Vashon sailed to the West Indies, and for the next three years he taught at College Faustin, Port-au-Prince, Hayti. Returning to the United States in the fall of 1850, he contributed to a number of periodicals and engaged in the practice of his profession at Syracuse, N. Y.; but before long he became principal of the one school for Negro children in Pittsburgh, Penn. To that school came as a teacher Susan Paul Smith, who was the daughter of Elijah W. Smith, a musician prominent in Boston, and whose training had been in the best New England tradition. The two were married in 1857 and became the parents of seven children. The *Pittsburgh Daily Dispatch* of October 11, 1878, says that Vashon's application to be admitted to the bar in Pittsburgh was denied on account of his color, that later he went to Washington and was admitted, that he served as a professor in Howard University and finally went to Mississippi. He was in that state at the time of the yellow fever epidemic in the fall of 1878 and died at Rodney on October 5. His wife, who was several years younger than himself, was from 1872 to 1880 principal of the Thaddeus Stevens School in Washington, and later lived in St. Louis, surviving until 1912. See, aside from *Pittsburgh Daily Dispatch* referred to, General *Catalogue of Oberlin College*, Oberlin,

[261]

O.; *The Condition, Elevation, Emigration, and Destiny of the Colored People of the United States,* by Martin R. Delany, Philadelphia, 1852, pp. 119-120; and *Homespun Heroines,* by Hallie Q. Brown, Xenia, O., 1926, pp. 133-134.

Vashon's poem "Vincent Ogé" was contributed in abridged form to the first number of *Autographs for Freedom.* It shows the author as attempting a more ambitious theme than had been used by any American Negro before him, and as having a genuine sense of poetic values. He does not give a straightforward narrative, but uses the rhythmic, discursive, and frequently subjective manner of Byron and Scott, sometimes with surprising effect. Ogé himself was a prominent figure in Hayti in the revolutionary era, and his story is graphically told by Wendell Phillips in the oration on Toussaint L'Ouverture. He was a mulatto, a native of Hayti, but educated in France. For generations the mulattoes on the island had held an anomalous position between the white slave owners on one hand and the black peasants on the other. They could own property, but they could not hold office, were forced to pay special taxes, and were subject to other indignities in their civic and social life. When then the storm broke in France in 1789, they met, sent to the National Convention in Paris a gift of six million francs, pledged one-fifth of their income to the payment of the national debt, and asked only in return that they be relieved of all proscription. The Convention hastened to express its gratitude, and Ogé, a friend of Lafayette, was asked to carry the message of democracy to the island. The decree of the National Convention was laid on the table of the General Assembly; and then, as Phillips tells us, one old planter seized it, tore it in fragments, and swore by all the saints that he would never respect it. An elderly mulatto, worth a million, who had done nothing more than ask for his rights, was hanged; and the white lawyer who drafted the petition was hanged with him. Ogé himself was broken on the wheel, ordered to be drawn and quartered, and the four parts of his body were hung up in the four leading cities of the island. It was on March 12, 1791, that he died for what was called an insurrectionary effort but what was really the prelude to the exploits of Toussaint L'Ouverture.

Naturally he has since been regarded as one of the chief martyrs in the history of his country.

"A Life-Day" is to be found in *The Semi-Centenary and the Retrospection of the African Methodist Episcopal Church*, by Daniel A. Payne, Baltimore, 1866, pp. 172-175.

VINCENT OGÉ

There is, at times, an evening sky—
    The twilight's gift—of sombre hue,
All checkered wild and gorgeously
    With streaks of crimson, gold and blue;—
A sky that strikes the soul with awe,
    And, though not brilliant as the sheen,
Which in the east at morn we saw,
    Is far more glorious, I ween;—
So glorious that, when night hath come
And shrouded in its deepest gloom,
We turn aside with inward pain
And pray to see that sky again.
Such sight is like the struggle made
When freedom bids unbare the blade,
And calls from every mountain-glen—
    From every hill—from every plain,
Her chosen ones to stand like men,
    And cleanse their souls from every stain
Which wretches, steeped in crime and blood,
Have cast upon the form of God.
Though peace like morning's golden hue,
    With blooming groves and waving fields,
Is mildly pleasing to the view,
    And all the blessings that it yields
Are fondly welcomed by the breast
    Which finds delight in passion's rest,

That breast with joy foregoes them all,
While listening to Freedom's call.
Though red the carnage,—though the strife
Be filled with groans of parting life,—
Though battle's dark, ensanguined skies
Give echo but to agonies—

    To shrieks of wild despairing,—
We willingly suppress a sigh—
Nay, gaze with rapture in our eye,
Whilst "Freedom!" is the rally-cry
    That calls to deeds of daring.

      *   *   *   *   *

The waves dash brightly on thy shore,
    Fair island of the southern seas!
As bright in joy as when of yore
    They gladly hailed the Genoese,—
That daring soul who gave to Spain
A world—last trophy of her reign!
Basking in beauty, thou dost seem
A vision in a poet's dream!
Thou look'st as though thou claim'st not birth
While sea and sky and other earth,
That smile around thee but to show
Thy beauty in a brighter glow,—
That are unto thee as the foil
    Artistic hands have neatly set
Around Golconda's radiant spoil,
    To grace some lofty coronet,—
A foil, which serves to make the gem
The glory of that diadem!

      *   *   *   *   *

If Eden claimed a favored haunt,
    Most hallowed of that blessed ground,
Where tempting fiend with guileful taunt

A resting-place would ne'er have found,—
As shadowing it well might seek
    The loveliest home in that fair isle,
Which in its radiance seemed to speak
    As to the charmed doth Beauty's smile,
That whispers of a thousand things
For which words find no picturings.
Like to the gifted Greek who strove
    To paint a crowning work of art,
And from his ideal Queen of Love,
    By choosing from each grace a part,
Blending them in one beauteous whole,
To charm the eye, transfix the soul,
And hold it in enraptured fires,
Such as a dream of heaven inspires,—
So seem the glad waves to have sought
    From every place its richest treasure,
And borne it to that lovely spot,
    To found thereon a home of pleasure;—
A home where balmy airs might float
    Through spicy bower and orange grove;
Where bright-winged birds might turn the note
    Which tells of pure and constant love;
Where earthquake stays its demon force,
And hurricane its wrathful course;
Where nymph and fairy find a home,
And foot of spoiler never come.

   * * * * *

And Ogé stands mid this array
    Of matchless beauty, but his brow
Is brightened not by pleasure's play;
    He stands unmoved—nay, saddened now,
As doth the lorn and mateless bird
That constant mourns, whilst all unheard,

The breezes freighted with the strains
Of other songsters sweep the plain,—
That ne'er breathes forth a joyous note,
Though odors on the zephyrs float—
The tribute of a thousand bowers,
Rich in their store of fragrant flowers.
Yet Ogé's was a mind that joyed
    With nature in her every mood,
Whether in sunshine unalloyed
    With darkness, or in tempest rude
And, by the dashing waterfall,
    Or by the gently flowing river,
Or listening to the thunder's call,
    He'd joy away his life forever.
But ah! life is a changeful thing,
    And pleasures swiftly pass away,
And we may turn, with shuddering,
    From what we sighed for yesterday.
The guest, at banquet-table spread
With choicest viands, shakes with dread,
Nor heeds the goblet bright and fair,
Nor tastes the dainties rich and rare,
Nor bids his eye with pleasure trace
The wreathed flowers that deck the place,
If he but knows there is a draught
Among the cordials, that, if quaffed,
Will send swift poison through his veins.
    So Ogé seems; nor does his eye
With pleasure view the flowery plains,
    The bounding sea, the spangled sky,
As, in the short and soft twilight,
    The stars peep brightly forth in heaven,
And hasten to the realms of night,
    As handmaids of the Even.

*   *   *   *   *

The loud shouts from the distant town,
 Joined in with nature's gladsome lay;
The lights went glancing up and down,
 Riv'ling the stars—nay, seemed as they
Could stoop to claim, in their high home,
 A sympathy with things of earth,
And had from their bright mansions come,
 To join them in their festal mirth.
For the land of the Gaul had arose in its might,
And swept by as the wind of a wild, wintry night;
And the dreamings of greatness—the phantoms of power,
Had passed in its breath like the things of an hour.
Like the violet vapors that brilliantly play
Round the glass of the chemist, then vanish away,
The visions of grandeur which dazzlingly shone,
Had gleamed for a time, and all suddenly gone.
And the fabric of ages—the glory of kings,
Accounted most sacred mid sanctified things,
Reared up by the hero, preserved by the sage,
And drawn out in rich hues on the chronicler's page,
Had sunk in the blast, and in ruins lay spread,
While the altar of freedom was reared in its stead.
And a spark from that shrine in the free-roving breeze,
Had crossed from fair France to that isle of the seas;
And a flame was there kindled which fitfully shone
Mid the shout of the free, and the dark captive's groan;
As, mid contrary breezes, a torch-light will play,
Now streaming up brightly—now dying away.

   *   *   *   *   *

 The reptile slumbers in the stone,
  Nor dream we of his pent abode;
 The heart conceals the anguished groan,
  With all the poignant griefs that goad
   The brain to madness;

Within the hushed volcano's breast,
   The molten fires of ruin lie;—
Thus human passions seem at rest,
   And on the brow serene and high,
      Appears no sadness.
But still the fires are raging there,
Of vengeance, hatred, and despair;
And when they burst, they wildly pour
   Their lava flood of woe and fear,
And in one short—one little hour,
   Avenge the wrongs of many a year.

     *   *   *   *   *

And Ogé standeth in his hall;
   But now he standeth not alone;—
A brother's there, and friends; and all
   Are kindred spirits with his own;
For mind will join with kindred mind,
As matter's with its like combined.
They speak of wrongs they had received—
Of freemen, of their rights bereaved;
And as they pondered o'er the thought
Which in their minds so madly wrought,
Their eyes gleamed as the lightning's flash,
Their words seemed as the torrent's dash
That falleth, with a low, deep sound,
Into some dark abyss profound,—
A sullen sound that threatens more
Than other torrent's louder roar.
Ah! they had borne well as they might,
   Such wrongs as freemen ill can bear;
And they had urged both day and night,
   In fitting words, a freeman's prayer;
And when the heart is filled with grief,
   For wrongs of all true souls accurst,

In action it must seek relief,
　　Or else, o'ercharged, it can but burst.
Why blame we them, if they oft spake
Words that were fitted to awake
The soul's high hopes—its noblest parts—
The slumbering passions of brave hearts,
And send them as the simoon's breath,
Upon a work of woe and death?
And woman's voice is heard amid
　　The accents of that warrior train;
And when has woman's voice e'er bid,
　　And man could from its hest refrain?
Hers is the power o'er his soul
　　That's never wielded by another,
And she doth claim this soft control
　　As sister, mistress, wife, or mother.
So sweetly doth her soft voice float
　　O'er hearts by guilt or anguish rifen,
It seemeth as a magic note
　　Struck from earth's harps by hands of heaven.
And there's the mother of Ogé,
　　Who with firm voice, and steady heart,
And look unaltered, well can play
　　The Spartan mother's hardy part;
And send her sons to battle-fields,
　　And bid them come in triumph home,
Or stretched upon their bloody shields,
　　Rather than bear the bondman's doom.
"Go forth," she said, "to victory;
Or else, go bravely forth to die!
Go forth to fields where glory floats
In every trumpet's cheering notes!
Go forth to where a freeman's death
Glares in each cannon's fiery breath!

Go forth and triumph o'er the foe;
Or, failing that, with pleasure go
To molder on the battle-plain,
Freed ever from the tyrant's chain!
But if your hearts should craven prove,
Forgetful of your zeal—your love
For rights and franchises of men,
My heart will break; but even then,
Whilst bidding life and earth adieu,
This be the prayer I'll breathe for you:
'Passing from guilt to misery,
May this for aye your portion be,—
A life, dragged out beneath the rod—
An end, abhorred of man and God—
As monument, the chains you nurse—
As epitaph, your mother's curse!' "

*   *   *   *   *

A thousand hearts are breathing high,
And voices shouting "Victory!"
    Which soon will hush in death;
The trumpet clang of joy that speaks,
Will soon be drownèd in the shrieks
    Of the wounded's stifling breath,
The tyrant's plume in dust lies low—
Th' oppressed has triumphed o'er his foe.
But ah! the lull in the furious blast
May whisper not of ruin past;
It may tell of the tempest hurrying on,
To complete the work the blast begun.
With the voice of a Syren, it may whisp'ringly tell
    As a moment of hope in the deluge of rain;
And the shout of the free heart may rapt'rously swell,
    While the tyrant is gath'ring his power again.

Though the balm of the leech may soften the smart,
 It never can turn the swift barb from its aim;
And thus the resolve of the true freeman's heart
 May not keep back his fall, though it free it from shame.
Though the hearts of those heroes all well could accord
With freedom's most noble and loftiest word;
Their virtuous strength availeth them nought
With the power and skill that the tyrant brought.
Gray veterans trained in many a field
Where the fate of nations with blood was sealed,
In Italia's vales—on the shores of the Rhine—
Where the plains of fair France give birth to the vine—
Where the Tagus, the Ebro, go dancing along,
Made glad in their course by the Muleteer's song—
All these were poured down in the pride of their might,
On the land of Ogé in that terrible fight.
Ah! dire was the conflict, and many the slain,
Who slept the last sleep on that red battle-plain!
The flash of the cannon o'er valley and height
Danced like the swift fires of a northern night,
Or the quivering glare which leaps forth as a token
That the King of the Storm from his cloud-throne has spoken.
And oh! to those heroes how welcome the fate
Of Sparta's brave sons in Thermopylae's strait;
With what ardor of soul they then would have given ,
Their last look at earth for a long glance at heaven!
Their lives to their country—their backs to the sod—
Their hearts' blood to the sword, and their souls to their God!
But alas! although many lie silent and slain,
More blest are they far than those clanking the chain,
In the hold of the tyrant, debarred from the day;—
And among these sad captives is Vincent Ogé!
  * * * * *

Another day's bright sun has risen,
And shines upon the insurgent's prison;
Another night has slowly passed,
And Ogé smiles, for 'tis the last
He'll droop beneath the tyrant's power—
The galling chains!   Another hour,
And answering to the jailor's call,
He stands within the Judgment Hall.
They've gathered there;—they who have pressed
Their fangs into the soul distressed,
To pain its passage to the tomb
With mock'ry of a legal doom.
They've gathered there;—they who have stood
Firmly and fast in hour of blood,—
Who've seen the lights of hope all die,
As stars fade from a morning sky,—
They've gathered there, in that dark hour—
The latest of the tyrant's power,—
An hour that speaketh of the day
Which never more shall pass away,—
The glorious day beyond the grave,
Which knows no master—owns no slave.
And there, too, are the rack—the wheel—
The torturing screw—the piercing steel,—
Grim powers of death all crusted o'er
With other victims' clotted gore.
Frowning they stand, and in their cold,
Silent solemnity, unfold
The strong one's triumph o'er the weak—
The awful groan—the anguished shriek—
The unconscious mutt'rings of despair—
The strainèd eyeball's idiot stare—
The hopeless clench—the quiv-ring frame—
The martyr's death—the despot's shame.

The rack—the tyrant—victim,—all
Are gathered in that Judgment Hall.
Draw we the veil, for 'tis a sight
But friends can gaze on with delight.
The sunbeams on the rack that play,
For sudden terror flit away
From this dread work of war and death,
As angels do with quickened breath,
From some dark deed of deepest sin,
Ere they have drunk its spirit in.

* * * * *

No mighty host with banners flying,
  Seems fiercer to a conquered foe,
Than did those gallant heroes dying,
  To those who gloated o'er their woe;—
Grim tigers, who have seized their prey,
Then turn and shrink abashed away;
Quail 'neath the flashing of the eye,
Which tells that though the life has started,
The will to strike has not departed.

* * * * *

Sad was your fate, heroic band!
Yet mourn we not, for yours the stand
Which will secure to you a fame,
That never dieth, and a name
That will, in coming ages, be
A signal word for Liberty.
Upon the slave's o'erclouded sky,
  Your gallant actions traced the bow,
Which whispered of deliv'rance nigh—
  The meed of one decisive blow.
Thy coming fame, Ogé is sure;
Thy name with that of L'Ouverture,
And all the noble souls that stood

With both of you, in times of blood,
Will live to be the tyrant's fear—
Will live, the sinking soul to cheer!

A LIFE-DAY

(The following poem, written in 1864, is founded upon incidents which took place in one of our Southern states. The judge referred to, has recently figured as a provisional governor in President Johnson's plan of reconstruction. Pittsburgh, March 5th, 1866.   G. B. V.)

MORNING

The breeze awakes with morn's first ray,
Like childhood roused from sleep to play;
The sunshine, like a fairy sprite,
Comes to undo the wrong of night;
And earth is jocund with the glee
That swells from hill and vale and tree.
It echoes music fitly set
For mocking-bird and paroquet;
And, joyous as a ransomed soul,
It hears the notes of the oriole.
The murmur of the wide-swept cane
Hymneth the rapture of the plain,
And mingles with the brooklet's song,—
    A mirthful brook with fitful gleam,
    Hasting to Mississippi's stream,
And glad'ning both its banks along;
Surely, to be mid scenes like this
Doth render life a dream of bliss—
A treasure-house without alloy;—
Here's Joy's alive, and Life is joy.
Oh! what a joy it is to him

Who for this scene has left the room
Where sickness, hollow-eyed and grim,
    Hath held, for years, its court of gloom,—
Whose shrunken limbs too clearly own
That there the monster had his throne!
They tell not all his tale of woe,—
    How friends and brothers from him fled,
And left him to the fever's glow,
    The ulcered frame, the throbbing head,
With no defense against the grave
Save this—the care of one poor slave.
That faithful one is by his side;—
What more of bliss can now betide?
What matter that the earth is fair?
    What matter that the glad birds sing?
His pleasure is that she doth share
    The balmy breeze's welcoming.
Her sweet smile is the sunshine bright
That floods the landscape wide with light;
Her gladsome youth the genial morn
That doth his happy day adorn,
And her soft voice the music sweet
With which no warbler can compete.
And now that Life and Hope again
Ope to him paths long closed by pain,—
Now, while her tawny cheek, her eye,
Are bright with modest ecstasy,
The hushed shades of the orange grove
Smilingly hear his tale of love.

NOON

How swiftly glide our mortal years,
    When Love doth wing each blissful hour,—
When all our hopes, and all our fears,

Are minions of his magic power!
Twelve years! Twelve moments in her life,
Since she became a happy wife!
All chains are riven save the tie
Which links her to his destiny.
What cares he for the glance of scorn
    That mocks him in his daily walk?
What, that each coming night and morn
    Echoes his neighbors' gibing talk?
She, once his slave and now his bride,
Outvalues all the earth beside.
And 'neath the orange-trees he strays
With her, as in their younger days;
But not with her alone; for now
His hand doth press a maiden's brow
Whose flaxen curls and eyes of blue
From her fond sires have caught their hue.
Beside them stands a dark-eyed boy,
Whose laugh rings out his infant joy,
As, now and then, comes flashing by
The many-colored butterfly.
Oh! with such pledges of fond love
    As thou dost mark in either boon,
Say, mother, hath not He above
    Granted thy morn a fitting noon?

NIGHT

Alas! that noon should yield to night
Its treasured joys of life and light!
Alas! that sun-bright happiness
Should be o'clouded by distress!
The noble soul who gladly gave
A wife's name to his faithful slave,
Hath passed away, and those who fled

In horror from his stricken bed,
Have come, like vultures to the dead,—
Have come to batten on the store
 He left to those he held so dear—
To claim them in their anguish sore,
 As born thralls to a bondage drear.
And one whose guilty deeds hurl shame
 On white-robed Justice' sainted name,
Holding no sacred thing in awe,
 Dared to proclaim the marriage tie
 Shielding them with its purity,
A fraud upon the slaver's law.
A wailing comes upon the breeze,
That sighs amid the orange trees;
 And she is there, and all alone.
Oh, linger, night! for with the day
Her children will be far away—
Her children! Ah! no more her own!
O, mother! mourning by the spot
 Hallowed by sweetest memory,
And bidding fancy shape the lot
 Each little one is doomed to see.
Alas! thy poor heart knows too well
What to itself it dares not tell!
Hundred of boys as gently born
 As he who was thy joy and pride,
Have by the cruel lash been torn,
 And 'neath its bloody scourgings died.
Hundreds of maidens full as fair
 As she whose little life you gave,
Know what a dowry of despair
 Is beauty in a female slave.
And thou, lorn mother!—thy sole part
Is weeping, till it breaks thy heart.

Shades of the heroes, long since gone!
   Was this your glory's end and aim
Was it for this, O Washington!
   That, welcoming the rebel's name,
Halter and battle you defied?
For this, O Warren! that you died?

JAMES MADISON BELL

JAMES MADISON BELL was born in Gallipolis, Ohio, April 3, 1826. When he was sixteen years of age he went to Cincinnati to live with a brother-in-law, and there he became a plasterer. In his twenty-second year he married. A man of strong feeling, he soon adopted a radical attitude toward slavery; from 1854 to 1860 he lived in Canada; and he became a personal friend of John Brown, giving assistance in getting men for the raid of 1859. In 1860 he went to California, but at the close of the Civil War he removed his family from Canada to Toledo, Ohio. He then traveled in the East, giving aid to the freedmen; in 1868 he was elected to the Republican convention in Ohio; and he was a delegate from the state to the national convention that nominated Grant for a second term. He died in 1902. Bell was an able speaker, and often read his poems with strong effect; but nothing that he wrote is of high technical excellence. Of some pieces of more than usual length, *The Progress of Liberty* especially shows the influence of Byron, while generally representative is *The Day and the War*, inscribed to the memory of John Brown. See *The Poetical Works of James Madison Bell, with a biographical sketch by Bishop B. W. Arnett*, Lansing, Mich., 1901.

THE DAY AND THE WAR

Sacred to the Memory of the Immortal
Captain John Brown,
The Hero, Saint, and Martyr of Harper's Ferry,
The following poem is most respectfully inscribed,
by one who loved him in life, and in death
would honor his memory

Introductory Note

The Poet laments the long years of enslavement of his race, but rejoices that the Emancipation Proclamation is the harbinger of the good time coming, and has at length given him

> "A fitting day to celebrate."

He shows how this wicked Rebellion, instituted to perpetuate Slavery, will cause "the final abolition" of the accursed institution.—The colored people are incited to prove themselves worthy of the position they must assume, by patriotism, fortitude, and virtue.

The deceitful policy of the European Governments is examined and criticized—their jealousy of the growing power of the American Union; their sympathy with the Rebels; the material aid and comfort they render unto the Confederacy, and their desire to effect the dismemberment of the Republic. England, remembering the loss of the colonies, is covertly aiding the Rebellion, and, while professing neutrality, is supplying them with ships and munitions of war.

He next sings of the heroism of the colored troops— their deeds of valor at Milliken's Bend—bravery of Miller's men, of which company all save one were either slain or wounded—and of the heroic achievements of the Black Brigade.

He relates a vision of the War, and portrays in vivid colors the horrors of a battlefield after the fight. An angel appears, who announces the advent of Peace. The warrior returns from the carnage of battle; his sword is turned into a plowshare, his spear into a reaping-hook, and a "real Republic" is formed.

In conclusion, he eulogizes the God-approved act of President Lincoln in issuing the great Emancipation Proclamation, and predicts that when posterity is enumerating the benefactors of mankind, "great Lincoln's name will lead the host."

P. A. BELL.

Twelve score of years were long to wait
A fitting day to celebrate:
'Twere long upon one native's soil
A feeless drudge in pain to toil.
But time that fashions and destroys,
And breeds our sorrows, breeds our joys;
Hence we at length have come with cheer,
To greet the dawning of the year—
The bless'd return of that glad day,
When, through Oppression's gloom, a ray
Of joy and hope and freedom, burst,
Dispelling that insatiate thirst
Which anxious years of toil and strife
Had mingled with the bondman's life.

A fitting day for such a deed,
But far more fit when it shall lead
To the final abolition
Of the last slave's sad condition:
Then when the New Year ushers in,
A grand rejoicing shall begin;
Then shall Freedom's clarion tone
Arouse no special class alone,
But all the land its blast shall hear,
And hail with joy the jubilant year;
And maid and matron, youth and age,
Shall meet upon one common stage,
And Proclamation Day shall be
A National Day of Jubilee
No longer 'neath the weight of years—
No longer merged in hopeless fears—
Is now that good time, long delayed,
When right, not might, shall all pervade.
Drive hence despair—no longer doubt,

Since friends within and foes without
Their might and main conjointly blend
To reach the same great, glorious end—
The sweeping from this favored land
The last foul chain and slavish brand.

No longer need the bondman fear,
For lo! the good time's almost here,
And doubtless some beneath our voice
Shall live to hail it and rejoice;
For almost now the radiant sheen
Of freedom's glad hosts may be seen;
The ear can almost catch the sound,
The eye can almost see them bound,
As thirty million voices rise
In grateful paeans to the skies.

But of the present we would sing,
    And of a land all bathed in blood—
A land where plumes the eagle's wing,
    Whose flaming banner, stars bestud—
A land where Heaven, with bounteous hand,
    Rich gifts hath strewn for mortal weal,
Till vale and plain and mountain grand
    Have each a treasure to reveal:
A land with every varying clime,
    From torrid heat to frigid cold—
With natural scenery more sublime
    Than all the world beside unfold,
Where vine-clad France may find a peer,
    And Venice an Italian sky,
With streams whereon the gondolier
    His feather'd oar with joy may ply.
O heaven-blest and favored land,
    Why are thy fruitful fields laid waste?

Why with thy fratricidal hand
    Hast thou thy beauty half defaced?
Why do the gods disdain thy prayer?
    And why in thy deep bitterness
Comes forth no heaven-clothed arm to share
    A part, and help in the distress?

    Hast thou gone forth to reap at noon,
And gather where thou hadst not strewn?
Hast thou kept back the hireling's fee
And mocked him in his poverty?
Hast thou, because thy God hath made
Thy brother of a different shade,
Bound fast the iron on his limb,
And made a feeless drudge of him?
Hast thou, to fill thy purse with gold,
The offsprings of his nature sold?
And in thy brutal lust, beguiled
His daughter and his couch defiled?

    For all this wrong and sad abuse,
Hast thou no offering of excuse?
No plea to urge in thy defense
'Gainst helpless, outraged innocence?
Then fearful is thy doom indeed,
If guilty thou canst only plead.
Thy sin is dark, and from the law
No dint of pity canst thou draw.
If thou are charged, 'twill hear thy suit;
If guilty, swift to execute,
Eye for an eye and tooth for tooth;
Yet, Oh! forbid it, God of truth:
Let not thine arm in anger fall,
But hear a guilty nation's call;
And stay the vial of wrath at hand;

Pour not its contents on the land;
Should they the last dregs in the cup
Of bitterness be called to sup,
And all the contents of the vial
Of thy just wrath be poured the while,
With all the tortures in reserve,
'Twould scarce be more than they deserve,
For they have sinned 'gainst thee and man.
But wilt thou not, by thy own plan,
Bring them past this sea of blood,
Ere they are buried 'neath its flood?

America! I thee conjure,
By all that's holy, just and pure,
To cleanse thy hands from Slavery's stain,
And banish from thy soil the chain.
Thou canst not thrive, while with the sweat
Of unpaid toil thy hands are wet,
Nor canst thou hope for peace or joy
Till thou Oppression doth destroy.

*   *   *   *   *

Though Tennyson, the poet king,
    Has sung of Balaklava's charge,
Until his thund'ring cannons ring
    From England's center to her marge,
The pleasing duty still remains
To sing a people from their chains—
To sing what none have yet assay'd,
The wonders of the Black Brigade.
The war had raged some twenty moons,
Ere they in columns or platoons,
To win them censure or applause,
Were marshal'd in the Union cause—
Prejudged of slavish cowardice,

While many a taunt and foul device
Came weekly forth with Harper's sheet,
To feed that base, infernal cheat.

But how they would themselves demean,
Has since most gloriously been seen.
'Twas seen at Milliken's dread bend,
Where e'en the Furies seemed to lend
To dark Secession all their aid,
To crush the Union Black Brigade.
The war waxed hot, and bullets flew
Like San Francisco's summer sand,
But they were there to dare and do,
E'en to the last, to save the land
And when the leaders of their corps
Grew wild with fear, and quit the field,
The dark remembrance of their scars
Before them rose, they could not yield:
And, sounding o'er the battle din,
They heard their standard-bearer cry—
"Rally! and prove that ye are men!
Rally! and let us do or die!
For war, nor death, shall boast a shade
To daunt the Union Black Brigade!"

And thus he played the hero's part,
Till on the ramparts of the foe
A score of bullets pierced his heart;
He sank within the trench below.
His comrades saw, and fired with rage,
Each sought his man, him to engage
In single combat. Ah! 'twas then
The Black Brigade proved they were men!
For ne'er did Swiss, or Russ, or knight,
Against such fearful odds arrayed,

With more persistent valor fight,
   Than did the Union Black Brigade!

As five to one, so stood their foes,
When that defiant shout arose,
And 'long their closing columns ran,
Commanding each to choose his man!
And ere the sound had died away,
Full many a ranting rebel lay
Gasping piteously for breath—
Struggling with the pangs of death,
From bayonet thrust or shining blade,
Plunged to the hilt by the Black Brigade.

   And thus they fought, and won a name—
None brighter on the scroll of Fame;
For out of one full corps of men,
But one remained unwounded, when
The dreadful fray had fully past—
All killed or wounded but the last!

   And though they fell, as has been seen,
Each slept his lifeless foes between,
And marked the course and paved the way
To ushering in a better day.
Let Balaklava's cannons roar,
   And Tennyson his hosts parade,
But ne'er was seen and never more
   The equals of the Black Brigade!

     *   *   *   *   *

   With one allusion, we have done
The task so joyously begun:
It is to speak, in measured lays,
Of him the Nation loves to praise.
   When that inspired instrument,

The subject of this great event,
Forth from the Halls of Congress came,
With even justice as its aim,
'Twas deem'd by some a fiendish rod,
But otherwise adjudged of God,
Who, turning earthward from His throne,
Beheld great Lincoln all alone,
With earth-bent brow, in pensive mood,
Pondering o'er some unsubdued
And knotty problem, half dissolved,
And half in mystery yet involved.

The interest of a continent,
All broken up by discontent—
His own dear land, land of his love,
The fairest 'neath the realms above—
Weighed down his form and rack'd his brain,
And filled his patriot heart with pain.
But when his mind conceived the thought
To Write Four Million Captives Free!
An angel to his conscience brought
Approving smiles of Deity;
And ere he had with flesh conferr'd,
He gave the bright conception birth,
And distant nations saw and heard,
And bless'd his mission on the earth.

And we today reiterate,
With warmth of heart and depth of soul,
God bless America's Magistrate!
Long may he live to guide, control;
Long may that arching brow and high—
That spiritual and piercing eye:
That tall, majestic, manly form—
Live, our rainbow 'midst the storm;

And when the roar of battle's pass'd,
When vain Secession's breath'd his last,
When peace and order are restored,
And freedom sits at every board,
And when the Nation shall convene
In mass, as ne'er before was seen,
And render eulogistic meeds
To worthy heroes' noble deeds,
A lengthened train shall claim their boast,
But Lincoln's name shall lead the host!
His name shall grow a household word,
Where'er the human voice is heard;
And tribes and people yet unborn,
Shall hail and bless his natal morn.

EMANCIPATION IN THE DISTRICT OF COLUMBIA

APRIL 16, 1862

Unfurl your banners to the breeze!
    Let Freedom's tocsin sound amain,
Until the islands of the seas
    Re-echo with the glad refrain!
Columbia's free!   Columbia's free!
    Her teeming streets, her vine-clad groves,
Are sacred now to Liberty,
    And God, who every right approves.

Thank God, the Capital is free!
    The slaver's pen, the auction block,
The gory lash of cruelty,
    No more this nation's pride shall mock;
No more, within those ten miles square,
    Shall men be bought and women sold;

Nor infants, sable-haired and fair,
   Exchanged again for paltry gold.

To-day the Capital is free!
   And free those halls where Adams stood
To plead for man's humanity,
   And for a common brotherhood;
Where Summer stood, with massive frame,
   Whose eloquent philosophy
Has clustered round his deathless name
   Bright laurels for eternity.

Where Wilson, Lovejoy, Wade, and Hale,
   And other lights of equal power,
Have stood, like warriors clad in mail,
   Before the giant of the hour,—
Co-workers in a common cause,
   Laboring for their country's weal,
By just enactments, righteous laws,
   And burning, eloquent appeal.

To them we owe and gladly bring
   The grateful tributes of our hearts;
And while we live to must and sing,
   These in our songs shall claim their parts.
To-day Columbia's air doth seem
   Much purer than in days agone;
And now her mighty heart, I deem,
   Hath lighter grown by marching on.

FRANCES E. W. HARPER

FRANCES ELLEN WATKINS was born of free parents in Baltimore in 1825. Losing her mother before she was three years old, she was cared for by an aunt, and for some years she attended a school kept by an uncle; but when not more than thirteen she had to work to earn her living. About 1850 she left Maryland for Ohio, and taught domestic science at Union Seminary in Columbia, the principal of the institution being John M. Brown, later bishop in the A. M. E. Church. Three years later she was in Little York, Penn.; but by this time she had become interested in the Underground Railroad and had begun her work as a lecturer against slavery. "About the year 1853," she said, "Maryland had enacted a law forbidding free people of color from the North to come into the state on pain of being imprisoned and sold into slavery. A free man who had unwittingly violated this infamous statute had recently been sold into Georgia and had escaped thence by secreting himself behind the wheel house of a boat bound northward; but before he reached the desired haven he was discovered and remanded to slavery. It was reported that he died soon after from the effects of exposure and suffering. . . . Upon that grave I pledged myself to the anti-slavery cause." Feeling thus Miss Watkins visited Philadelphia, New Bedford, and Boston, and on September 28, 1854, was engaged as a permanent lecturer by the Anti-Slavery Society of Maine. Her gifts now became more widely recognized. She traveled much in the East and worked so hard that her health was threatened. In 1860, in Cincinnati, she married Fenton Harper, but he died four years later. After the issuing of the Emancipation Proclamation she was in great demand, and in the troublous years after the war she spent much time in the South, often traveling and speaking under trying circumstances. Her work was now that of a representative of the Women's Christian Temperance Union. Grace Greenwood, writing in the *Independent* after one of her addresses, said: "She has a noble head, this bronze muse; a strong face, with a shadowed glow upon it indicative of thought and of a nature most femininely sensitive, but not in the least morbid. She stands quietly beside her desk and speaks without notes, with gestures few and fitting. Her manner is marked by dignity and composure. She is never assuming, never theatrical." Phebe A. Hanaford said in *Daughters of America* (1882): "Frances E. W. Harper is one of the most eloquent women lecturers in the country. As one listens to her clear, plaintive, melodious voice, and follows the flow of her musical speech in her logical presentation of truth, he can but be charmed with her oratory and rhetoric. . . . She is one of the colored women of whom white women may be proud, and to whom the abolitionists can point and declare that a race which can hold such women ought never to have been held in bondage." Mrs. Harper died February 22, 1911. In 1922 her memory was honored by the World's Women's Christian Temperance Union at its meeting in Philadelphia when her name was placed in the Red Letter Calendar with those of Frances E. Willard, Lady Henry Somerset, and other distinguished workers in the cause.

Frances E. W. Harper's booklets sold tens of thousands of copies, but she was distinctly a minor poet, and her success is largely to be accounted for by the vitality of her subject-matter and her ability to read her lines effectively. She is earnest but hardly ever stirs the deeper springs of poetry. The loose and flowing meters show the influence of Longfellow. The earliest booklet seems to have been one entitled *Forest Leaves*, but of this no copy has been preserved. *Poems on Miscellaneous Subjects* appeared in Boston in 1854; three years later the booklet was issued with additions in Philadelphia, and there seem to have been numerous other reprintings. *Moses, a Story of the Nile* was in the second edition in 1869. Small collections entitled simply *Poems* appeared in 1871 and 1900; and *Sketches of Southern Life* (largely concerned with the experiences of "Aunt Chloe"), issued in 1872, was enlarged in 1896. All of these booklets except the first were published in Philadelphia. There was also a novel, *Iola Leroy, or Shadows Uplifted*, Philadelphia, 1892. See sketches in *Men of Maryland*, by George F. Bragg, Baltimore,

1925, and *Homespun Heroines*, by Hallie Q. Brown, Xenia, O., 1926, and the Introduction to *Iola Leroy* by William Still.

BURY ME IN A FREE LAND

Make me a grave where'er you will,
In a lowly plain, or a lofty hill;
Make it among earth's humblest graves,
But not in a land where men are slaves.

I could not rest if around my grave
I heard the steps of a trembling slave;
His shadow above my silent tomb
Would make it a place of fearful gloom.

I could not rest if I heard the tread
Of a coffle gang to the shambles led,
And the mother's shriek of wild despair
Rise like a curse on the trembling air.

I could not sleep if I saw the lash
Drinking her blood at each fearful gash,
And I saw her babes torn from her breast,
Like trembling doves from their parent nest.

I'd shudder and start if I heard the bay
Of bloodhounds seizing their human prey,
And I heard the captive plead in vain
As they bound afresh his galling chain.

If I saw young girls from their mothers' arms
Bartered and sold for their youthful charms,
My eye would flash with a mournful flame,
My death-paled cheek grow red with shame.

I would sleep, dear friends, where bloated might
Can rob no man of his dearest right;

My rest shall be calm in any grave
Where none can call his brother a slave.

I ask no monument, proud and high,
To arrest the gaze of the passers-by;
All that my yearning spirit craves,
Is bury me not in a land of slaves.

ETHIOPIA

Yes, Ethiopia yet shall stretch
    Her bleeding hands abroad;
Her cry of agony shall reach
    Up to the throne of God.

The tyrant's yoke from off her neck,
    His fetters from her soul,
The mighty hand of God shall break,
    And spurn the base control.

Redeemed from dust and freed from chains,
    Her sons shall lift their eyes;
From cloud-capt hills and verdant plains
    Shall shouts of triumph rise.

Upon her dark, despairing brow
    Shall play a smile of peace;
For God shall bend unto her woe,
    And bid her sorrows cease.

'Neath sheltering vines and stately palms
    Shall laughing children play,
And aged sires with joyous psalms
    Shall gladden every day.

Secure by night, and blest by day,
    Shall pass her happy hours;

Nor human tigers hunt for prey
   Within her peaceful bowers.

Then, Ethiopia, stretch, O stretch
   Thy bleeding hands abroad!
Thy cry of agony shall reach
   And find redress from God.

Vashti

She leaned her head upon her hand
   And heard the King's decree—
"My lords are feasting in my halls;
   Bid Vashti come to me.

"I've shown the treasures of my house,
   My costly jewels rare,
But with the glory of her eyes
   No rubies can compare.

"Adorn'd and crown'd I'd have her come,
   With all her queenly grace,
And mid my lords and mighty men
   Unveil her lovely face.

"Each gem that sparkles in my crown,
   Or glitters on my throne,
Grows poor and pale when she appears,
   My beautiful, my own!"

All waiting stood the chamberlains
   To hear the Queen's reply.
They saw her cheek grow deathly pale,
   But light flash'd to her eye:

"Go, tell the King," she proudly said,
   "That I am Persia's Queen,

And by his crowds of merry men
    I never will be seen.

"I'll take the crown from off my head
    And tread it 'neath my feet,
Before their rude and careless gaze
    My shrinking eyes shall meet.

"A queen unveil'd before the crowd!—
    Upon each lip my name!—
Why, Persia's women all would blush
    And weep for Vashti's shame!

"Go back!" she cried, and waved her hand,
    And grief was in her eye:
"Go, tell the King," she sadly said,
    "That I would rather die."

They brought her message to the King;
    Dark flash'd his angry eye;
'Twas as the lightning ere the storm
    Hath swept in fury by.

Then bitterly outspoke the King,
    Through purple lips of wrath—
"What shall be done to her who dares
    To cross your monarch's path?"

Then spake his wily counsellors—
    "O King of this fair land!
From distant Ind to Ethiop,
    All bow to thy command.

"But if, before thy servants' eyes,
    This thing they plainly see,
That Vashti doth not heed thy will
    Nor yield herself to thee,

"The women, restive 'neath our rule,
    Would learn to scorn our name,
And from her deed to us would come
    Reproach and burning shame.

"Then, gracious King, sign with thy hand
    This stern but just decree,
That Vashti lay aside her crown,
    Thy Queen no more to be."

She heard again the King's command,
    And left her high estate;
Strong in her earnest womanhood,
    She calmly met her fate,

And left the palace of the King,
    Proud of her spotless name—
A woman who could bend to grief
    But would not bow to shame.

PRESIDENT LINCOLN'S PROCLAMATION OF FREEDOM

It shall flash through coming ages;
    It shall light the distant years;
And eyes now dim with sorrow
    Shall be clearer through their tears.

It shall flush the mountain ranges;
    And the valleys shall grow bright;
It shall bathe the hills in radiance,
    And crown their brows with light.

It shall flood with golden splendor
    All the huts of Caroline,
And the sun-kissed brow of labor
    With lustre new shall shine.

It shall gild the gloomy prison,
  Darken'd by the nation's crime,
Where the dumb and patient millions
  Wait the better coming time.

By the light that gilds their prison,
  They shall seize its mould'ring key,
And the bolts and bars shall vibrate
  With the triumphs of the free.

Like the dim and ancient chaos,
  Shrinking from the dawn of light,
Oppression, grim and hoary,
  Shall cower at the sight.

And her spawn of lies and malice
  Shall grovel in the dust,
While joy shall thrill the bosoms
  Of the merciful and just.

Though the morning seemed to linger
  O'er the hill-tops far away,
Now the shadows bear the promise
  Of the quickly coming day.

Soon the mists and murky shadows
  Shall be fringed with crimson light,
And the glorious dawn of freedom
  Break refulgent on the sight.

FIFTEENTH AMENDMENT

Beneath the burden of our joy
  Tremble, O wires, from East to West!
Fashion with words your tongues of fire,
  To tell the nation's high behest.

Outstrip the winds, and leave behind
   The murmur of the restless waves;
Nor tarry with your glorious news,
   Amid the ocean's coral caves.

Ring out! ring out! your sweetest chimes,
   Ye bells, that call to prayer and praise;
Let every heart with gladness thrill,
   And songs of joyful triumph raise.

Shake off the dust, O rising race!
   Crowned as a brother and a man;
Justice to-day asserts her claim,
   And from thy brow fades out the ban.

With freedom's chrism upon thy head,
   Her precious ensign in thy hand,
Go place thy once despiséd name
   Amid the noblest of the land.

O ransomed race! give God the praise,
   Who led thee through a crimson sea,
And 'mid the storm of fire and blood,
   Turned out the war-cloud's light to thee.

ALEXANDER CRUMMELL

FOR A LONG time the life of Alexander Crummell was a baffling quest. Dr. DuBois has well set forth the threefold temptation he had to meet, of Hate, Despair, and Doubt, and the victory he won. He was born in New York City, March 3, 1819. His paternal grandfather was the son of a West African chief and his mother's people had been free for generations. After availing himself of the meagre facilities offered at the time in the schools of New York, he and Henry Highland Garnet and Thomas S. Sidney went in 1835 to Canaan, New Hampshire, five miles from Hanover, where an academy had been opened by some abolitionists. The principal was kind, but the attitude of the neighbors was hostile. Feeling rose to a high pitch when the Negro boys took part in the speaking on the Fourth of July, and the next month a mob hitched up ninety-five yoke of oxen and dragged the school building from its place to a swamp. To appease their temper still further, the people fired a salute at the departure of the youths from the vicinity. Crummell with his companions rode back to New York on the top of the stage coach. The next year he went to the well known Oneida Institute, Oneida County, N. Y., of which the abolitionist, Beriah Green, was president, and there he remained three years. Then succeeded a period that was enough to conquer all but the most dauntless spirit. In 1839, on recommendation of Rev. Peter Williams of St. Philip's, the young student applied to the General Theological Seminary of the Protestant Episcopal Church, but was refused admission. He fared better in Boston, however, and at length, in December, 1844, was ordained priest in Philadelphia. For a while he served in Providence, but there were not many Negro people in the city and his best efforts went for naught. Feeling that he should try again in a community that gave better promise, he went to Philadelphia with a letter to Bishop Henry U. Onderdonk. The bishop refused to receive him in his diocese except on terms that he could not accept, and he went again to New York. There he worked with a small group in the old church of his family, frowned upon by the proslavery men in control of the Episcopal Church in New York.

In 1847, on the suggestion of a few influential friends, Crummell went to England to solicit funds for a church that he hoped to build in New York. The trip marked the turning-point in his life. He talked with distinguished liberals and men of letters; and some men of the clergy, having the discernment to see his promise, assisted in his going to Queen's College, Cambridge. There he remained from 1851 to 1853, graduating with the A.B. degree. As his health was threatened and he felt the need of a warmer climate, he did not go' back to New York but turned toward Africa. The next twenty years he spent in Liberia and Sierra Leone, working with all his might, speaking with the force of an oracle, and returning only twice to the United States for brief visits. In 1873, however, he came back to stay and was placed in charge of St. Mary's Mission, Washington, D. C. There his long experience told in rich fruition, and he worked with such power that he could soon erect St. Luke's Protestant Episcopal Church, where he labored for nearly twenty-two years. In March, 1897, he led in founding the American Negro Academy. He died while sojourning at Point Pleasant, N. J., September 10, 1898. He had lived a life without reproach, that of a scholar and a gentleman, thinking only noble thoughts and expressing himself in graceful English. Cromwell said: "In his manner he was austere, fearless, and dignified; yet he was as easy to approach as a child. Tall, erect, majestic, and noble in his carriage, he was a distinguished man in any social gathering, and on the public highway; his natural stride and his commanding appearance gave him a most striking individuality, pointing him out in any assemblage."

Crummell was intensely interested in matters of scholarship and racial justice, and he expressed himself with an optimism not possessed by many men of his time. When not more than twenty-seven years of age, he delivered a eulogy of Clarkson that gave some indication of his future style and that was published as *The Man: the Hero: the Christian! A Eulogy on the Life and Character of Thomas Clarkson: Delivered in the City of New*

York, December, 1846 (New York, 1847). *The Duty of a Rising Christian State* (London, 1856) was the annual oration before the Common Council and the Citizens of Monrovia on the anniversary of their independence, July 26, 1855. It was a strong and well organized plea for soul freedom on the part of the Liberians, reflecting the speaker's English training, and was included with other addresses in *The Future of Africa* (New York, 1862), from which the selection below is taken. Later collections were *The Greatness of Christ, and Other Sermons* (New York, 1882) and *Africa and America* (Springfield, Mass., 1891). Some of the later addresses of Crummell, published singly, received wide circulation. When Rev. J. L. Tucker, a white Protestant Episcopal minister of Jackson, Miss., spoke slanderously about the Negro before the Church Congress of 1882 in Richmond, he replied with *A Defense of the Negro Race in America* (Washington, 1883). *The Black Woman of the South: Her Neglects and her Needs* was a remarkable address before the Freedman's Aid Society of the Methodist Episcopal Church at Ocean Grove, N. J., August 15, 1883. It is said that half a million copies of this were necessary to satisfy the demand.

For the facts of Crummell's life and a personal impression, see *The Negro in American History,* by John W. Cromwell, Washington, 1914, pp. 130-138. A keen and sympathetic interpretation is in *The Souls of Black Folk,* by W. E. Burghardt DuBois, Chicago, 1903, pp. 215-227. For a careful review of the published writings see *The Negro Author,* by Vernon Loggins, New York, 1931, pp. 199-209.

Hope for Africa

(Selection from a sermon with this title preached on behalf of the Ladies Negro Education Society at Hotwell's Church, Clifton, Bristol, England, April 21, 1852, from the text, "Ethiopia shall soon stretch out her hands unto God.")

I am well aware that it is the part of a wise man not to be too sanguine. I know, too, that, looking at the untold, the unknown millions in Central Africa, upon whom the eyes of civilized man have never fallen, the work is yet but begun. But when I note the rapidity of God's work during the brief period I have mentioned, and know that God allows no obstacles to stand against Him and His cause, whether it be a pestilential shore, or a violent population, or a sanguinary king, or vindictive slave-dealers, or a slave-trading town like that of Lagos; when I see these things, I cannot but believe that we are now approaching the fulfilment of this prophecy. When I see, moreover, how this great continent is invested on every side by the zealous ardent missionary or the adventurous traveler; how, almost weekly, something is brought to our ears across the ocean, of new discovery, or of startling incident; how that now there is every probability that soon the very heart of that continent, and all its centuries of mystery, will be revealed to the gaze and scrutiny of the civilized world; and then, that by the common road, by trade, by commerce, by the flying wings of steamers, by caravans, by converted Africans, by civilized and pious Negroes, from the West Indies or America, the Bible, the Prayer-Book, and tracts, and the Church in all her functions and holy offices, will almost at once be introduced among the mighty masses of its population;—when I see these things, my heart is filled with confident assurance; I cannot but believe that the day of Africa's redemption fast draweth nigh! And vast and extensive as the work may be, it seems that it will be a most rapid one; everything gives this indication: for first, you will notice, that since the abolition of the slave trade, this race, in all its homes, has been going forward: it has had nowhere any retrograde movements. And next, you will notice, that the improvement of this race, social, civil, and religious, has been remarkably quick, and has been, almost all, included in a very brief period; and therefore I think that the work of evangelization in this race will be a rapid one. So God, at times, takes "the staff of accomplishment" into His own hand, and fulfils His ends with speed. The children of Israel were thirty-nine years performing a journey, which could have been accomplished in a few days: but in the fortieth year they marched a longer distance than all the years preceding, and entered, in a few weeks, at once, into the Promised Land. So God, now, unseen to human eyes, may be leading on His hosts to a mighty victory over Satan; and in the briefest of all the periods of the Church's warfare, may intend to accomplish the most brilliant and consummate of all His triumphs. And this is my conviction with regard to Africa. In my soul I believe that the time has come. I have the strongest impression of the nigh approach of her bright day of deliverance. The night, I am convinced—the night of forlornness, of agony and desolation—is far spent; the day is at hand! The black charter of crime and infamy and blood, which for nigh three centuries has given up my fatherland to the spoiler, is about to be erased! The malignant lie, which would deliver up an entire race, the many millions of a vast continent, to rapine and barbarism and benightedness, is now to be blotted out! And if I read the signs of the times aright, if I am not deceived in supposing that now I see God's hand graciously opened for Africa, if to my sight now appear, with undoubted clearness,

"the baby forms
Of giant figures yet to be,"

what a grand reversal of a dark destiny will it not be for poor bleeding Africa! What a delightful episode from the hopeless agony of her unmitigated, unalleviated suffering! For ages hath she lain beneath the incubus of the "demon of her idolatry." For ages hath she suffered the ravages of vice, corruption, iniquity, and guilt. For ages hath she

been "stricken and smitten" by the deadly thrusts of murder and hate, revenge and slaughter. Fire, famine, and the
sword have been her distressful ravaging visitations. War,
with devastating stride, has ravaged her fair fields, and peo-
pled her open and voracious tombs. The slave trade—that
fell destroyer!—has sacked her cities, has turned the hands
of her sons upon each other, and set her different communities at murderous strife, and colored their hands with fraternal blood! Yes, everything natural has been changed into
the monstrous; and all things harmonious turned into dis-
cord and confusion. Earth has had her beauty marred by
the bloody track of the cruel men who have robbed my fatherland of her children; and the choral voice of ocean, which
should lift up naught but everlasting symphonies in the ears
of angels and of God, has been made harsh and dissonant, by
the shrieks and moans and agonizing cries of the poor victims, who have either chosen a watery grave in preference
to slavery, or else have been cast into its depths, the sick and
the emaciated, by the ruthless slave-dealer! And then, when
landed on the distant strand—the home of servitude, the seat
of oppression—then has commenced a system of overwork
and physical endurance, incessant and unrequited—a series
of painful tasks, of forced labor, of want and deprivation,
and lashings, and premature deaths, continued from generation to generation, transmitted as the only inheritance of
poor, helpless humanity, to children's children!

But now there is a new spirit abroad—not only in the
Christian world, but likewise through the different quarters
of her own broad continent. There is an uprising of her
sons from intellectual sloth and spiritual inertness; a seeking
and a stretching forth of her hands, for light, instruction,
and spirituality, such as the world has never before seen;
and which gives hopes that the days of Cyprian and Augustine
shall again return to Africa; when the giant sins and the

deadly evils which have ruined her, shall be effectively stayed; and when Ethiopia, from the Atlantic to the Indian Ocean, from the Mediterranean to the Cape, "shall stretch out her hands unto God!"